The Seven Laws of Presidential Leadership

An Introduction to the American Presidency

Charles W. Dunn

PEARSON

Prentice
Hall

UPPER SADDLE RIVER, NEW JERSEY 07458

Library of Congress Cataloging-in-Publication Data

Dunn, Charles W.
  The seven laws of presidential leadership : an introduction to the American presidency /
Charles W. Dunn.
    p. cm.
  Includes bibliographical references and index.
  ISBN 0-13-934290-7
    1. Presidents–United States. 2. Political leadership–United States. 3. Executive
power–United States.

JK516.D86 2007
352.23'60973–dc22

2005056638

VP/Editorial Director: Charlyce Jones Owen
Executive Editor: Dickson Musslewhite
Editorial Assistant: Jennifer L. Murphy
Executive Marketing Manager: Emily Cleary
Director of Production & Manufacturing:
Barbara Kittle
Managing Editor: Lisa Iarkowski
Production Editor: Jean Lapidus
Copy Editor: Laura A. Lawrie
Image Permission Coordinator: Nancy Seise
Manufacturing Manager: Nick Sklitsis
Assistant Manufacturing Manager:
Mary Ann Gloriande
Prepress & Manufacturing Buyer:
Mary Ann Gloriande
Cover Design: Bruce Kenselaar

Cover Credits: Top photo: President Bush meeting with the National Security Council. Bottom Row (left to right): Portrait of George Washington; Thomas Jefferson (1743–1826); President Lincoln in 1864; Franklin D. Roosevelt; John F. Kennedy chats with outgoing President Dwight D. Eisenhower on the way to the inaugural ceremony on January 20, 1961; Vice-President Lyndon B. Johnson is sworn into the Office of President aboard Air Force One in Dallas, Texas. He is flanked left by Kennedy's widow, Jacqueline Bouvier Kennedy.
Compositor: GGS Book Services
Printer/Binder: R. R. Donnelley/Harrisonburg
Cover Printer: R. R. Donnelley/Harrisonburg

Pearson Education LTD.
Pearson Education Singapore, Pte. Ltd
Pearson Education, Canada, Ltd
Pearson Education–Japan

Pearson Education Australia PTY, Limited
Pearson Education North Asia Ltd
Pearson Educación de Mexico, S.A. de C.V.
Pearson Education Malaysia, Pte. Ltd

10 9 8 7 6 5 4 3 2 1
ISBN 0-13-934290-7

Contents

Preface

Combining tradition and innovation is the goal of *The Seven Laws of Presidential Leadership*. Every course in the American presidency must deal with a certain body of knowledge, including history, rhetoric, politics, Congress, the Courts, and other subjects. The advantage of *The Seven Laws of Presidential Leadership* is that it allows for the presentation of this traditional information through an innovative method that sparks student interest and increases teaching options for the instructor. The gain is obvious: All the "nuts and bolts" are present. But they are not simply arranged in neat traditional compartments. All of the traditional components of presidency texts appear in *The Seven Laws of Presidential Leadership*, but with a fresh approach, offering a new way of thinking about the world's most prestigious public office.

What inspired this book? After some 30 years of teaching and writing about the presidency at Florida State University, the University of Illinois (Urbana), Clemson University, Grove City College, and Regent University, I wanted to distill into one book the general laws that govern presidential leadership. The title, *Seven Laws*, came from a series of new lectures, which I delivered at Clemson University. I noticed then that in response to those lectures, students listened more intently, took notes more thoroughly, and responded with more questions than ever before. The students' response increasingly prompted me to think about how a book could capture the same high level of student interest.

Accordingly *readability* and *memorability* stand out as the bywords of *The Seven Laws of Presidential Leadership*, which:

1. Synthesizes scholarship on the presidency and presidential leadership into a memorable set of seven laws; and
2. Uses a crisp, jargon-free writing style.

The goal: A book that students will want to keep in their libraries rather than to sell it on the used-book market.

Some texts feature presidential leadership in relationship to one facet of the presidency, such as policy making, power, and character; others focus on the dilemmas and problems of presidential leadership; still others present a theory of presidential leadership; and some concentrate on presidential history. *The Seven Laws of Presidential Leadership* merges these approaches into seven laws, which integrate and synthesize the concepts and structures, history and politics of presidential leadership. Functioning like coat hangers on which students can hang their knowledge and understanding of the presidency, **the *laws* refer to the enduring norms, principles, and standards that govern and explain presidential leadership**.

Before the 1960s, the presidency appeared as part of college courses on the Chief Executive. Then as scholarship developed, especially during the 1960s and 1970s, the presidency itself became a course, usually known as the American Presidency. Finally, scholars turned their attention to presidential leadership, which sometimes became the new title, notably during the 1980s and 1990s. Now in the 21st century both the American Presidency and Presidential Leadership are standard titles for courses on the presidency. *The Seven Laws of Presidential Leadership* fits courses with either title.

Despite the substantial bibliography available on the presidency, no text on the presidency offers an extensive topical bibliography at the end of the text. Some offer brief end-of-chapter bibliographies, whereas others offer either short or long alphabetical bibliographies at the end of the book. *The Seven Laws of Presidential Leadership* remedies this deficiency by presenting an extensive topical bibliography at the end of the text. Various pedagogical advantages and opportunities emerge from this bibliography, including ideas for assigned or extra credit reading, research projects, and classroom activities, such as round table discussions and debates.

All too often and to all too great an extent, presidential biographies and autobiographies are the stepchildren of presidency texts. Long overlooked as effective teaching and learning tools, they deserve their rightful place in classes on the presidency. Biographies and autobiographies tell stories, pedagogically a sound way to engage and to expand student interest in the subject. *The Seven Laws of Presidential Leadership* singles out autobiographies and biographies in the comprehensive topical bibliography by offering a selection of important books by or about each president. Professors can use autobiographies and biographies as assigned or extra credit reading, or as reading for research projects, and students may deliver oral reports or participate in round table discussions about their reading of autobiographies and biographies.

According to President Franklin D. Roosevelt, "The presidency is preeminently a place of moral leadership." But all textbooks overlook what he considered paramount. *The Seven Laws of Presidential Leadership* rectifies this serious oversight by examining the critical differences between personal and public policy morality and how presidents should handle moral crises and questions. Among the cases explored are: (1) Franklin Roosevelt's affairs, (2) Harry Truman's dilemmas with dropping the bomb on Hiroshima and Nagasaki, (3) Dwight Eisenhower's slack leadership on civil rights issues, (4) John F. Kennedy's sexual escapades, (4) Lyndon Johnson's Vietnam trauma, (5) Richard Nixon's Watergate ordeal, (6) Gerald Ford's pardon of Nixon, (7) Jimmy Carter's loss of trust among the American people, (8) Ronald Reagan's Iran-Contra problem, (9) George Bush's reversal of his "Read My Lips" pledge, (10) Bill Clinton's Whitewater and related scandals, and (11) George W. Bush's difficulties in the "War on Terrorism."

Featuring seven advantages not found in other texts, *The Seven Laws of Presidential Leadership*:

1. Presents *seven distinct laws of presidential leadership* as synthesized from presidential scholarship;
2. Uses the seven laws as both *pedagogical and substantive tools* to enhance *memorability* and *learning retention*;
3. Explores in depth the various *theories of presidential leadership*;
4. Examines the *impact of culture* on presidential leadership;
5. Probes the relationships between morality, moral issues and presidential leadership;
6. Provides a *comprehensive topical bibliography* to guide the development of reading and research assignments, and classroom projects; and
7. Presents a carefully selected bibliography of *autobiographies and biographies* on each president to engage and expand student interest in the presidency through reading about the persons who have held the office.

Many people provided superb help over many years in developing the ideas for *The Seven Laws of Presidential Leadership*. Among the many students who have sharpened my insights into presidential leadership, several merit special mention: Heidi Ault, Travis Barham, Rebecca Bragg, Rebecca Dannecker, Matthew Divelbiss, Meghan Graves, Jennifer Hopkins, Ryan Teague, Chris Koon, Roberta Knowles, Jennifer Mahurin, Natalie McDaniel, David Page, Tommy Strickland, and Amanda Tharpe. Of particular note, I could hardly have completed this project without the able assistance of Barbara M. Jones, and the steadfast encouragement of my wife, Carol, who has lifted me up during those down times faced by every author. Finally, our younger son, Josh, who has taught American government and politics, including the presidency, at the University of Virginia, William & Mary, and the University of Colorado (Colorado Springs), has provided keen insights.

The author also thanks the following reviewers for their helpful suggestions: J. David Fairbanks of the University of Houston, Downtown; Phillip Warf of The University of Arizona; Dennis Simon of The Southern Methodist University; Fiona Ross of The University of Bristol; and Jeff Fox of Fort Lewis College.

No author succeeds without the vision of a superb editorial director and the diligent work of a production editor along with many other behind-the-scenes staff, who are the unsung heroes of every book. In all of my writing I have worked with none better than those at Pearson/Prentice Hall, including Charlyce Jones Owen, Vice President and Editorial Director, and Jean Lapidus, Production Editor.

Throughout the many years of writing *The Seven Laws of Presidential Leadership*, I have desired to write a user-friendly book, helping faculty with their teaching and students with their learning. Whether successful in the endeavor, I leave to the judgment of you, the reader.

Now, at the end, I once again echo sentiments sometimes attributed to Robert Louis Stevenson: "I hate to write. I love to have written." The book is now in your hands.

CWD

Chapter One

The Law of History

The Irony of Power and Promise

The tyranny of the legislature is really the danger most to be feared, and will continue to be for many years to come. The tyranny of the executive power will come in its turn, but at a more distant period.

—Thomas Jefferson, Letter to James Madison (March 15, 1789)

INTRODUCTION TO THE LAW OF HISTORY

> The American presidency, a magnetically powerful attraction for presidents, presidential candidates, press corps, and public, is simultaneously potent and impotent. Assured of their power, but frustrated by their weaknesses, presidents must perform a tight-wire act in the center ring of American politics.

Thomas Jefferson understood that presidential power and presidential leadership are like an optical illusion. They are not what they seem. The Founders appeared to create a presidency constrained by strict constitutional boundaries, but the Executive Article actually created opportunities for expanding presidential power and leadership.

As with Isaac Newton's first law, the law of inertia, the Founders set in motion an object, presidential power, whose momentum gradually increased until the 1930s, when it began to accelerate. Although outside forces have acted to check presidential power, notably during the scandals of the Nixon and Clinton presidencies, presidents remain preeminent in American politics. Presidents more than anyone else determine the national agenda, setting priorities and proposing policies.

Although seated at the summit of power, presidents are vulnerable. Rising popular expectations make them vulnerable to public distrust and dissatisfaction when their leadership fails to produce satisfactory results. Economic, political, and social conditions cause people to look to the president for leadership, but in leading the president divides, satisfying some and alienating others. As though playing a game of chess, presidents constantly face checkmate from Congress, the bureaucracy, the courts, the press corps, and interest groups. It is as though the power and promise of presidential leadership outstrips performance. The American Founders sowed the seeds of this irony of power and promise during the Constitutional Convention of 1787.

CONSTITUTIONAL CREATION[1]

Modern Americans, who could hardly imagine their president as anything less than the preeminent leader of their nation and the world, have lost sight of the presidency's constitutional origins. Conceived shortly after the bitter and violent reaction to the executive tyranny of the English Crown and King George III's colonial governors, the presidency occupied second place to the Congress in the Constitution's Articles. Fashioning the presidency as a constitutional fraction of one-third of the federal triangle to check legislative and judicial power, the Founders' intentions reflected reality.

Did the Founders look on the president as the national leader or as the party leader or as the world leader? Hardly. As an infant nation, the United States lacked a well-developed idea of nationhood. In politics, political parties neither existed nor did the Founders believe in them. Internationally, the United States was a mere prop on the apron of the stage and not an actor on center stage.

Although balancing power more evenly among the three branches than in the Articles of Confederation, the American Constitution retained an imbalance of power in favor of the legislative branch. Guided more by separation of powers than sharing of powers, the Founders did not paint a picture of the president exercising a broad range of legislative and judicial powers. The Founders could not have understood Clinton Rossiter, who said in 1956 that the president is like a "magnificent lion who can roam widely and do great deeds." But, wittingly or unwittingly, the Founders set in motion an object, presidential power, which ultimately justified Rossiter's colorful characterization.

Although credited for their imagination and innovation in drafting the Constitution, the Founders' realism restrained their reforms. Squeezed in a vise between the strong and tyrannical executive power of the English Crown and royal governors, whom they despised, and the weak and ineffective executive power in the Articles of Confederation and State Constitutions, which they disliked, the Founders balanced the pendulum of reform between the extremes of *executive tyranny* and *legislative supremacy*.

Because legislative supremacy scarcely proved more virtuous than executive tyranny, the Founders compromised, planting the seeds of an active president in the Constitution's fertile topsoil. James Madison, for example, condemned state constitutions for their undue emphasis on preventing an "overgrown and all-grasping prerogative of an hereditary magistrate," blinding people to "danger from legislative usurpation, which, by assembling all power in the same hands, must lead to the same tyranny as is threatened by executive usurpations" (*Federalist* No. 48).

The challenge? Create an executive who could act without activating the opposition of those who feared executive tyranny. The Founders believed that an ineffective executive would translate into ineffectual government and that an unduly strong executive would doom ratification of the Constitution.

The answer? Adopt the ideas of Montesquieu and Locke. In *The Spirit of the Laws*, Montesquieu argued for a "balanced constitution" to preserve liberty through power checking power:

> When the legislative and executive powers are united in the same person, or in the same body of magistrates, there can be no liberty, because apprehensions may arise lest the same monarch or senate should enact tyrannical laws, and execute them in a tyrannical manner.

In his *Two Treatises on Government* (N.B. Chapter 14 of his second treatise), Locke argued that the executive should have broad, discretionary, and residual power.

> . . . the good of the society requires that several things should be left to the discretion of him that has the executive power. . . . For the legislators not being able to foresee and provide by laws for all that may be useful to the community, the executor of the laws, having the power in his hands, has by the common law of Nature a right to make use of it for the good of society.

Montesquieu and Locke conceived of separate branches of government, each able to defend its prerogatives from the others' intrusions. *Separation of powers* served as a defense against the undesirable extremes of executive tyranny and legislative supremacy. Locke's notion of an executive's *residual power* not only reinforced its ability to resist legislative intrusion but also ultimately to assert its own separate and independent agenda, even developing powers not expressly stated in the Constitution.

Successfully performing a tight-wire act, the Founders balanced the need for a more powerful executive with the need to restrain the excessive exercise of that power. Experience with the Articles of Confederation and state constitutions made the case for a strong executive, but experience with the English Crown and royal governors countered those arguments. Montesquieu and Locke showed the Founders how to balance the competing pressures.

Political delicacy dictated that the Founders write a brief and imprecise Executive Article, allowing time and circumstance to shape the presidency's development. The Founders' successful tight-wire act created an enduring tug-of-war between advocates of an active and a passive presidency. No one contributed more to this tug-of-war than Alexander Hamilton, whose writings in *The Federalist* advocated an *energized executive*:

> A feeble Executive implies a feeble execution of the government. A feeble execution is but another phrase for a bad execution; and a government ill executed, whatever it may be in theory, must be, in practice, bad government. Taking it for granted, therefore, that all men of sense will agree in the necessity of an *energetic Executive* [emphasis supplied], it will only remain to inquire, what are the ingredients which constitute this energy?
>
> The ingredients which constitute energy in the Executive are unity; duration; adequate provision for its support; and competent powers. (*Federalist* No. 70)

Hamilton believed that the United States needed a single chief executive, who could serve for extended terms, with sufficient personnel and powers to conduct the presidency's business. Initial support for Hamilton's idea at the Convention came primarily from delegates in states with more powerful governors, namely, New York and Pennsylvania. Charles Pinckney (South Carolina) joined James Wilson (Pennsylvania) and Alexander Hamilton (New York) in leading the Convention to adopt an *energized executive*, which evolved after a protracted series of negative and positive decisions in the Convention. From the seeds of an *energized executive* grew today's presidency.

Negative Decisions

Delegates from New Jersey and Virginia, who quickly presented the Convention with proposals for a divided and weak executive, called for a plural or multiheaded executive and for legislative election of the executive.

After abandoning these proposals in the New Jersey and Virginia Plans, the Convention adopted a single executive with an electoral constituency independent of the legislative branch. A single executive allowed one person to act on behalf of the executive branch, whereas nonlegislative election strengthened the executive's independence from the legislature. Later, when the Convention created the Electoral College, the executive could secure a national constituency by appealing to the voters to win a majority of Electoral College votes. Ultimately these negative decisions ensured that the president became not only the sole leader of the executive branch but also of the nation and of the president's party.

Positive Decisions

But a single executive with a national constituency needs something more: sufficient time and adequate powers to develop, promote, and implement policies. In many states, then, governors served for only one year with no right of succession and with only limited powers. By granting the president a four-year term with the right of succession, the Convention allowed sufficient time for the achievement of a presidential agenda. Through endowing the president with adequate powers, the president could aggressively fight for policies. Lacking precise restrictions, these broadly worded powers permitted presidents to extend the boundaries of their office.

Power to Appoint. Authority to nominate and appoint personnel allows presidents to (1) establish personnel and budgetary controls over the bureaucracy, (2) influence the judiciary's direction, and (3) guide foreign policy. Only two limitations restrain a president's power to nominate: senatorial confirmation and the inability to remove judges and quasi-judicial officials, including members of independent regulatory agencies. No limitations pertain to the appointing power, such as naming members of the White House staff.

Power to Faithfully Execute the Laws. Departments and agencies in the executive branch, a president's principal means for implementing and enforcing the laws, report directly to the president, except for independent regulatory agencies. Because presidents may exercise some discretion in the implementation and enforcement of laws, they have both expressed and implied powers based on the Constitution and Supreme Court decisions.

With only rare exceptions, the courts have upheld a president's implied powers, which spring from two sources: the president's discretionary authority and the constitutional declaration that "executive power shall be vested in a president of the United States." *Implied powers*, according to the U.S. Supreme Court, mean that the enforcement and implementation of laws by the president include not only statutes enacted by Congress, but also "any obligation fairly and properly inferable from [the Constitution], or any duty . . . to be derived from the general scope of . . . duties under the laws of the United States." In the same case, *In re Neagle* (1890), the U.S. Supreme Court said that executive power is not "limited to the enforcement of acts of Congress . . . according to their express terms" but also includes "the rights, duties and obligations growing out of the Constitution itself, our international relations, and all the protection implied [emphasis supplied] by the nature of the government under the Constitution."

One of the best-known efforts to check a president's power to faithfully execute the laws occurred during the 1970s when politics and ideology inspired passage of the Budget Impoundment and Control Act (1973). After President Richard M. Nixon, a Republican, refused to spend funds appropriated by a Democratically controlled Congress, it retaliated by setting up procedures to curb this traditional exercise of the impoundment power, first used by President George Washington.

Power as Commander in Chief. Today, would any presidential power surprise the Founders more than commander in chief? Evoking little discussion at the Convention and drawing scant attention in Federalist Number 69, this power has undergone great transformation. Federalist Number 69 calmly says the power of commander in chief "would amount to nothing more than the supreme command and direction of the military and naval forces, as first General and Admiral of the Confederacy." Growing from this simple power of military command, the power of commander in chief now refers to a broad and largely undefined exercise of power during emergencies.

Congress, reacting to alleged abuses of this power during the Vietnam War, passed the War Powers Act (1973) to restrict presidential action during emergencies. Congress required presidents to obtain congressional approval for military action extending beyond 30 days. Ironically, rather than weakening the power of commander in chief, the War Powers Act may strengthen it, because a president can commit troops for 30 days without congressional approval, which places Congress in an awkward position. Politically, could Congress afford to mandate the troops' immediate return when almost always the public rallies to support the president during such emergencies? Proponents of the War Powers Act say it forces presidents to consider the consequences of a military commitment should Congress want to disapprove of it. Realistically, however, presidents have considered these consequences anyway.

Power to Negotiate Treaties. Presidential determination of foreign policy rests on the powers to negotiate treaties, to appoint personnel, and to faithfully execute the laws. Although the Senate has the power to ratify treaties, presidents liberally circumvent this power by using executive agreements, which do not require Senate ratification. Executive agreements between another nation and the United States call for judicious use, however, lest Congress and the public react critically, creating an embarrassing situation for a president and the nation.

Fusion of Powers

The Executive Article illustrates flexibility, America's widely acclaimed constitutional virtue. Accommodating myriad demands and many interpretations, the executive article has allowed presidential power numerous opportunities for expansion. In addition to its unclear and imprecise limits, the executive article along with the legislative and judicial articles instituted not so much a doctrine of *separation of powers* as *fusion of powers*. A doctrine of strict separation of powers would have clearly defined the limits of executive power. The more accurate doctrine, fusion of powers, has allowed the presidency to develop legislative, judicial, and executive responsibilities. Today's presidents are not passive participants, watching and checking the legislative and judicial branches, but active influences in shaping what they do. Flexibility, achieved through fusion of powers, has placed presidents at the apex of influence in American government. Stretched like elastic, presidential power has expanded to meet the needs of changing times and circumstances.

DEFINING MOMENTS AND TURNING POINTS

Congressional domination of American government, Woodrow Wilson's conclusion in *Congressional Government* (1885), held sway until early in the 20th century, but long before then precedents emerged for a more powerful presidency. Although not permitting the eclipse of legislative power, the Constitution revealed possibilities for the advance of presidential power. For example, President George Washington, aided by his Secretary of the Treasury, Alexander Hamilton, established a foundation for presidential reverence. Not only Washington's commanding presence but also his decisive action on such issues as the Whiskey Rebellion stimulated presidential respect. Then, three other developments soon contributed to the ultimate growth of presidential power:

- Evolution of the party system and the president's role as party leader under Thomas Jefferson;
- Growth of a president's national constituency under Andrew Jackson when he rallied a new constituency to win office; and the

- Exercise of emergency powers during the Civil War by Abraham Lincoln, who set aside the *writ of habeas corpus* and made other commanding decisions.

These developments showed that a president could influence public opinion, challenge Congress, and take decisive action through a president's implied powers. Major advancements in presidential power, however, awaited the 20th century, beginning with Theodore Roosevelt and Woodrow Wilson, who called for an activist presidency. Their call signaled a changing America and a changing view of presidential power against the backdrop of a deliberative, slow-moving, and methodical Congress.

Changing America

America's agrarian society and legislative dominance of the national government made a good match until the 20th century. Unhurried communication, leisurely transportation, and a simple economy fit a slow-moving Congress. However, as economic development quickened, conditions rapidly changed, calling for prompt governmental responses to new, different, and complex problems. Additionally, the crisis atmosphere of modern America, which since 1940 has produced several wars and many military actions, triggered congressional deference to presidential leadership. Domestic emergencies, notably those associated with the Depression and civil rights, also intensified the spotlight on the president. Only the president appeared to have the leadership capacity vital to responding quickly in crises.

Changing Conceptions of Presidential Power

Early in the 20th century, tension mounted between two ideas about presidential power. Advocates of an *activist presidency* believe in the expansive exercise of presidential power arguing that the Constitution does not restrict presidents to precisely defined powers but allows them to act in the national interest based on their implied powers. Proponents of a *passive presidency* insist that specific constitutional or congressional authorization must support presidential action.

Presidents holding the more legal and restricted view of presidential power maintained ascendance until the early 20th century, when Theodore Roosevelt and Woodrow Wilson made the case for a more expansive and unrestricted exercise of presidential power. Roosevelt asserted that only specific constitutional restrictions or specific restrictions imposed by Congress under its constitutional powers limit presidential action. Woodrow Wilson advanced the case for an activist presidency even more.

- His office is anything he has the sagacity and force to make it. . . .
- The Constitution . . . is a vehicle of life, and its spirit is always the spirit of the age.
- The President . . . [can] be as big a man as he can. His capacity will set the limit.[2]

Franklin D. Roosevelt laid the capstone for the activist presidency, declaring that it ". . . is preeminently a place of moral leadership" and that "[W]ithout leadership alert and sensitive to change, we are bogged up or lose our way . . . "[3] Since Roosevelt, the activist view has either guided or influenced presidents, even those who appeared more passive, such as Dwight D. Eisenhower and Gerald R. Ford. No longer merely a legal executive, performing specifically delineated functions, presidents now serve as head of state, opinion molder, legislative leader, chief administrator, and party leader.

The scales of presidential greatness tilt toward activist presidents. All presidents rated *great* or *near great* performed as activist presidents, including Abraham Lincoln, Theodore Roosevelt, Woodrow Wilson, Franklin Roosevelt, Harry Truman, and Ronald Reagan. Scholars, journalists, and the public at large rate activist presidents higher, except when major scandal or policy setbacks tarnish their records, which the Vietnam War did to Lyndon Johnson. More passive presidents, such as William Howard Taft and Herbert Hoover, normally rate no higher than *average* or *fair* on a scale of *great, near great, average, fair,* and *poor.*

The presidency attracts attention like a lightning rod. Liberal and progressive interests merit most of the credit for the expansion of presidential power since the New Deal, as they fought to enlarge the national government's role in American society. But, for example, two conservative Republican presidents, Richard M. Nixon and Ronald Reagan, exercised the presidency's expanded powers to pursue conservative policy objectives, fighting to reduce the national government's power and to restore power to the states.

Because both conservatives and liberals can use presidential power to achieve their goals, it serves as a means to an end. Sometimes, however, its misuse provokes controversy. Lyndon Johnson's escalation of the Vietnam War led to the deaths of some 58,000 Americans, and Richard Nixon's cover-up of the Watergate break-in produced a constitutional crisis. The presidency's enhanced powers make occupancy of the office even more important for conservatives and Republicans, liberals and Democrats, who want the upper hand in setting the national agenda. Ideological and political interests not in control of the presidency expose abuses in the exercise of that power to improve their prospects for winning the office. Most recently Presidents Clinton and Bush have faced the ire of the opposition regarding their alleged abuses of power.

Congressional Deliberation

Compared to the presidency, Congress changes methodically and responds to crises slowly. As a deliberative body with no one person to represent it, Congress moves at a measured pace whether to streamline the legislative process or to act on critical policy issues. Presidents need only call a press conference or issue a statement or propose a piece of legislation to spell out the executive's policy positions. In the public eye, presidents appear more responsive since congressional action on policies requires the approval of two houses and their respective committees and subcommittees. Not surprisingly, public opinion polls reveal more trust and confidence in the president than in Congress.

Although Congress often serves as the incubator of new ideas, it rarely receives credit. History books focus on presidencies and eras, such as Franklin Roosevelt and the New Deal, even though members of Congress may have developed a president's policy ideas long before his election. History credits Richard Nixon for the policy of revenue sharing between the national and state governments, but members of Congress introduced bills embodying this idea a decade earlier. Similarly President Ronald Reagan receives credit for supply-side economics and George W. Bush for various educational reforms, but members of Congress introduced those ideas well in advance of their presidencies.

The president's built-in advantages put Congress on the defensive as a reactor to the president's role as initiator. Presidents have increasingly used Executive Orders to implement their policies, especially when confronting Congressional opposition. Presidents Bush Sr., Bill Clinton, and George Bush Jr. used Executive Orders on such issues as homosexuality in the military and affirmative action. William G. Howell calls this *Power without Persuasion*, and Kenneth Mayer, *With the Stroke of a Pen*.[4]

The Courts and Presidential Power

On balance, Supreme Court decisions have generally confirmed expanded uses and protections of presidential power. In foreign affairs, for example, *U.S. v. Curtiss Wright Corporation* (1936), *U.S. v. Pink* (1942), and *Goldwater v. Carter* (1979) affirmed, respectively, that presidents possess the constitutional author-ity (1) to represent the United States as its organ or voice in international affairs, (2) to execute Executive Agreements with other nations, and (3) to unilaterally abrogate treaties without Senate approval. In domestic affairs, the Supreme Court upheld the president's power to remove executive branch appointees in *Myers v. U.S.* (1926), but not appointees to regulatory bodies in *Humphrey's Executor v. U.S.* (1935). Although presidents can exercise the right of executive privilege against divulging confidential communications within the executive branch, *U.S. v. Nixon* (1974) held that they may not do so in criminal proceedings against themselves nor as in *Clinton v. Jones* (1997) can they shield themselves from liability in the performance of nonofficial actions. Then in presidential-congressional relations, when Congress tried to eclipse presidential power through the legislative veto, which would have allowed Congress to reverse presidential actions in implementing legislation, the Supreme Court ruled that action unconstitutional in *I.N.S. v. Chadha* (1983), but in another case, *New York v. Clinton* (1998), the Supreme Court declared the line-item unconstitutional as a violation of separation of powers. These decisions are but a few of the many that show on the whole the rise in judicial support of presidential powers.

THE PARADOX OF PRESIDENTIAL POWER

If presidential power has increased, popular expectations of presidential performance have surged. Popular expectations now surpass the reach of presidential power. Or, stated differently, the promise of power now exceeds the performance of power. Disparity between promise and performance produces a breach between perception and reality. When the public expects more than a president can deliver, a credibility gap emerges. Why the breach? How does it affect the presidency?

Pedestal of Prominence

By the 1960s, American scholars and journalists had put the presidency on a pedestal of prominence far above the Founders' intentions, ascribing to presidents and the presidency these accolades:

- "the great engine of democracy;"
- "the American people's one authentic trumpet;"
- "a superb planning institution;" and
- "the pulpit of the nation."[5]

Several decades earlier, Woodrow Wilson foreshadowed this exalted reverence of the presidency, but his bold promise for the presidency failed to foresee the performance of Lyndon Johnson in Vietnam, Richard Nixon in Watergate, Bill Clinton in Whitewater and its attendant scandals, and George Bush Jr. in Iraq.

> The nation as a whole has chosen him, and is conscious that it has no other political spokesman. His is the only national voice in affairs. Let him once win the admiration and confidence of the country, and no other single force can withstand him, no combination of forces will easily overpower him. His position takes the imagination of the country. He is the representative of no constituency, but of the whole people. When he speaks in his true character, he speaks for no special interest. If he rightly interprets the national thought and boldly insists upon it, he is irresistible; and the country never feels the zest for action so much as when its President is of such insight and caliber.[6]

Sometimes presidents face "no-win" situations, not because of who they are but because of the built-in conflict between the public's demands and presidential limitations. Although the public easily identifies the president as the national leader, it does not know that presidents must attempt to avoid many landmines that would torpedo their efforts to lead: an intransigent bureaucracy, an intractable Congress, a cynical press, warring interest groups, economic surprises, and international crises.

Insulation and Isolation

Traveling in presidential limousines, Marine Corps helicopters, and Air Force One, surrounded by the Secret Service and fawning aides, and introduced by the sound of "Hail to the Chief," presidents lose touch with real life. As government programs expanded, especially during and after the New Deal, personnel increases paralleled the rise in presidential power, creating large executive branch bureaucracies. In 1939, their growth prompted creation of the Executive Office of the President, including the White House Staff, to improve presidential administration. Ironically, these well-intentioned efforts backfired. Rather than improving a president's outreach to the public, they often insulated and isolated him, causing presidents and their staffs to look like a king and his court. The staffs, protecting a president from direct and meaningful interaction with the public, provide him with their view of reality.

Before the upsurge of presidential power during the New Deal, Congress and political parties exercised greater restraint on presidential action. For much of American history, presidents neither addressed the Congress nor attended their party conventions, and before the advent of public opinion polling, they relied on congressional and party leaders to interpret public opinion. Now presidents serve as party leader and scriptwriter of the congressional agenda.

Presidential isolation threatens two fundamental purposes of the American political tradition: keeping political power within legitimate political boundaries and providing a clear view of reality. The reluctant and begrudging responses of Presidents Richard M. Nixon and William Jefferson Clinton to judicial and Congressional inquiries during their respective scandals challenged these two purposes. Claiming the doctrine of executive privilege allowed them to withhold information from Congress and the courts, Presidents Nixon and Clinton attempted to shield themselves from probes of unlawful activity. The courts, which generally rejected their claims of executive privilege, reduced presidential power by limiting the use of this doctrine. Ironically, in asserting presidential prerogatives, Nixon and Clinton left a weakened presidency.

Presidential Job Description

What if President Lyndon B. Johnson were only remembered for his Great Society domestic programs and not for the Vietnam War? What if President Richard M. Nixon were only remembered for his foreign policy in opening the door to China and not for the Watergate scandal? What if President George H. Bush were remembered for his foreign policy in the Gulf War and not for his lack of vision in domestic policy? When presidents do not perform well in both domestic and foreign policy, their records risk reduced stature on the pages of history.

The skills and times necessary for achievement in domestic policy do not coincide with those in foreign policy. Lyndon B. Johnson, perhaps the most skilled legislative strategist among all presidents, not only lacked understanding in foreign affairs but also served during the turbulent 1960s, which shortened the leash on presidential action in military operations. By contrast, Richard Nixon, one of history's most skilled presidents in foreign affairs, faced a Congress controlled by Democrats, who limited his potential for success in domestic policy. George H. Bush, who enjoyed unparalleled popularity and performance ratings through masterminding an international coalition against Iraq's Saddam Hussein, offered little or no vision in domestic policy. A complex presidential job description, broadly divided between domestic and foreign policy, tests effective performance on both fronts.

Changing popular demands may alter the presidential job description. President William Jefferson Clinton successfully challenged President George H. Bush's failure to provide vision in domestic policy during the 1992 campaign. Then, in the 2000 campaign, President George W. Bush connected

Vice President Al Gore with the moral scandals of the Clinton administration. Although one of history's brightest presidents, Clinton had to survive repeated moral challenges to his presidency, which limited his potential for success. Presidents Franklin D. Roosevelt and John F. Kennedy committed deeds comparable to President Clinton's, but the press did not probe their indiscretions.

Analysis of 20th-century presidents reveals a cycle or an ebb and flow between active and less active presidents. For example, following a period of more active presidents comes a period of less active presidents. Typically, the more active presidents maintain a more vigorous pace and pursue a more aggressive and expansive policy agenda. To illustrate, following the turbulent period of World War II, the Great Depression, and the Korean War with the active presidencies of Franklin D. Roosevelt and Harry S. Truman, the American public turned to a less active president, Dwight David Eisenhower. Then, after the tumultuous 1960s and early 1970s and the active presidencies of John F. Kennedy, Lyndon B. Johnson, and Richard M. Nixon, two less active presidents came on the scene, Jimmy Carter and Gerald R. Ford.

PRESIDENTIAL STYLE

Years	More Active	Less Active
1905–09	Roosevelt	
1909–13		Taft
1913–21	Wilson	
		Harding
		Coolidge
		Hoover
1933–53	Roosevelt	
	Truman	
1953–61		Eisenhower
1961–74	Kennedy	
	Johnson	
	Nixon	
1974–80		Ford
		Carter
1981–88	Reagan	
1989–92		Bush
1993–00	Clinton	
2001–	Bush	

Active presidents occasionally face judicial challenges, such as when the U.S. Supreme Court struck down portions of the New Deal early in Franklin D. Roosevelt's administration. Roosevelt fought back, however, and the Court capitulated by upholding his New Deal programs, a change now known as a "switch in time that saved nine." The Court recognized its weakness at the bar of public opinion to which Roosevelt had appealed.

The Iron Triangle and Bureaucratic Intransigence

How does a president manage a bureaucracy with its close ties to the Congress and interest groups? Presidents serve only four to eight years, but they must lead an enduring bureaucracy. Although constitutionally and theoretically the chief executive, presidents face Civil Service restrictions, which limit them to filling only 2,500 or so policy-making positions in a bureaucracy of several million personnel. Facing the bureaucracy's entrenched policy interests, civil service protection, and well-developed ties to Congress and interest groups, presidents have limited latitude as chief executive. For example, the late FBI Director J. Edgar Hoover served six presidents. Although some wanted to remove him, none did, because he had cultivated political strength with key members of Congress and interest groups.

Because the bureaucracy has enjoyed its greatest growth during liberal and Democratic administrations, conservative and Republican presidents claim another obstacle in leading the bureaucracy: ideological and political intransigence. Their argument goes like this: Bureaucrats, who gained office when liberal and Democratic policies expanded the bureaucracy, will naturally resist divergent presidential policy directions. Believing that the bureaucracy had opposed his policies during his first administration, President Richard M. Nixon decided to extend his outreach into the bowels of the bureaucracy by transferring White House loyalists to key bureaucratic positions during his second administration. The Watergate scandal short-circuited that effort. Democrats, however, also distrust the bureaucracy. Presidents Franklin D. Roosevelt and Lyndon B. Johnson created new bureaucratic agencies rather than place their new programs in the hands of existing departments and agencies. Johnson, for example, located his Great Society Program in the Executive Office of the President rather than in such Departments as Labor and Health, Education, and Welfare (forerunner of the Departments of Education, Housing and Urban Development, and Health and Human Services).

Campaigning and Governing: A Disconnect

Campaigning for the White House and governing in the White House differ. The criteria and background necessary for winning do not guarantee a successful presidency. Or otherwise said: A good candidate may not make a good president.

The U.S. Congress, especially the Senate, and state governorships serve as principal training grounds for presidents. From 1932 through 2000, all presidents, save one, General Dwight David Eisenhower, had served in either the U.S. Senate, the U.S. House of Representatives, or as a state governor. Harry S. Truman, John F. Kennedy, Lyndon B. Johnson, and Richard M. Nixon served in the Senate, whereas Gerald R. Ford and George H. Bush served in the U.S. House of Representatives. Five members of Congress also served as vice president before their election as president: Harry S. Truman, Lyndon B. Johnson, Richard M. Nixon, Gerald R. Ford, and George H. Bush. Governors elected president since 1932 include Franklin D. Roosevelt, Jimmy Carter, Ronald Reagan, William Jefferson Clinton, and George W. Bush.

Congressional experience offers many opportunities for presidents and presidential candidates: (1) familiarity with the ways of Washington; (2) knowledge of foreign affairs, especially in the Senate; (3) understanding of the legislative process; (4) leadership on major issues; and (5) exposure in the national media. But legislative and presidential leadership differ. Successful legislators emphasize negotiation and compromise to advance their ideas and bills through the complex machinations of the Congress. Successful presidents emphasize the direction and execution of policies contained in their agenda for the nation.

President Lyndon B. Johnson brought his superior legislative skill to the White House, where it failed him. In the Senate, he won by getting the votes of a majority of members, often doing that by wooing the whales, that is, the more important Senators, knowing that the minnows, that is, the less important Senators, would follow in their wake. As president, he attempted to win the public's support for such policies as Vietnam by winning the support of major labor, industrial, religious, and other national leaders, thinking that their constituencies would fall in line. Although presidents must do what Lyndon Johnson did, they also must successfully make their case to the public. On balance, winning the votes of a majority of fellow legislators spells success for a legislator, whereas winning the public's support is more likely to spell success for a president.

Governors come to the White House with administrative experience. They have learned how to develop and promote an agenda through popular and press appeal, interest group backing, and legislative support. But they lack the advantages of members of Congress, especially Senators: exposure to foreign affairs, access to the national media, and experience in Washington.

Candidate appeal and job training do not guarantee a successful presidency. John F. Kennedy had candidate appeal and congressional experience, but he lacked administrative preparation, which revealed itself in the Bay of Pigs debacle early in his presidency. Although he recovered from this fiasco, his early decision making showed insufficient command of the executive branch in foreign affairs. Jimmy Carter brought administrative experience as a governor to the White House, but he lacked knowledge of Washington. For at least two years, his administration stumbled without skillful political leadership to marshal support in Congress and elsewhere.

Presidential Honeymoons

Presidents take office for a *honeymoon*: a time of unknown duration when political leaders, the press, and others avoid intensive examination and criticism of their performance. Ironically, just when the political environment appears most favorable to their leadership, presidents may lack the administrative and political experience to convert that to their advantage. Then as their experience mounts, the political environment becomes more challenging.

President William Jefferson Clinton constantly faced political and ideological animosity and adversity throughout his administration. In fact, he may have had the shortest honeymoon of any president during the 20th century. Within the first hours of his administration, he issued two controversial Executive Orders to repeal President George H. Bush's restrictions on abortions and on military service by homosexuals. Immediate hostile reaction foreshadowed the hyperhostile environment he faced on health care, impeachment, and other issues. President George W. Bush, who assumed the presidency in a supercharged environment of Democratic and Republican attacks and counterattacks, had to deftly avoid stepping on political landmines to preserve his honeymoon. Despite Bush's efforts, six months into his administration most of his 2,500 nominations for senior policy positions in the bureaucracy remained unfilled. Threats from Senate Democrats to Bush nominees delayed his attempts to lead the executive branch.

The Permanent Campaign

The dust hardly settles on one presidential campaign before the next begins. A failed run for the presidency or a party's nomination may only set the stage for the next. Among those who ran and lost and ran again: Thomas E. Dewey (1944, 1948); Adlai E. Stevenson (1952, 1956); Richard M. Nixon (1960, 1968); Ronald Reagan (1976, 1980); and George W. Bush (1980, 1988). Rivals for the presidency begin to tout their policy ideas and put together their campaign organizations several years before the campaign and election.

President William Jefferson Clinton, however, added another dimension: Performing as president like a presidential candidate, he continued in campaign mode for eight years. Recognizing that the best defense is a good offense, the *permanent campaign* maintains a frenzied pace of public appearances and the constant advocacy of new ideas. Presidential aides must remain alert to their mission and the politics essential to its achievement. Reelection considerations dominate White House thinking and decision making. President George W. Bush has followed President Clinton's precedent of the permanent campaign.

Because the permanent campaign focuses on reelection, public opinion polls become exceedingly important. The extensive use of daily tracking polls by Presidents Ronald Reagan and William Jefferson Clinton raised serious questions. To what extent should daily tracking polls govern White House decision making? Should presidents govern in the national interest or in the interest of reelection? Admittedly, public opinion should influence presidential decision making, but how much? The permanent campaign tempts presidents and their advisors to rely unduly on public opinion and daily tracking polls, causing them to think less about what is right and more about what will advance the cause of reelection.

Balkanization

Supposedly, a president unifies the country as the nation's only elected leader, but as the head of his party and as the principal architect of national policies, he divides. As party leader and as an advocate of policies, a president automatically receives opposition from the other party and from those who oppose his policies. Furthermore, two factors worsen these divisions. First, since the mid-1960s, the public's declining trust in government and public officials has left presidents without a large and consistent reservoir of support for presidential leadership. Second, the balkanization of American society into an intensely competitive society diminishes deference to presidential leadership. In part these factors have contributed to President George W. Bush's generally lower job performance ratings, which have typically ranged between 45 and 55 percent.

America of the 1950s had fewer and less intense divisions: not so many interest groups, greater cooperation between the political parties, and only a mild conservative–liberal divide. During the 83rd Congress, 1953–54, the death of a Republican Senator reduced Republicans to a minority in the Senate, but Democrats did not make themselves the majority party. Contrast that with 2001 when a Republican Senator, James Jeffords (VT), became an Independent, costing Republicans their majority status. Democrats quickly moved to assert their standing as the majority party. Or consider the collegial relationship between the House Democratic and Republican leaders throughout the 1940s and 1950s. The only two men who served as Speaker then,

Democrat Sam Rayburn (TX) and Republican Joe Martin (MA), were close personal friends. By the 1990s, when Republican Newt Gingrich (GA) became Speaker, political animosity reigned. He and Democratic Leader Richard Gephardt (MO) hardly spoke to one another.

Ideology and Presidential Power

During the 20th century, most liberals argued for a stronger presidency, whereas most conservatives opposed them. Viewing the president as the catalyst for achieving the social and economic objectives of the New Deal, Fair Deal, New Frontier, and Great Society, liberals premised the nation's welfare on electing presidential activists. During these times, conservatives found themselves in opposition to their programs. Conservatives and Republicans, reacting to Franklin D. Roosevelt's election to four terms, successfully fought for ratification of the 22nd Amendment (1951) to limit presidential tenure to two terms or no more than 10 years. Ironically the 22nd Amendment precluded Presidents Eisenhower and Reagan from seeking third terms, which they would likely have won.

The election of activist, conservative Republican presidents, however, put the shoe on the other foot. Then conservative Republicans wanted activist presidents to turn back the advances of liberal public policies and to adopt conservative policies. So, perhaps whether conservatives and liberals favor activist presidents depends on "whose ox is being gored." Both conservatives and liberals appear more concerned with the use of presidential power to achieve ideological aims than they are with the proper constitutional exercise of that power. Thus, the ends of presidential power now play a major role in its justification.

The Expectations Game

Although expectations of presidents are now higher, presidents assume office with differing levels of expectations. Taking office as a minority president, having lost the popular vote, President George W. Bush benefited from lower expectations. To the surprise of many he significantly exceeded those expectations within the first six months of his administration by winning congressional passage of a major tax-reduction bill and by exceeding the critics' expectations for his first European trip. The partisan divide in Washington together with his lack of congressional and foreign policy experience lowered performance expectations. Later, still in an environment of lower expectations, he obtained passage of such key legislation as "No Child Left Behind," the Central American Free Trade Agreement, and a new energy policy. His successes in an environment of lower expectations made his performance look better. By contrast, high expectations can harm a president's public standing as it did for President George H. Bush, who failed to perform up to the level of popular anticipation after his extraordinary success in the Gulf War.

Trust versus Distrust

Presidents stand in a cross fire between conditions that generate power and others that diminish public trust. Recessions, depressions, inflation, and other critical social and economic problems focus more attention on the president and often initiate increases in presidential power. Asserting their power in response to the public's cry for action, presidents propose major policy initiatives. But their exercise of power may boomerang.

- Facing critical economic inflation, Gerald R. Ford passed out WIN (Whip Inflation Now) buttons, which quickly became a laughing stock, when his policies failed to produce results. His policy, failing to measure up to his power, resulted in lost trust.

- Reacting to problems in the healthcare industry, William Jefferson Clinton proposed major reforms, which would have created a large governmental bureaucracy. To support his proposals, he delivered an outstanding speech to a Joint Session of Congress. In spite of initial widespread public support, Clinton's reform proposals lost the battle for public opinion during congressional committee hearings and through critical media exposure. His proposals, unable to withstand political and popular scrutiny, lowered for a time the public's trust in his presidency.

- Early in his administration, George W. Bush lost public trust on environmental issues. Inheriting a nonexistent national policy on energy, he proposed an ambitious program to satisfy energy needs through expansion of the coal, oil, and nuclear energy industries. His energy proposals, however, conflicted with the public's perception of environmental needs, and damaged his popular standing. He had campaigned for office as an environmentalist, but he had also received substantial financial backing from coal, oil, and nuclear energy interests. The public wanted action on energy, but not at the expense of the environment. To shore up weakened public trust, President Bush scurried to curry favor with the environmental lobby, acting to increase pollution emission standards for the coal and automobile industries. Finally, during his second administration, Congress responded favorably to his call for a national energy policy.

Although popular expectations demand the exercise of presidential power to solve national problems, public trust does not always follow. With the best of intentions and after careful study of issues, presidents may act to solve problems only to find that the public sees matters differently. Presidents face the age-old conundrum: "Damned if you do, damned if you don't."

Reform and Its Limitations

When time appears most ripe for reform to reduce presidential power, why does little or no reform occur? Or if reform occurs, why may it backfire? Few times appeared more ripe for reform than during the scandal-prone Nixon and Clinton presidencies. Both presidents faced intense congressional investigations over several years, including impeachment charges. Richard M. Nixon resigned from office rather than face the likelihood of Senate action to remove him from office. William Jefferson Clinton, impeached by the Republican-controlled House of Representatives, won a Senate vote against conviction when in a closely divided Senate Democrats voted for him, preventing the necessary two-thirds majority for conviction.

Why did these presidencies fail to produce major lasting reforms to limit presidential power? Both prompted many calls for reform, but when the crises subsided, the push for reform died. American history documents that crises usually precede reforms, but the momentum for reform recedes when the crisis dies.

Among proposals to rectify the imbalance of power between the president and Congress during the Nixon and Clinton scandals were these: (1) require that the president report to Congress on steps he has taken to implement new laws, (2) limit the scope of executive privilege, and (3) appoint an independent prosecutor to investigate abuses of power in the executive branch.

Ironically, through its existing powers, especially the power of oversight, Congress already possesses authority: (1) to investigate the executive branch to determine presidential compliance with congressional intent concerning the implementation of all laws and to investigate presidential malfeasance, misfeasance, and nonfeasance in office; (2) to cite the president for contempt if he fails to provide requested information; and (3) to bring suit in federal court seeking a court order to provide the information.

Following the Watergate scandal, Congress passed the Ethics in Government Act of 1978, which allowed the Attorney General to request that the federal courts name an *independent counsel*, sometimes called a special prosecutor, to investigate and prosecute violations of federal law by the president and other senior officials. Later, this act troubled both Democrats and

Republicans. Democrats did not like independent counsel Kenneth Starr's investigation of William Jefferson Clinton, whereas Republicans thought that Attorney General Janet Reno should have requested an independent counsel to investigate alleged violations of campaign finance laws by President Clinton and others. In 1999 Congress let the act die.

The issue is not whether Congress can check presidential power but whether it has the will.

In defense of Congress, however, history shows that it faces two major challenges, particularly with respect to campaign finance reform: drafting laws (1) that close all the loopholes and (2) that do not violate the First Amendment, which mandates that "Congress shall make no law . . . abridging the freedom of speech or of the press." Campaign finance reforms invite circumvention, as candidates, parties, and contributors look for loopholes around a reform. Limiting campaign funding and spending without violating the First Amendment challenges the most artful of legislative bill drafters.

Some ambitious reforms are stillborn. Because change in American politics generally occurs incrementally or slowly, typically major and abrupt changes do not receive favorable consideration. For example, Congress would likely never consider seriously the British vote of no confidence. Allowing Congress to vote no confidence in a president would lead to a new election, thus permitting Congress to undermine a president's popular election and changing the Constitution's separation of powers. Of course, as a constitutional amendment such a reform would require two-thirds approval by both houses of Congress, and by three-fourths of state legislatures or state ratifying conventions.

Efforts to investigate and impeach Presidents Nixon and Clinton consumed the Congress for many months, diverting its attention from other pressing issues and also from reforms introduced to limit presidential power. But even after prolonged investigations, many members of Congress said they did not want to weaken the presidency but only to check the behavior of these individual presidents.

CONCLUSION

According to Isaac Newton's first law, the law of inertia, an object once in motion will continue in motion unless acted upon by outside forces. In 1787 the Founders set in motion an object, presidential power, whose momentum has gradually accelerated, creating a force far more powerful than the Founders' intentions. As power increased, so did expectations. The combination of increasing power and rising expectations generated friction as outside forces acted to limit presidential power and as presidential performance failed to live up to expectations. Simply put, the history of the presidency reveals a disparity between the power and promise of presidential leadership and presidential performance.

Notes

[1]See generally, Edward S. Corwin, *The President: Office and Powers, 1787–1957* (New York: New York University Press, 1957); and Max Farrand, *The Framing of the Constitution of the United States* (New Haven, CT: Yale University Press, 1913).

[2]Woodrow Wilson, *Constitutional Government in the United States* (New York: Columbia University Press, 1911): 69–71, 77–79.

[3]Anne O'Hare McCormick, "Roosevelt's View of the Big Job," *New York Times Magazine* (September 11, 1932): 2.

[4]See: William G. Howell, *Power Without Persuasion* (Princeton, NJ: Princeton University Press, 2003); and Kenneth Mayer, *With the Stroke of a Pen: Executive Orders and Presidential Power* (Princeton, NJ: Princeton University Press, 2002).

[5]For a full assessment of these and other quotations about the American presidency, see Thomas E. Cronin, "The Textbook Presidency and Political Science," *Congressional Record* (October 5, 1970): S17102–S17115.

[6]As cited in James MacGregor Burns, *Presidential Government* (Boston: Houghton Mifflin Company, 1965): 96.

Chapter Two

The Law of Rhetoric

The Stagecraft of Presidential Leadership

The overlap of the electoral campaign with the process of governing means that the distinction between campaigning and governing is being effaced.

—Jeffrey K. Tulis[1]

INTRODUCTION TO THE LAW OF RHETORIC

> Successful presidential leadership requires the merger of good campaigning with effective governing and the recognition that presidential rhetoric is much more than the spoken word. To effectively communicate their ideas and policies to the public, presidents must properly stage their rhetoric as in a campaign, recognizing that the substance of excellent ideas and policies requires an appropriate style of presentation. So, just as campaigning and governing must come together so, too, must style and substance.

Jeffrey K. Tulis concludes that as soon as presidential candidates win office, they must translate their campaign skills into governing the nation. Campaigning and governing are now like a seamless garment. Credited with being the first to govern by campaigning, President Clinton's White House schedule looked like a campaign schedule always running in high gear. President George W. Bush's White House merely refined the art and science of campaigning while governing. Clinton and Bush bonded campaigning and governing by turning the White House into "campaign central," preparing their schedules as though they were on the campaign trail. Since the nation's founding, rhetoric properly staged has gradually evolved into the essence of both good campaigning and effective governing.

ERAS OF RHETORICAL CHANGE

From George Washington to George W. Bush, nothing about the presidency has changed more than rhetoric, and nothing has changed the presidency more than rhetoric. Changes in the presidency and presidential rhetoric occurred gradually, evolving alongside changes in society and government. As both society and government changed, moving from simplicity to complexity, rhetoric became more important to presidential leadership.[2]

Historically the evolution of rhetorical leadership passed through three eras—constitutional, conventional, and contemporary—with rhetorical leadership differing in each era. All of this raises important questions. Why did rhetoric become the catalytic agent of change? How has rhetoric changed the presidency? Are these changes healthy for American democracy?

The Constitutional Era

Congressional Government, the title of Woodrow Wilson's classic explanation of American government in 1883,[3] cast Congress on center stage in the leading role of American government—a role only rarely played by presidents from George Washington through William McKinley. Not only in power and influence but also rhetorically presidents played a subordinate role to the Congress.

Daniel Webster, Henry Clay, and John C. Calhoun, who never served as presidents, enjoyed far better rhetorical reputations than any presidents of their times. Because the Congress, particularly the U.S. House of Representatives, played the role prescribed by the Founders as the "people's branch of government," presidents delivered few public addresses and with only rare exceptions maintained a substantial distance from the electorate. Congressional debates and not presidential addresses generally produced not only greater quantity but also a higher quality of rhetoric. Only rarely would the rhetoric of a Lincoln capture the hearts of Americans, and even then, recognition of his rhetorical success occurred more after his death than during his presidency.

Alexander Hamilton was among the few Founders who wanted an active presidency. Most wanted a passive presidency, which reacted and responded to congressional action rather than an active presidency, which initiated action and communication with the Congress. They also believed that presidential power centered in the office of the presidency, not in individual presidents. According to the Founders, the office of the presidency rather than individual presidents would serve as the primary unifying force of the nation. Thus, although presidential rhetoric was not unimportant, its importance centered in unifying the nation through the office of the president, not in establishing governing coalitions for individual presidents. Only later when the focus of presidential power shifted from the office of the president to individual presidents did presidential rhetoric begin to play a consistently major role in American public life.

Andrew Jackson, normally considered the first to use rhetoric to fashion direct popular appeals and to form a popular mandate for an individual president, stands out as a rare exception to the norm in the Constitutional Era. Using rhetoric to build a new governing coalition, Jackson stirred the populace to support him and his ideas of "Jacksonian Democracy." This emphasis on establishing a popular tie between president and populace evolved gradually between the presidencies of Andrew Jackson and Theodore Roosevelt. For the most part, however, presidents in the Constitutional Era used rhetoric in accord with the Founders' intentions.

The Conventional Era

Theodore Roosevelt and Woodrow Wilson shifted the bedrock of presidential power from the Constitution and statutory law to popular support. By appealing directly to the people in support of their policy initiatives, presidents in the Conventional Era often pressured Congress to respond to popular opinion, making rhetoric a presidential weapon in separation-of-power conflicts with the Congress.

Franklin D. Roosevelt expanded on the precedents of Theodore Roosevelt and Woodrow Wilson, who had assumed major new roles by personally leading their political parties, publicly delivering the State of the Union and other addresses to Congress, and promoting their positions on important issues, such as child labor and the League of Nations. By perfecting the use of presidential press conferences, speaking directly to the people through radio addresses, which his calming "fireside chats" made famous, and traveling often to the hinterland to connect with the public directly, Franklin D. Roosevelt transformed the presidency into the focal point of American government.

What Franklin D. Roosevelt was to the era of radio, John F. Kennedy became to the era of television, which magnified even more the presidency as the vital center of American government. Kennedy opened presidential press conferences to live televised coverage and allowed television cameras into the White House to film him and his family. After Kennedy, no longer would newspaper reporters dominate the White House press corps. Television newscasters, technicians, and camera crews became a major, often dominant, part of the White House press corps. Before television's matriculation at the White House, newspaper reporters never rivaled presidents for media attention, but after television arrived, anchors on network newscasts and White House correspondents for the networks became fixtures in the public eye.

Ronald Reagan, as no other, personified the presidency of the Conventional Era, placing himself at the center of high drama as events allowed. When earthquakes, floods, hurricanes, and tornadoes devastated the land, television fed the footage of his trips to the tragedy-torn areas into the public's living room. When American soldiers gave their last ounce of devotion on foreign soil, he was there at Andrews Air Force Base to receive their remains, to console their loved ones, and to comfort the nation. No one was more adept at feeling the pain and sorrow of Americans on such occasions than Ronald Reagan. Sometimes known as "The Great Communicator," he exuded passion and compassion on center stage. But his presence on center stage was not daily. Like a great actor, he spoke his lines on center stage with maximum effect and then moved off stage.

The Contemporary Era

William Jefferson Clinton and George W. Bush defined a new era of rhetorical leadership. While the spoken word dominated the Conventional Era, image governs the Contemporary Era. Rhetorical leadership is now much more than speech. As television expanded through countless cable outlets and as the Internet commanded increased public attention, creating a successful presidential image more and more dictated the direction of White House planning. Besides wanting presidents to command center stage with the spoken word, White House staffs also want to surround them with appropriate props. So now the White House is the choreographer of presidential rhetoric, staging events to fashion the image of presidential leadership.

When President George W. Bush flew an S-3B "Viking" fighter plane from California to the U.S. *Abraham Lincoln* to mark the cessation of major hostilities in Iraq in early May 2003, he spoke to over 5,000 sailors and marines on deck. Who can remember the president's words? But who has forgotten his breathtaking arrival on the fighter plane, his dramatic disembarking in a pilot's uniform, and the spectacular stage on deck for his speech? Pictures eclipsed words in power and memorability with one fateful exception. "Mission Accomplished," the large banner unfurled behind the president on the aircraft carrier, came back to haunt him when hundreds of American troops soon fell prey to insurgent attacks. Events overtook rhetoric as they did for his father, who proclaimed, "Read my lips" during his successful 1988 campaign. When he compromised on his word before the 1992 campaign, voters connected the dots and removed him from office.

President William Jefferson Clinton's staff also staged happenings. When he announced plans for using federal funds to add 100,000 police officers in America's municipalities, several rows of police officers in their blue uniforms stood behind and around him. This law-enforcement image overshadowed the words President Clinton spoke on that occasion. Given his soft-on-crime image, he welcomed this picture on television news and on the front pages of newspapers.

Presidents in the Contemporary Era must compete with many other newsmakers for a precious few seconds on news stories. Because presidential rhetoric is not only what presidents say but also the images they convey, when, where, and with whom they say something becomes as important as what they say. Presidents must fight hard to stay ahead of the news curve. To fall behind the news curve or even to stay even with it conveys an image of poor leadership.

So presidents must remain nimble of foot, constantly looking for ways to lead rather than to react to the news, especially negative news. Rather than to await the passing of a downward economic spiral early in his administration, President George W. Bush announced plans for tax reductions to stimulate an economic rebound. His economic recovery package became the centerpiece of political discussion nationally and in the Congress. In 1995, rather than let congressional Republicans shut down the national government during a budgetary impasse between the president and Congress, President William Jefferson Clinton aggressively announced plans to keep key offices open to assist the American public.

The Contemporary Era requires presidents to become the initiator-in-chief of news stories. In effect, the White House is now its own 24-hour-cable news channel. Not only do presidents in the Contemporary Era deliver more speeches, but they also travel to more places to deliver them. Presidential speeches have become more "sound bite" than substance. To command the lead story on the evening news, presidents must present an image, complete with a captivating "sound bite" and an appealing backdrop to attract the attention of television news directors. The perception of leadership has become as important as the reality of leadership or, simply put, looking like a leader is now as important as being a leader, and perhaps sometimes more so.

Rhetorical leadership in the Contemporary Era is both image-motivated and impulse-driven. Whereas the Kennedy and Reagan presidencies were image-motivated during the Conventional Era, those of Bill Clinton and George W. Bush added impulse-driven to image-motivated during the Contemporary Era. Ironically, despite their ideological and other differences, Presidents Clinton and Bush used the same rhetorical strategy and tactics to govern. Myriad quick and calculated rapier-like appearances on the stage of national and international news mark their presidencies. What the "no-huddle" offense is to football, presidential rhetoric is to the Contemporary Era. Or, put another way, presidential rhetoric is like currency, which presidents spend quickly and in large sums.

RHETORICAL CURRENCY

Just as Mr. Clinton used the rhetoric of a "New Democrat" to appeal to the heartland of America, Mr. Bush employed "compassionate conservatism" to resonate with the concerns and values of Middle America. Because Middle America perceived the Democratic Party as too liberal and the Republican Party as too conservative, Messrs. Clinton and Bush had to lead their respective parties to the center. "New Democrat" and "Compassionate Conservative" became the rhetorical currency they spent to achieve this aim.

Rhetorical Change Agents

Theodore Roosevelt's "New Nationalism," Franklin Roosevelt's "New Deal," Harry Truman's "Fair Deal," John F. Kennedy's "New Frontier," and Lyndon Johnson's "Great Society" stand out among the great presidential campaign slogans. But they bear an important difference from "New Democrat" and "Compassionate Conservatism." As the center of gravity of power in the Democratic and Republican Parties shifted to the left and right, respectively, beginning during the 1960s, the two parties found themselves out of sync with most Americans, who are centrist and not ideologically attracted to the left and right. Increasingly, candidates for presidential nominations in the Democratic and Republican parties felt compelled to move to the left and right, respectively, to win the nomination, but then obliged to move to the middle to appeal to mainstream America. When candidates, such as Republican Barry Goldwater in 1964 and Democrat George McGovern in 1972, failed to shift gears, they lost landslide elections.

Clinton and Bush, however, recognizing the need to broaden their electoral appeal, crafted rhetorical slogans to reduce negative popular perceptions of their parties and to broaden their popular appeal. Because the public perceived Bill Clinton and his party as soft on crime, he fashioned rhetoric to toughen their image, including calls for federal funds to add 100,000 police officers on American streets. By contrast, recognizing that the public felt Republicans lacked empathy for the less fortunate, Bush crafted such rhetoric as "no child left behind" to counter the public's negative perceptions. Rhetoric now serves to harden and to soften popular images of the parties and their candidates as they counter negative popular perceptions and appeal to middle America.

Rhetorical Opportunism

Presidents and presidential candidates sometimes benefit from the rhetorical *faux pas* and behavior of their predecessors. To emphasize his opposition to tax increases, President George Bush Sr. said: "Read my lips," but later he failed to keep his word. Then, as the economy lay dormant, a photographer snapped his picture on a yacht off the coast of Maine, hardly an endearing picture to Americans out of work. In both instances, then-presidential candidate William Jefferson Clinton rhetorically capitalized on President Bush's mistakes.

When broken promises and scandals rocked the administration of President Clinton, President Bush Jr. inherited an excellent political opportunity to paint an ethical contrast with his predecessor. Whereas scandals plagued Mr. Clinton throughout his administration, Mr. Bush found his first year filled with international conflicts, such as the downed plane in China and the events of September 11, 2001. Forced into the role of commander in chief, Mr. Bush encouraged Americans as he led diplomatic and military actions around the world. Then the Iraqi War in 2003 manifestly multiplied his rhetorical opportunities, not only setting up even more opportunities to use his rhetorical skill and popular appeal but also challenging his rhetorical abilities as the War wore on.

By expanding the agenda of his rhetorical slogan, "compassionate conservatism," he crafted a pragmatic and progressive conservatism: showcasing the benefits of democracy and capitalism to the world; expanding welfare reform; reforming expensive and expansive entitlement programs; eliminating partial-birth abortion; fighting for "no child left behind" initiatives; standing for "faith-based" initiatives; and advocating tax relief. That is precisely what his father failed to do. President George Herbert Walker Bush inherited high popularity ratings from the 1991 Gulf War, but he failed to translate them into rhetorical advances in pursuit of policy objectives, thus allowing his challenger in 1992, William Jefferson Clinton, to make a creditable case against him as disengaged and out of touch.

Although Mr. Clinton did not face the same challenges and in turn experience the same opportunities for presidential greatness, the scandals of his personal life degraded his opportunities to play a larger role on the political and international stage. For much of his eight years, Clinton found himself in a defensive posture, swimming against the high tide of personal scandal. Seeking to keep afloat by redefining the meaning of such simple words as *is* and *alone* in the Monica Lewinsky saga, Clinton left a legacy that created rhetorical opportunities for Bush.

When asked under oath in grand jury testimony if he had had any "sex of any kind, in any manner, shape or form" with a White House intern, Monica Lewinsky, Mr. Clinton said: "It depends on what the meaning of the word 'is' is." Then when asked if the two of them had ever been alone, he compounded his obfuscation by saying: "it depends on how you define 'alone.'"

The Clinton scandal was as much an outgrowth of the dramatic change in morals as the misbehavior of one man in office. Clinton attempted to govern under the premise that the only truth is private truth, believing that without a unified public truth he would never be condemned for any action as along as he denied knowledge or responsibility. Ultimately America's historic understanding of a unified public truth caught up with him.

The dark cloud of a criminal indictment swirled like a tornado ready to touch down until the day before he left office. On January 19, 2001, he avoided the possibility of a criminal indictment by agreeing to make two admissions: (1) confessing to false statements under oath about his relationship with Ms. Lewinsky; and (2) consenting to give up his law license for five years.

Clinton's rhetorical obfuscation set the stage of Bush's rhetorical simplification. Bush resolved to assign clear meanings to words, to restore traditional morality to presidential rhetoric, clearly contrasting good and evil, right and wrong, truth and falsehood. The backdrop of Clinton's behavior and the events of September 11, 2001, and the War Against Terrorism combined to give Bush these opportunities, allowing him to use such language as "axis of evil" to describe Iraq, Iran, and North Korea.

Devaluation of Rhetorical Currency

Harry S. Truman delivered fewer than 100 speeches per year during his presidency, but not so with Presidents Clinton and Bush, whose speeches easily exceed 500 per year. Presidents now rush breathlessly from speech to speech and event to event. Not only are presidential speeches greater in number today but they are also so shorter in length. In these shorter speeches, sound bites and slogans dominate rather than reasoned consideration of complicated issues. Presidents now produce more rhetoric, but with less value.

Spectacle is more important than speech. Speeches, even if worthy of the term *speech*, have become part of presidential image making. The value of presidential rhetoric now rests less in what a president says and more in how and where he says it, making form more important than substance. Presidents do not so much contribute to a substantive dialogue on major issues as they seek to control the dialogue through style. Speeches are like accent pieces on a table rather than the centerpiece. Or put another way, they accent presidential presence more than they define the essence of a president's policies.

Adlai E. Stevenson's presidential candidacies in 1952 and 1956 left behind a legacy of superior rhetoric in well-reasoned speeches, which addressed major public issues. In 1968 presidential candidate Richard M. Nixon delivered lengthy policy addresses via radio, often on radio time purchased by his campaign. In the Contemporary Era, however, candidates are more likely to issue position papers than to deliver major policy addresses. Like blitzkrieg warfare, presidential campaigns require swift and continuing movement, hardly the setting for thoughtful and lengthy analysis of issues.

The same is true of presidential speechmaking, where blitzkrieg rhetoric helps to keep opponents on the defensive and off balance. Even before President Bush left the aircraft carrier *Abraham Lincoln*, where he announced the cessation of major hostilities in Iraq, political opponents had already begun to decry his use of that stage. But before their criticisms could take hold in the public mind, he flew off to other events the very next day, even changing the subject from the war to the economy.

Presidential speeches are now more ceremonial and less deliberative, and the stage is more important than the lines spoken on stage. Even the best and most memorable presidential addresses suffer from being overshadowed by their staging. Because presidential speeches are less likely to have memorability over time and in the flow of history, presidents do not so much speak to the ages as they do to the moment.

Great presidents have left behind great contributions to political rhetoric, including Abraham Lincoln's "Four score and seven years ago" from his Gettysburg Address, Theodore Roosevelt's "A Square Deal for every man and every woman in the United States" from his Address to the Boys' Progressive League, Franklin D. Roosevelt's "The only thing we have to fear is fear itself" from his First Inaugural Address, and John F. Kennedy's "Ask not what your country can do for you; ask what you can do for your country" from his Inaugural Address. Contemporary presidents may speak great lines, but they are more likely to get lost in the fast pace of American life and the strategy of blitzkrieg rhetoric.

RHETORICAL STRATEGY

Machiavelli's *The Prince* appropriately uses this title, "How a Prince Must Act in Order to Gain Reputation" to discuss the critical importance of a leader's image.[4] Today, Machiavelli could title this chapter "How a President Must Act in Order to Gain Reputation." Looking presidential, the image, has become exceedingly important for contemporary presidents, especially as they face an adversarial media and a divided society. Presidents and their staffs must follow a strategy that will keep them out in front of adversarial attacks, knowing that the best defense is a good offense, and they must attempt to build national unity in an increasingly divisive society. Planning to stage the spoken word now occupies considerable time in the White House. Influencing the success of these plans are 13 factors.

Maintaining Movement and Momentum

Knowing that a moving target is more difficult to hit than a stationary target, presidential rhetoric plays an important role in creating a presidential image of positive action and policy initiatives. By announcing new appointments and heralding new policy initiatives, presidents can keep the opposition on the defensive, creating in the public's mind the image of a president producing solutions to their problems while opponents obstruct his efforts.

President George W. Bush did this in many ways, including the well-publicized judicial nominations of Miguel Estrada, Charles Pickering, and Priscilla Owens, which Senate Democrats filibustered, thus enabling him to paint them as obstructionists. In each instance, he appealed not only to his conservative base but also to Hispanics with Estrada, Southerners with Pickering, and women with Owens. In like manner, President Clinton maintained movement and momentum by regularly announcing new programs, especially on issues that would peel off popular support from Republicans, such as increased funding for judicial and criminal justice programs, and welfare reform.

Countering Negative Images

Successful rhetorical strategy requires overcoming negative personal images. President Clinton, suffering from his negative image as a playboy president, announced that he would have three leading clergymen serve as his spiritual counselors. Also when he went to church, he carried a Bible with him as he exited the front door of Foundry United Methodist Church. President Bush, suffering from the harsh image of uncaring conservatism, added *compassionate* to *conservatism* and proposed many initiatives to demonstrate that he was caring.

Also he made a special point of reaching out publicly to groups estranged from conservatism. During his very first Sunday in office in January 2001, he publicly attended a large black church in Washington.

Other presidents have acted in similar ways. President Eisenhower, a five-star general, left office by warning Americans of the danger of the "military-industrial complex." John F. Kennedy lessened the sting of his Roman Catholic identity by boldly appearing before several thousand Southern Baptist pastors, declaring that he would conduct his presidency independent of Roman Catholic and Vatican interests. Wanting to shed his racist image as a Southerner, Lyndon B. Johnson became the foremost champion of civil rights, claiming credit for the two most far-reaching pieces of civil rights legislation since the Civil War, the Civil Rights Act of 1964 and the Voting Rights Act of 1965. Richard M. Nixon, a hard-core anticommunist, opened the door to China.

Displaying Vigor and Strength

Because softness and weakness never appear on any list of successful leadership attributes, presidents and presidential candidates must take precautions to avoid these traits. If they do not, they may fatally flaw their presidency or presidential candidacy. For example, in 1972 the odds-on favorite to win the Democratic presidential nomination, U.S. Senator Edmund Muskie (D, ME), appeared on the front cover of *Time* magazine as the likely winner of the Democratic nomination, but later he made the mistake of crying on the front steps of the *Manchester Union-Leader* (New Hampshire) newspaper after it had personally attacked his wife. When the public interpreted his weeping as weakness, his campaign plummeted. In 1976 President Gerald Ford refused to exercise strong leadership and remove his Secretary of Agriculture Earl Butz, who had made racist comments. In 1980, President Jimmy Carter lost to Ronald Reagan in part because the public perceived him as weak and soft in the conduct of foreign and military policy.

Presidents and presidential candidates must appear resolute and steadfast. Indeed, sometimes they win while losing so long as their image exudes firmness and tenacity. President Richard Nixon fought hard, but lost two Senatorial confirmation votes on nominees from the South for U.S. Supreme Court Justice, but he won while losing. Because he wanted to strengthen his appeal and that of his party in the South, the Senate's votes against two Southerners added luster to his southern appeal, contributing in the long run to what was then the emerging Republican majority in the South.

By far the best-known example of this tactic occurred in 1948 when President Harry S. Truman called the Republican-controlled 80th Congress into Special Session and charged them with an agenda, which they promptly refused to act upon. He then took a whistle-stop tour throughout America, calling the Republican Congress a "Do-Nothing Congress," which catapulted him to victory. Truman was at his lowest point in personal popularity when he called Congress into session. Likewise, so was President Clinton when House Speaker Newt Gingrich (R, GA) attempted to shut down the national government in 1995. By not caving in to this effort, he began his political recovery, which ultimately led to his easy reelection in 1996. President Bush also established strength by refusing to cave in to Democrats and the General Accounting Office in their efforts to force his release of the names of energy industry officials who met with Vice President Dick Cheney while he formulated the Bush administration's energy policy. President Bush's refusal to buckle to Senate Democrats in fights for his judicial nominees and for John Bolton to serve as Ambassador to the United Nations also stood him in good stead as a leader of conviction.

Vetoing or threatening to veto a bill stands out as one of a president's best weapons to negate the appearance of softness and weakness. Many presidents, such as Nixon and Ford, have used this tactic, especially when facing a Congress controlled by the other party. Historically, in perhaps the best-known example of vetoing or threatening to veto bills, President Truman challenged the Republican-controlled 80th Congress from 1947 to 1949. This type of leadership can enable a president to make a forceful case to the public and to put the opposing party on the defensive.

Understanding Consensus and Conviction

President Lyndon B. Johnson wrapped himself in the mantle of a popular consensus leader after his landslide victory in 1964, using his popularity to gain Congressional enactment of his bold vision for a Great Society, but when his popular support faded during the Vietnam War, he claimed conscience and conviction as the motive of his actions. Because presidents ride on the roller coaster of public opinion, they face differing needs when riding high than when nose-diving. Presidents with high popularity ratings, such as George W. Bush had immediately after the wars in Afghanistan and Iraq, can wear the mantle of a popular consensus leader, but when their popular support wanes, as President Bush's did during the protracted War on Terrorism, they often eschew consensus leadership, seeking to claim the mantle of "a profile in courage."

Traveling to Avoid Political Difficulties

When facing political trouble at home, presidents beginning with Woodrow Wilson have traveled widely to distract attention from their difficulties. Wilson traveled extensively overseas to build support for his proposed League of Nations and then he traveled throughout America to sell it to the public. As the political fires of Watergate singed President Nixon's reputation, he traveled overseas more frequently. Similarly, during the Clinton administration, when various scandals threatened his reputation, he became the most widely traveled president in American history. Inasmuch as the Constitution gives presidents almost unilateral responsibility for foreign and military affairs, they can shift their focus from the domestic to the international arena to distract attention from their domestic difficulties where constitutionally their power is much weaker.

Centralizing Praise and Decentralizing Blame

Centralizing praise and decentralizing blame is an important White House calling card. Command center stage when events and policies go well, but move off stage when they do not. In modern times, no one did this more effectively than President Reagan, who earned the title of "The Teflon President," because he deftly decentralized blame. For example, serious problems in two Departments, Interior and Energy, never touched him, because he kept them at arm's length, tying them to the Secretaries in those Departments. Similarly international scandals in Iran and Nicaragua hardly touched him, but they did affect such subordinates as Oliver North.

Presidents need to occupy center stage when events go well for them but shift the blame to others when they do not. The wars in Afghanistan and Iraq, which far exceeded expectations for quick and precise endings, allowed President Bush to bask in the limelight of their success. However, when poll numbers decline and events turn sour, presidents need scapegoats, which President Bush also used when the economy was not doing so well and trouble surfaced at the Securities and Exchange Commission and in the Department of the Treasury. He quickly arranged for replacing the Chairman of the SEC and the Secretary of Treasury with new faces. Then he attacked Democrats in Congress as obstructionists for failing to act promptly on his economic recovery package, including tax reductions.

Being Open and Approachable

Presidents sometimes struggle with being open and approachable to others, especially under duress. The more the Vietnam War produced bad results, the more withdrawn President Lyndon B. Johnson became. The same was true of President Richard M. Nixon during Watergate. In both instances, their withdrawal made them appear less democratic and less responsive to public opinion. Interestingly, both started out with the appearance of an open and an accessible style. Lyndon Johnson was known for his love of "pressing the flesh" on the campaign trail and in other public events throughout the country, so much so that the Secret Service expressed concern for his safety and security. Then Richard Nixon, inheriting the presidency from what had become Lyndon Johnson's closed and unapproachable style, subtly presented the opposite image. Where Lyndon Johnson had stood behind a massive lectern with a large presidential seal on the front and a score or so of media microphones on top, Richard Nixon stood behind a single microphone on a simple stand with no massive lectern or presidential seal in front of him, creating the image of openness. Although Richard Nixon won one of the greatest landslide elections in 1972, his high popularity plummeted in the face of Watergate tribulations.

Capitalizing on a Predecessor's Image Problems

President Jimmy Carter, assuming office after the debacles of Vietnam and Watergate and their closed presidencies, set about to create an open presidency. Carter walked in his 1977 Inaugural Parade, held "Town Meetings" for citizens to talk directly with the President, forbade the Marine Corps Band from playing "Hail to the Chief," reduced the amount of limousine service for White House personnel, and removed large numbers of television sets from the White House. Capitalizing on a predecessor's image problems is commonplace. John F. Kennedy, who played more golf than Dwight D. Eisenhower, had the putting green removed from outside the Oval Office, because Eisenhower had the reputation of spending too much time on the putting green and at the Burning Tree Country Club.

Playing the Expectations Game

President George W. Bush benefited as perhaps no other president from the expectations game. From his 2000 campaigns for nomination and election and throughout his presidency, he benefited from a low bar of expectations, which he consistently exceeded. After his loss to U.S. Senator John McCain in the New Hampshire primary, pundits thought his campaign was unraveling, but he convincingly defeated McCain in the South Carolina primary and went on to win the nomination easily. Then during his race for the presidency with Vice President Al Gore, critics thought Bush could not stand up to Gore in debate, but he did. During his tenure, especially before major speeches and critical decisions, experts lowered the bar of expectations, thinking he might fail, but each time he confounded their prognostications, getting major legislation passed and defying doubters in Iraq and Afghanistan.

Another president written off by the media, Harry S. Truman inherited the office with little or no preparation on the death of President Franklin D. Roosevelt in 1945. Defying the pundits' odds, he made several of the most important foreign and military policy decisions ever made by any president. He decided to drop the atomic bomb on Hiroshima and Nagasaki and to create the Truman Plan, Marshall Doctrine, and the North Atlantic Treaty Organization (NATO) for the rebuilding and protection of Europe. Then in 1948 hardly a soul thought he could win when he not only faced a formidable Republican challenger, Thomas E. Dewey, but also confronted two third-party candidates from his own party.

Whether with Bush or Truman or other candidates facing a low bar of expectation, rhetoric customarily plays a part in their ability to rise above the low bar. Bush's speeches received substantial praise, even from his critics, while Truman had the ability to motivate people with his down-to-earth manner and rhetoric. Bush's speechwriting team merits much credit for crafting language appropriate to his style of speaking. Although Truman did not have a speechwriting team, he had advisors and his own intuitive judgment, which enabled him to craft such slogans and sayings as "The Do-Nothing Congress" and "The buck stops here."

Among those who failed in part because of a high bar of expectations was George Romney (R, MI), who was the odds-on favorite to win the Republican nomination in 1968. But after returning from a trip to inspect progress in the Vietnam War, Romney said the generals had "brainwashed" him. And from that point on his campaign unraveled. Republicans did not want to support a candidate the generals could outsmart. Also in 1968 Lyndon Johnson decided not to seek reelection after his stand-in in the New Hampshire primary lost while winning. His stand-in won the primary, but not by the margin of victory set by the press.

Offsetting Society's Divisions

President Franklin D. Roosevelt could almost always depend on a stable coalition of the Solid South, Big Cities and Big Unions to guarantee electoral victories and majority support for his New Deal program. Gradually, however, the Democratic Party lost its popular support, which had exceeded 50 percent of the public. Today Democrats, Republicans, and Independents divide popular support into about one-third each. Divisions do not stop here, however. Immigration has brought many more nationalities to the United States, and the White-Anglo-Saxon-Protestant majority no longer holds sway.

Now presidents must govern in the face of a host of divisions—ideological, political, racial, ethnic, and others.

Within the Republican Party, social and economic conservatives vie for favorable presidential attention. President Ronald Reagan successfully balanced these competing interests, but not without criticism from social conservatives who thought he had sold out some of their positions, such as abolishing the U.S. Department of Education. His successor, President George Herbert Walker Bush could not balance those competing interests, which led to two serious independent or third-party candidacies in 1992. His son, President George W. Bush, generally finessed his party divisions more successfully. But not without problems. For example, social conservatives did not like President Bush's concessions to homosexuals, who received appointments to positions in his administration. President Bill Clinton succeeded in welfare reform against significant opposition by bringing together a majority of Republicans and reform-minded Democrats under the slogan of "Mend It. Don't End It."

Speechwriters and the Policy Process

An entourage of full-time presidential speechwriters now plays a role every bit as important as policy thinkers, legal counsel, and press secretary. Because they determine how a president states his policies, style and substance merge in their hands. The nuance and subtlety of language and its use make their role exceedingly important. Full-time speechwriting gradually developed as the presidency grew in size and as presidents delivered more speeches. Presidents Clinton and Bush not only employed several full-time speechwriters but also turned to others inside and outside the White House for help in crafting language. *Wordsmiths*, a synonym for speechwriters, translate a president's policies and vision into convincing style. Before the rise of full-time wordsmiths, other persons inside and outside the White House doubled as speechwriters. For example, under President John F. Kennedy, his principal speechwriter, Ted Sorenson, doubled as a legal adviser.

"Crafted Talk" and Public Opinion Polling

Critics often charge that presidents shift their policies to the prevailing winds of public opinion, using public opinion polls to determine what policies they will advocate and how they will advocate them. Lawrence R. Jacobs and Robert Y. Shapiro[5] refute this criticism. In *Politicians Don't Pander: Political Manipulation and the Loss of Democratic Responsiveness*, they conclude that presidents use polling more to determine how to craft their messages to sell their policies than to determine their policies. Contrary to common perception, they argue, changing the public's mind about their policies is more important than enabling the public mind to influence their policies. Democracy may suffer in either extreme. If presidents always bow to the prevailing winds of public opinion in determining public policy, then political convenience trumps personal conviction. But, by contrast, if they always use the public as a rubber stamp for their policies, the public merely becomes a pawn on the chessboard of presidential politics. Aristotle would probably say of this conundrum that "Virtue is the golden mean between two extremes." In the final analysis, wise presidents do both, either responding to or directing public opinion as the situation dictates.

Freedom from Parties and Institutions

The rhetorical currency of the Contemporary Era creates greater freedom and independence for presidents and presidential candidates from parties and institutions. By virtue of their ability to use contemporary rhetorical devices to control both the medium and the message, presidents and presidential candidates can generate their own issues and ideas without as much restraint from their parties and other institutions. They can use this independence to build their own coalitions and force their parties and other institutions to get in line with them. Public opinion rather than party and institutional opinion becomes much more important to presidents and presidential candidates.

CONCLUSION

Proper rhetorical staging enables candidates and presidents to communicate their messages effectively to the American people, who can then judge whether they approve of those messages. Candidates and presidents, even the well financed, who fail to stage their rhetoric properly, falter along the political wayside. For example, in 2004 former Vermont Governor Howald Dean had more than ample resources to win the Democratic nomination, but faulty rhetorical staging fatally wounded his candidacy, beginning with his feverishly frenetic, apparently uncontrollable response to defeat in the Iowa Caucuses.

Thinking that presidents should govern, not campaign, people may react negatively to the idea of a seamless garment of campaigning and governing, which smacks of just more politics. On the positive side, however, the seamless garment benefits democracy through the effective communication of messages between leaders and followers. Consideration of rhetorical staging in presidential campaigns reveals other benefits to democracy. As the best simulation of the presidency itself, the presidential campaign tests whether candidates can organize and communicate their ideas to the people. For example, presidential candidates, whose staffs can stage a successful National Convention, signal that they may have the necessary leadership skill to lead the nation through merging campaigning and governing.

Recent national conventions have served as successful stages for gaining rhetorical advantage in presidential campaigns, including Jimmy Carter in 1976, Ronald Reagan in 1980, George Herbert Walker Bush in 1988, and Bill Clinton in 1992. In 2004 before John F. Kerry could mount an effective campaign against George W. Bush, he had to unify the disparate elements of the Democratic Party, create an image of himself as warm and approachable, counter his image as a "flip-flopper" on issues, and present the Democratic Party as reasonably centrist and moderate rather than radically left-wing. The Democratic Convention in Boston became the stage for achieving these four goals. Controlling all aspects of the Convention environment, the Kerry campaign left nothing to chance, approving all speeches, video clips and floor signs. By the time he ended his acceptance speech on the fourth day, critics concluded that he had succeeded on all counts. As the Democratic Party left the Convention unified more than anyone could reasonably expect, his image had become fatherly, his positions more clearly stated, and the Party's perceived ideological posture more mainstream. Although those achievements alone could not spell success for his campaign, they benefited democracy by helping to ensure a more competitive campaign and by enabling the public to make clearer judgments between the candidates.

In the seamless garment of campaigning and governing, which separates successful candidates and presidents from the unsuccessful, proper rhetorical staging serves as a critical test of leadership.

Notes

[1]Jeffrey K. Tulis, *The Rhetorical Presidency* (Princeton, NJ: Princeton University Press, 1987): 183.

[2]Among the important books on presidential rhetoric are Wayne Fields, *Union of Words: A History of Presidential Eloquence* (New York: Free Press, 1996); Jeffrey K. Tulis, *The Rhetorical Presidency* (Princeton, NJ: Princeton University Press, 1987); Samuel Kernell, *Going Public* (Washington, DC: CQ Press, 1997); and Martin J. Medhurst, *Beyond the Rhetorical Presidency* (College Station: Texas A& M University Press, 1996).

[3]Woodrow Wilson, *Congressional Government: A Study in Politics* with an introduction by William F. Connelly (Somerset, NJ: Transaction Publishers, 2002).

[4]Nicolo Machiavelli, *The Prince*, translation by Harvey Mansfield (Chicago: University of Chicago Press, 1998).

[5]Lawrence R. Jacobs and Robert Y. Shapiro, *Politicians Don't Pander: Political Manipulation and the Loss of Democratic Responsiveness* (Chicago: University of Chicago Press, 2000).

Chapter Three

The Law of Theory

The Paradoxes of Presidential Leadership

An effective human being is a whole that is greater than the sum of its parts.[1]

—Ida P. Rolf

INTRODUCTION TO THE LAW OF THEORY

> Presidential leadership is not only bigger than the sum of its parts, but also bigger than any single theory. Presidents cannot rely upon any one theory of presidential leadership to ensure a successful presidency. Moreover, successful presidents may differ as to which theories benefit them more. Since individual theories of presidential leadership only address parts of the whole, they are like pieces of a puzzle.

Based on her understanding of effective human beings, Ida P. Rolf could rightly conclude that effective presidential leadership is greater than the sum of its parts. A paradox, indeed. Theories about effective presidential leadership abound. But in each instance, they explain only a part and not the whole. On the artist's canvas of effective presidential leadership, theories constitute parts of the picture but not the whole picture. Taken individually, they help to explain the larger picture of presidential leadership, but they are not the picture itself. So theories selectively illumine our understanding of presidential leadership, but they do not explain the whole. At best, theories unveil the big picture of presidential leadership.

Theories about presidential leadership have addressed many questions. Among them are the following. From George Washington to George Bush, how many leadership styles have presidents had? How can we explain their different styles of leadership? What are the most effective leadership styles? Do common themes appear in the various leadership styles? Do some leadership styles work better than others? Should Americans prefer one leadership style to another? Should presidents try to emulate the successful leadership styles of their predecessors? Obviously no single theory can answer all of these and other questions.

Theories—like sex, drugs, and money—are good, if in their proper place. But if not, dangerous results may occur. Coming from the Greek *theoria*, the "act of viewing, contemplation, consideration," a theory reflects an idea or a scheme, a philosophy or a model used to explain a subject, such as presidential leadership. A theory draws on a limited body of evidence to explain the behavior of the whole. When stipulated as fact, however, theories may invite criticism, as they are at least in part indicative, suggestive, and speculative rather than inclusive, comprehensive, and definitive. Their primary value rests in partially explaining a subject.

What explains presidential leadership? Theorists about presidential leadership offer many different ideas, schemes, philosophies, and models. Among the many explanations, some focus on power; others on personality; and still others on history and circumstances. Although any one explanation has value, none fully explains presidential leadership.

Four themes typify theories about presidential leadership: (1) power, (2) the exceptional person, (3) history and culture and (4) paradox. All theories focus in some way on presidential power to classify presidents, concentrating particularly on the sources of power and how presidents use their power. Explicitly or implicitly these theories point to an ideal use of power in the hands of an exceptional president. Paradoxes emerge, however, when human nature and other factors challenge a theory's discrete categories and conclusions. Although theories enhance understanding of presidential leadership, they possess limitations.

PRESIDENTIAL POWER

Presidential power, a broad term and the most recurring theme among theories of presidential leadership, often bears a close relationship to persuasion, influence over others, influence on history, skillful management, leadership, and political skill. Theories about presidential power measure the level of presidential success or failure by the amount of power that presidents command and their success in exercising that power. Thus, successful presidents have more power and exercise it more effectively. The power of persuasion is the best-known theory of presidential power.

Power of Persuasion

President Harry S. Truman clearly stated the heart and soul of this theory:

> The President may have a great many powers given to him in the Constitution and may have certain powers under certain laws which are given to him by the Congress of the United States, but the principal power that the President has is to bring people in and try to persuade them to do what they ought to do without persuasion. That's what the powers of the President amount to.[2]

Developing this theme as a theory, Richard Neustadt defines presidential leadership as the power to persuade and rates presidents by their ability to influence others.

> His strength or weakness, then, turns on his personal capacity to influence the conduct of the men who make up government. His influence becomes the mark of leadership. To rate a President according to these rules, one looks into the man's own capabilities as seeker and as wielder of effective influence upon the other men involved in governing the country. . . . "Power" means his [the President's] influence.[3]

Presidential power derives from a president's ability to influence rather than from the Constitution's stated powers. As Neustadt says: "The probabilities of power do not derive from the literary theory of the Constitution."[4] Neustadt distinguishes between formal powers and real power. Although the Constitution grants a wide range of formal powers to presidents, real power springs from persuasion. Put another way, the successful exercise of formal powers depends upon the successful practice of persuasion.

> "Powers" are no guarantee of power; clerkship is no guarantee of leadership. The President of the United States has an extraordinary range of formal powers, of authority in statute law and in the Constitution. . . . Here is testimony that despite his status he does not get action without argument. *Presidential power is the power to persuade.*[5]

If persuasion is the essence of presidential power, then personal relationships determine the success of presidential leadership. Or, as Neustadt says: "The essence of a President's persuasive task is to convince such men that what the White House wants of them is what they ought to do for their sake and on their authority. Persuasive power, thus defined, amounts to more than charm or reasoned argument."[6] Presidents must know how to use their resources—"powers" and "power"—authority and logic—status and charm—to become truly powerful and successful. That is, the power of persuasion depends upon successful bargaining.

In the give-and-take of bargaining, presidents possess some advantages, such as superior status and authority, but these alone are insufficient to persuade others to accept their position.[7] The reciprocity of real power varies significantly, depending upon the organization, the issue at hand, the persons involved, and the circumstances presidents face.[8] As a president faces these unique conditions, he must learn how to convince others "to believe that what he wants of them is what their own appraisal of their own responsibilities requires them to do in their interest, not his."[9] Real or true power then requires a president to persuade others that what he wants them to do is in their best interest.

The power to persuade contrasts with the power to command. Constitutionally, a president may command others to do something but at great risk. President Truman had the constitutional power to dismiss General Douglas McArthur from his command during the Korean War, but he paid a high price in doing so. McArthur returned from Korea to a massive ticker-tape parade down New York City's Fifth Avenue and overwhelming support in Congress. Every subordinate, personal and institutional, has strengths, such as public popularity, support in Congress, and ties to interest groups. When presidents command subordinates to act contrary to their perceived interests, they risk a backlash from their supporters.

Both personal reputation and public popularity influence a president's ability to bargain successfully. For example, presidents known for their firmness and competence usually achieve more in the give-and-take of bargaining, whereas presidents with high popularity may use public opinion as a lever in the bargaining process. The two Bushes illustrate the positives and negatives of reputation and popularity. George Herbert Walker Bush suffered in the give-and-take of bargaining, because he did not enjoy a reputation for toughness and tenacity, and he also was either unable or unwilling to use his high popularity after the Gulf War to bargain for important policy objectives. George W. Bush, however, doggedly pursued his objectives on many policy fronts, such as education reform and tax relief, and he also used his high popularity immediately after early successes in the Iraqi War to pursue major policy objectives.

Because changing events and conditions may cause their popularity to rise and fall like a yo-yo, presidents need to ensure that regardless of their popularity they retain a reputation for firmness and competence, over which they have much more control. Loss of both popularity and reputation severely damages their power to persuade. Depending on the power of persuasion to achieve their objectives, successful presidents must work hard to develop and to retain their reputations.

Fields of Power

Clinton Rossiter in *The American Presidency* describes 10 constitutional and nonconstitutional presidential roles: (1) Chief or Head of State, (2) Chief Executive, (3) Commander in Chief, (4) Chief Diplomat, (5) Chief Legislator, (6) Chief of Party, (7) Voice of the People, (8) Protector of the Peace, (9) Manager of Prosperity, and (10) World Leader.[10] But only the first five are official constitutional roles. In each role, constitutional and nonconstitutional, successful presidents understand how to act appropriately in their exercise of power.

As Chief of State presidents perform their role of connecting to the public, which Rossiter says "may often seem trivial, yet it cannot be neglected by a President who proposes to stay in favor and, more to the point, in touch with the people, *the ultimate source of all power*."[11] Because the people elect presidents, they empower them to lead the nation.

In the role of Chief Executive, however, the Constitution's prescribed powers for presidents do not measure up to their duties, according to Rossiter: "The President . . . has more trouble playing this role successfully than he does any other. It is, in fact, the one major area of presidential activity in which his powers are simply not equal to his responsibilities."[12] To illustrate, whereas presidents have the power of appointment and removal, a vast bureaucracy with civil service protection limits their performance. Rossiter notes that "we cannot savor the fullness of the President's duties unless we recall that he is held primarily and often exclusively accountable for the ethics, loyalty, efficiency, frugality, and responsiveness to the public's wishes of the two and a third million Americans in the national administration."[13] Since Rossiter wrote his book during the 1950s, both the number of federal employees and demands on presidents have greatly increased. Presidents and the people they lead engage in a constant tug-of-war. Although presidents need the people as a principal source of their power, the people hold their presidents accountable for many more responsibilities than they can perform. These bureaucratic and popular limitations on presidents are but two of many limitations on the presidential role of Chief Executive.

Commander in Chief, the third role of presidents, puts them in charge of the American military worldwide, which Rossiter observes that: "'when the blast of war blows in our ears,' the President's power to command the forces swells out of all proportion to his other powers. All major decisions of strategy, and many of his tactics as well, are his alone to make or to approve."[14] But the constitutional power to command is more than that. Lincoln, Wilson, Franklin Roosevelt, and now George W. Bush have interpreted this power to justify an "unprecedented series of measures that cut deeply into the accepted liberties of the people and the routine pattern of government."[15] Presidents hold a vast constitutional reservoir of military power, which wars, threats of war, terrorist threats, and terrorism serve as catalysts for enlargement.

As Chief Diplomat, presidents constitutionally possess "the very delicate, plenary and exclusive power . . . as the sole organ of government in the field of international relations."[16] For example, President Truman declared: "I make American foreign policy."[17] Although others, such as the Congress, may influence foreign policy, only the president as the constitutional representative of the whole country can speak on the nation's behalf. Others lack the constitutional position, sufficient access to information and the necessary personnel to challenge a president's diplomatic leadership. Rossiter argues that: "the role of Chief Diplomat has become the most important and exacting of all those we call upon the President to play."[18] Although the president may have exclusive power in this area, he needs all the power he can muster to meet the demands of modern diplomacy.

Constitutionally, presidents possess several powers in their role as Chief Legislator, including the right to deliver the State of the Union address and to veto legislation. Gradually, this role as Chief Legislator has expanded into one of persuasive leadership, wherein presidents in large measure set the legislative agenda for debate in Congress. Pundits assess presidential success in getting their proposals passed by the Congress. Presidents provide political guidance and practical unity to Congress on policy matters, as they link their proposals to the climate of the country. Rossiter points out that: "The refusal or inability of the President to point out the way results in weak or, at best, stalemated government."[19]

These five roles, explicitly given to presidents through the constitutional "job description," constitute their formal powers. Presidential success, however, depends equally as much on five informal roles, which the Constitution does not prescribe.

As Chief of Party, presidents play a unifying role as the primary articulators of party interests. As the principal representatives of their parties, presidents not only act to build and maintain party cohesion but also to lead their parties in policy disputes with the opposing party, especially in the Congress. Of this informal role, Rossiter notes its importance to Andrew Jackson, who used it to build a national political following: "By playing the politician with unashamed zest the first of these gave [Jackson's] epic administration a unique sense of cohesion."[20]

Second among the informal roles, the Voice of the People enables presidents to serve as "a moral spokesman for all."[21] Whereas presidents may serve as the political leader for some, they act as the prime voice for all in national affairs. Presidents in the words of Woodrow Wilson act as "the spokesman for the real sentiment and purpose of the country."[22] Wilson also asserted that "the President is the American people's one authentic trumpet, and he has no higher duty than to give a clear and certain sound."[23]

As Protector of the Peace, presidents work to maintain tranquility in the country. To wit, as Rossiter points out: "No man or combination of men in the United States can muster so quickly and authoritatively the troops, experts, food, money, loans, equipment, medical supplies, and moral support that may be needed in a disaster."[24] When challenged by natural catastrophes, presidents must respond substantively and symbolically, providing aid to victims of hurricanes and tornadoes and traveling to disaster areas to demonstrate their personal concern and compassion.

The role of Manager of Prosperity calls on presidents "to foster and promote free competitive enterprise, to avoid economic fluctuations or to diminish the effects thereof, and to maintain employment, production, and purchasing power."[25] Presidents who fail to play this role properly, such as Herbert Hoover, suffer consequences at the ballot box.

Globally, presidents serve as a World Leader, a role enabling them to influence international affairs because of the "power, drama, and prestige" of the presidential office.[26] Of this, Rossiter observes that presidential stature continues to increase in the world,[27] which in many ways now makes American presidents the world's premier leader.

All of the formal and informal roles are a package—interconnected and inseparable—as Rossiter points out:

> The president is not one kind of official during one part of the day, another kind during another part—administrator in the morning, legislator at lunch, king in the afternoon, commander before dinner, and politician at odd moments that come his weary way. He is all these things all the time, and any one of his functions feeds upon and into all the others.[28]

The combined and intertwined roles make presidents more powerful than they would otherwise be, as each role strengthens the others. Rightly put, the whole is greater than the sum of its parts.

On balance, presidents appear extraordinarily powerful, but restrictions on presidential power prevent presidents from becoming like a dictator or king. To justify this conclusion, Rossiter argues that: "The Presidency, like every other instrument of power we have created for our use, operates within a grand and durable pattern of private liberty and public morality, which means that it operates successfully only when the President honors the pattern by selecting ends and means that are 'characteristically American'."[29] Furthermore, he argues that "safeguards . . . keep the President's feet in the paths of constitutional righteousness."[30] Among the safeguards are the Congress, the Judiciary, the bureaucracy, political party system, state government system, free enterprise, allies overseas, and popular opinion, which is the most efficient and effective check.[31] In conclusion, Clinton Rossiter believes that presidents derive their power from the people, who in turn limit their exercise of that power.

Power as Political Skill

Strikingly similar to Richard Neustadt's theory of presidential power as that of persuasion is Barbara Kellerman's idea that presidential power comes from a president's influence over others. Successful presidents know how to use the people around them to enlarge their power, and they exhibit unusual determination in accomplishing tasks. In *The Political Presidency: Practice of Leadership*, Kellerman discusses how presidents must lead in many diverse ways to enhance their power.

> Most students of the presidency believe that the office allows and even encourages role-determining leaders who, to be effective, must draw to some degree on personal sources of power. Mainly, this resource consists of what I would label as interpersonal competence. There is the implicit suggestion that to be a directive leader, to accomplish at least some part of his own program, the president must be able to maneuver skillfully from within the world of other people. He must be able to use others for his own purpose.[32]

Kellerman then relates her theory to Clinton Rossiter's theory on the 10 roles of the president, simplifying and condensing those roles into two categories, headship and leadership. Headship roles stem from the constitutional authority of presidents, whereas leadership roles spring from a "president's skill as an interpersonal actor," wherein presidents engage in "crisis management, symbolic and morale-building leadership, recruitment leadership, legislative and political coalition building, program implementation, and evaluation." She notes that each of these requires "skill at building and maintaining good working relationships with others."[33]

Presidents exercise their power as interpersonal actors in four areas:

- Direction and Consequence: Control over the gains and costs to followers;
- Persuasion: Control by altering the perceptions held by followers;

- Affective Influence: Control by strengthening the desire of followers to act in accordance with their leader; and
- Manipulation: Control over the followers' environment.[34]

According to Kellerman, the best method for presidents to exert their power is transactional leadership: "trading of benefits rather than of punishment."[35] What are the characteristics of politically skillful presidents in the exercise of transactional leadership? Kellerman contends that presidential power as the exercise of skillful transactional leadership features the ability (1) to preempt problems before they become serious, (2) to provide advance notice about policy and personnel changes to subordinates and others, (3) to have a keen sense of timing in making decisions, (4) to use the cabinet wisely as surrogates, (5) to make compelling personal appeals, (6) to leverage personal access, (7) to bargain effectively, (8) to twist arms to accomplish objectives, (9) to reward with services and personal amenities, (10) to strike meaningful compromises, (11) to maintain an appropriate measure of detachment from others, and (12) to cultivate support by educating the public, by leading through effective images and impressions of good management, and by the ingratiation of others.[36]

Because presidential leadership depends substantially on securing the support and cooperation of others, Kellerman believes that transactional leadership reflects "the democratic ideal that power be shared."[37] In sum, transactional leadership benefits American politics and society by establishing relationships between presidents and the people they lead. Successful presidents build and maintain those relationships.

Power Struggle

In 1940, writing from his perspective as a British observer of American politics, Harold J. Laski penned one of the first books on the presidency, portraying the presidential office as one with dubious power. According to Laski, who mirrors a long-standing complaint about the presidency, especially among many scholars, the Constitution's division of powers impedes the necessary and proper exercise of presidential powers: "There are the forces inherent in the Constitution—an absolute division of powers, a system of checks and balances as between executive and legislative which gives to each an interest in the diminution of authority instead of in its consolidation, a tendency to destroy something of the president's prestige . . ."[38] Laski pinpoints the principal obstacles to presidential leadership.

First, Congress hinders presidential leadership. Laski claims that for presidents to exercise a substantial amount of power with Congress, crises are essential to get members to rally behind presidential leadership. He states that: "The president is at no point the master of the legislature. He can indicate a path of action to Congress. He can argue, bully, persuade, cajole; but he is always outside of Congress, and subject to a will he cannot dominate."[39]

Second, presidents find their control over policy limited. They can initiate policy but not control it.[40] Laski believes that: "This presents two issues of major magnitude in the context of the presidency. As things are, leadership can come from the president alone . . . there is no other source of direction which can secure the attention of the whole nation. But the forces which operate against continuity of presidential leadership are immense."[41]

Third, Laski maintains that a president who wishes to exert a great amount of power "is not only running counter to the purpose of the Constitution. He is also arraying against himself all the forces in American politics to whom his strength is bound to be obnoxious."[42]

Laski's main thesis—that the Constitution restrains the appropriate exercise of presidential power—means that presidents cannot perform their proper role of providing direction for the American democracy. He believes that: "Democracy needs clear direction, and it cannot get this unless the central motive force in a political system rests in the executive's hands . . . what is important is that the plans put into operation should essentially be plans for which he is willing to accept full responsibility."[43]

Viewing this as a serious internal flaw, Laski concludes that without relaxing the ties that bind presidential power, America will lack leadership that provides continuity in the direction of policy and in the definition of the national interest. As is, only when crises grip the country will Congress, the public, and politicians lay down their personal motives to support the president. Power for the president "on a big scale comes only because an emergency has to be surmounted. There is no provision for its continuity."[44]

Power Not Equal to Force

Of more recent vintage, the postmodern presidency refers in part to the president's changed role internationally. In *The Postmodern President*, Richard Rose says that successful postmodern presidents must act both effectively and responsively in an interdependent world.[45] To achieve success, they must properly apply power in three realms: Washington, nationally with the public-at-large, and internationally with other countries, international corporations, and other entities.

Rose, who credits Franklin D. Roosevelt with creating the modern presidency, says that the postmodern presidency has developed gradually over several presidencies. Although he notes especially the role of President

Ronald Reagan in the fall of communism in the Soviet Union and its satellites as an example of postmodern presidential leadership, he provides many other illustrations. Presidents in the postmodern era, he finds, must sometimes act in a nationally unpopular manner in order to act in an internationally responsible manner. For example, President Jimmy Carter incurred the wrath of many when he acted to abrogate the Panama Canal Treaty and America's unilateral interests there. President Bill Clinton also invited the antagonism of American labor unions in his pursuit of the North American Free Trade Act.

Echoing both Harold Laski and Richard Rose, David Barber in *The Presidential Character* believes that: "Americans vastly overrate the President's power—and they are likely to continue to do so. The logic of that feeling is clear enough: the President is at the top and therefore he must be able to dominate those below him."[46] Barber believes that the people see in their presidents the essence of life's struggles and themes. When presidents come out victorious in the drama of life, the people are likely to view them as powerful and successful. Popular perception, however, can actually harm presidential leadership if presidents let success "go to their head," forgetting that power and force are not equal and that persuasion is more effective than force.[47] Barber believes that:

> The most dangerous confusion in that connection is the equating of political power—essentially the power to persuade—with force. Such a President, frustrated in efforts at persuasion, may turn to those aspects of his role least constrained by the chains of compromise—from domestic to foreign policy, for instance, where the tradition of obedience holds. Then we may see a President, doubtful within but seemingly certain without, huffing and puffing with *machismo* as he bravely orders other men to die.[48]

Presidents exercise true or responsible power, according to Barber, when they resist the desire to cater to public acceptance and awe, and "buck[ing] the tide of [their] times in favor of some eternal purpose."[49] As presidents influence and do what is best—not what is popular—they live out the essence of proper presidential power.

Power Is in the Eye of the Beholder

The American presidency has fascinated many scholars over many years and from many points on the globe. Struggling to define what makes presidents truly good and truly great, they have focused on the sources and exercise of presidential power. If they agree on one thing, it is this: Power is not equivalent to force. After that scholars diverge in their coverage of different aspects of presidential behavior in the repertoire of presidential power, such as influence, persuasion, and political skill. Their consensus is that presidential power comes primarily from sources other than the Constitution, most notably the personal resources of presidents. This perception of presidential power focuses on an ideal type of president who has adequate power and uses it in the best manner.

THE EXCEPTIONAL PERSON

Intelligent. Hardworking. Optimistic, joyous, lighthearted. Sensitive. Loyal, appreciative, accepting, compassionate. *TRUTHFUL.* Devoted. Romantic, humorous. Attentive to detail. Wise. Committed, protective, self-esteem building, encouraging, understanding, loving. People loving, truth-loving, caring. Honest. Intriguing. Trustworthy. Built. Fatherly. Creative. Peaceful—spontaneous—steadfast. Goofy *and* Serious. Playful *and* responsible. Listening, humble, forgiving, sincere.

These are but some of the qualities jammed-packed onto a poster in a women's college dormitory titled, "Adjective for the Type of Man You Hope to Marry." One of the girls had written, "good sense of style." Next to it another had written, "good luck."[50]

Without exception, (no pun intended) these theories call for persons of near superhuman qualities to reside in the White House. Many wish lists, not unlike the one earlier, describe this ideal person. In his discourse on successful presidents, those who have the power to influence history, Rossiter prescribes that they must possess and cultivate the following qualities: affability; a stout and warm heart; cunning, in order to get the most out of their administrations; a sense of humor; a thick skin and a light heart; the "newspaper habit," which consists of clear channels to those outside the White House; not only a sense of History but also the power to influence it; political skill; the power of persuasion; and not only good health, but also the capacity to *thrive* on the rigors of the presidency.[51]

The Wish List Continued

In his book *Presidential Greatness,* Stephen Bailey called for a checklist of 43 items, including but by no means limited to the best of the following: achievement, administrative capacity, appointees, eloquence, industriousness, the absence of scandals and blunders, sensitivity.[52]

Charles W. Dunn has characterized the presidents and the presidency as "the apex of authority," the "peak of power," the "architect of progress," the "engineer of progress," the "contractor of public interest," the "decorator of the public interest," and the "catalytic converter in the engine of democracy."[53]

In *The American Presidency,* Harold J. Laski projects yet another list of qualities necessary for successful presidents. The list stipulates "the power to handle men," to "almost intuitively" use people for their purposes,[54] a realistic sense of direction for the country that balances personal aspirations with popular limitations, a rapid thinker and decision maker,[55] the ability to coordinate and delegate, a general "aloofness"[56] that is neither insensitive, nor subject to being shaken by criticism,[57] self-confidence, and seeing through "the eyes of the multitude."[58] A successful president, writes Laski, should be an "uncommon man with good opinions."[59]

Richard Neustadt writes that the President "plays every 'role,' wears every 'hat' at once."[60] Closely related to Neustadt's thinking, Barbara Kellerman argues that "Great leaders do more than just satisfy role requirements; like great actors, they recreate their roles . . . great leaders often change those very institutions that have created and refined the role the leader has inherited."[61] Kellerman considers four qualities essential to presidential leadership:

- First, the ability to assemble a team of both competent and committed staff and the political elite;
- Second, the ability to direct that team to develop policy and implement strategy;
- Third, the power and skill required to create a favorable national climate; and
- Fourth, the cunning to engage the political elite in two-way influence relationships so that policy becomes law.

Fred Greenstein in *The Hidden-Hand Presidency*, a study of General Eisenhower's presidency, proposes that presidential leadership bonds two opposites: (1) Chief or Head State, who as the symbol of national unity must represent the entire nation; and (2) Chief Executive, who as the nation's highest political executive must pursue progress, economically, politically, and socially both at home and abroad.[62] To serve as Chief of State, according to Greenstein, a person must have electability, well-developed political skills, and, at the same time, a credible reputation as a nonpolitician. However, to serve as Chief Executive, a person must understand and use diplomatic language, refuse to engage in personal attacks on others, pay close private attention to the personalities of others, and delegate selectively to key people.[63]

In a subsequent book, *The Presidential Difference*, Greenstein condenses his attributes for successful presidents to a list of six:

- public communicator;
- organizational capacity;
- political skill;
- vision;

- cognitive style or the ability to process a cascading flow of advice and counsel; and
- emotional intelligence.

Greenstein defines emotional intelligence as "the President's ability to manage his emotions and turn them to constructive purposes, rather than being dominated by them and allowing them to diminish his leadership."[64]

Emotional Intelligence

Greenstein ascribes the idea or theory of emotional intelligence to Harvard physiologist Howard Gardner and its popularization to Daniel Goleman,[65] who advanced the notion in his 1995 book, *Emotional Intelligence*, which suggests that the emotional makeup of people has as much influence on their advancement in life, personally and professionally, as do intellect or an Ivy League education.[66]

That same year, Gardner published his theoretical work, *Leading Minds: An Anatomy of Leadership*, wherein he emphasizes *minds*, as he "contrasts his theory [on leadership] with those of others by stressing that it is cognitive, rather than one that gives a central role to power, policies, the public, or the personality of the leader."[67] Rather than focusing on leaders in general, Goleman stresses the impact of emotional intelligence on professional success. Soon thereafter an avalanche of publicity emphasized the necessity of emotional intelligence in the workplace.

Training and Development—just one of many journals featuring articles on this new idea—published an article in 1996, which asked why the not-intellectual-giants Reagan and FDR are credited for leading the country better than other men considered to possess higher cognitive abilities, such as Nixon. The answer? Emotional intelligence.[68]

Four years later, in 2000, Greenstein applied emotional intelligence to presidential leadership in his book *The Presidential Difference*. After carefully surveying the six qualities that he deems most important to presidential leadership, he concludes in the very last sentence of his book that of the six qualities, cognitive and emotional intelligence are the two most essential, but, of these two, emotional intelligence is more important. Without emotional intelligence, he says, "all else may turn to ashes."[69]

Unraveling Emotional Intelligence

In "Leadership That Gets Results," Daniel Goleman provides insight into the importance of Greenstein's application of emotional intelligence to presidential leadership. Paradoxically and mysteriously, Goleman notes that effective leadership has long evaded many companies despite a large "cottage industry" on the subject. Now, however, he contends that new research-based information on emotional intelligence "takes much of the mystery out of effective leadership."[70]

Citing research on this subject, Goleman identifies six leadership styles, which have their roots in emotional intelligence.

- the *Coercive* style functions by "demand[ing] immediate compliance."
- the *Authoritative* style "mobilize(s) people toward a vision."
- the *Affiliative* style establishes emotional bonds and harmony.
- the *Democratic* style "build(s) consensus through participation."
- the *Pacesetting* style sets high standards and "expects excellence and self-direction."
- the *Coaching* style focuses on preparing people for the future.[71]

Skillful leaders, according to Goleman, use all six styles, "seamlessly" switching from style to style as situations dictate: supportive when necessary; demanding when required; and understanding and empathetic when needed. Their use of all six styles at the appropriate time strikes a note of *rightness*— a feeling of "Yes. That is the way it is supposed to be done."

Effective leaders use the *Coercive* style in times of crisis or significant change, when they must make command decisions under pressure. But in noncrisis situations that demand clear direction and vision, successful leaders shift to the *Authoritative* style, exhibiting enthusiasm, vision, and motivation. Goleman says that the successful leader in these circumstances "motivates people by making clear to them how their work fits into a larger vision for the organization."[72]

When the *Authoritative* style's top-down, command approach becomes overbearing, successful leaders will change to the *Affiliative* style or the *Coaching* style. Because people are the number one priority with the *Affiliative* style, successful leaders will place very high value on individuals and their emotions, building strong bonds with their followers by sensitively recognizing and rewarding their work. *Affiliative* leaders create a sense of belonging among their followers, even to the extent of building strong personal relationships.[73]

The *Coaching* style, like the *Affiliative* style, spotlights people rather than instantaneous progress. Its emphasis differs, however. An *Affiliative* leader works closely with followers to make changes, improvements, and advancements either for them or for the organization. This style of leadership does not work well when either followers resist change or leaders lack the ability to aid the progress of followers.[74]

When followers and subordinates possess high levels of competence and motivation, successful leaders will switch to the *Pacesetting* style, which stresses "doing things better and faster," and setting "extremely high performance standards." *Pacesetting* leaders must exemplify the same traits as their followers.[75]

The *Democratic* style works best when successful leaders must emphasize flexibility and trust. With this approach, successful leaders can build high morale by listening to followers, getting their ideas, and building mutual "trust, respect, and commitment."[76]

Goleman's descriptions swell in the heart of the reader as a warm feeling of rightness. Reading Goleman's answer to successful leadership is something like reading an Arthurian novel. The hero enters a forest thicket outnumbered six to one. No matter. He strikes one barbarian warrior with the blade of his sword and with one turn of his hand knocks another on-comer in the head with the sword's blunt handle. Jumping from the path of a hurdling hatchet in the nick of time, he in one swoop knocks the third adversary into the sword of a fourth. Instinctively, he turns to fight the man stealthily sneaking up behind him. Not without a suspense-filled fight, and our hero having lost his sword, he is able to unarm this foe, and use him as a shield against an oncoming arrow. As the two remaining warriors charge at him in fury, our hero grabs the hatchet, earlier intended for him but now stuck in the side of a tree, and hurls it at one while ducking a blow from the other and unsheathing a dagger from his boot. He stabs his attacker in the stomach. And there, after a series of one fluid move to another, stands our hero, unscathed, in the quiet of a forest thicket and six defeated foes.

Goleman asks those curious about the six styles of successful leadership to imagine a golfer's golf bag. Professional golfers pull the ideal club from the bag to make the best shot just as successful leaders choose the ideal leadership style to make the best decision.[77] While Goleman's analogy is appealing, it begs the question of just how successful leaders can choose the ideal leadership style.

Either You've Got It—Or You Don't

So, how is this done, really? Goleman answers: "Such leaders don't mechanically match their style to fit a checklist of situations—they are far more *fluid*." The most effective leaders "are *exquisitely sensitive* to the impact they are having on others and *seamlessly adjust* their style to get the best results."[78] Successful leadership reflects more of who you are than what you do.

"Hero," a 1933 radio hit, begins, "It was one of those great stories, that you can't put down at night. The hero knew what he had to do, and he wasn't afraid to fight." The chorus sings, "And the reason that she loved him was the reason I loved him too. He never wondered what was right or wrong, he just knew."[79] Goleman's hero just knows; he just *has* emotional intelligence.

Although emotionally intelligent leaders are apparently just born with it, Goleman holds out hope for others by asserting that "mastering the art of interpersonal communication, particularly in saying *just the right thing* or making the *apt* symbolic gesture at *just the right moment*" can be achieved by "those who work assiduously to increase their quotient of [emotional intelligence]."[80] He notes, however, that "Improving emotional intelligence isn't done in a weekend or during a seminar. . . . It takes diligent practice on the job, over several months."[81]

What is the correct view: "With-hard-work-and-the-help-of-an-expert-you-can-do-it" or "You've-got-it-if-you-were-born-with-it"? Although neither Goleman nor most presidential theorists answer categorically, they lean toward the latter. For example, biographies of the modern presidents in Greenstein's *The Presidential Difference*, which place great emphasis upon father–son relationships, leave the clear impression that the emotional intelligence of presidents has something to do with familial connections.[82]

Then in "What Makes for a Good President?"[83] about the Democratic and Republican presidential candidates in 2000, Greenstein briefly examines their emotional status. Commenting on Al Gore, he says that: "Mr. Gore was the dutiful son of a politically prominent father, even enlisting in the Army during a war he opposed in order not to damage his father politically." Greenstein writes further that "If the present-day Al Gore has an emotional failing, it is that he has often seemed excessively eager to comply with the demands of his political environment."

Regarding George W. Bush, Greenstein states the well-known facts that he is "the rebellious son of another politically prominent father," a son who "drifted from job to job during what he refers to as his 'nomadic' years and drank to excess—by his own confession—until early middle age." But after that, Greenstein allows that "[t]he George W. Bush of today has acquired impressive self-discipline."

To the extent that "you've-got-it-if-you-were-born-with-it" prevails over "with-hard-work-and-the-help-of-an-expert-you-can-do-it," familial relationships emerge as the primary determinant of the emotional intelligence of presidents.

Born with Emotional Intelligence

Greenstein is not alone in examining the backgrounds of presidents to explain their behavior. In *Presidential Character*, James David Barber states that: "the Presidency is much more than an institution. It is a focus on feelings."[84] Barber argues that Americans can anticipate the directions of presidents by understanding their "character, world view, and . . . style."[85] Barber believes that "Personality shapes performance," and that "As for personality, it is a matter of tendencies."[86] Barber defines "style" as "the President's *habitual* way of performing his three political roles: rhetoric, personal relations, and homework."[87] According to Barber, a president's worldview "consists of his primary, politically relevant beliefs, particularly his conceptions of social causality, human nature, and the central moral conflicts of the time." Thus, Barber simplifies it: "Style is his way of acting, world-view is his way of seeing."[88] Most important, perhaps, is Barber's definition of character, which he defines as "the way the President orients himself toward life."[89] Though no more simple, he also defines it as "the person's stance as he confronts life."[90] In short—the way a person *is*."

Much like Greenstein's emphasis on the early life, Barber states that "The best way to predict a President's character, world view, and style is to see how he constructed them in the first place." Barber believes that they have their "main development in childhood."[91] Character, developing so much in early life, determines the way a person is, providing "the main thrust and broad direction" for determining worldview, which develops mainly in adolescence, and style, which develops mainly in early adulthood.[92] According to Barber, they will continue to be shaped by cultural circumstances, the opportunities of life, and "historical accidents."[93]

Barber then uses this background to divide modern presidents into these categories: active and passive; positive and negative. Active presidents invest substantial energy in their work, whereas passive presidents invest much less energy.[94] Positive presidents reflect a happy and an enjoyable outlook on their political experiences, whereas negative presidents find theirs more sad and discouraging.[95]

These categories form four quadrants—active-positive, active-negative, passive-positive, and passive-negative—which Barber uses for distinguishing presidents:

- Active-Positive—Franklin D. Roosevelt, Truman, Kennedy, Ford, Carter, and George Herbert Walker Bush;
- Active-Negative—Wilson, Hoover, Johnson, and Nixon;
- Passive-Positive—Taft, Harding, and Reagan; and
- Passive-Negative—Coolidge and Eisenhower.[96]

Barber's bias for active-positive presidents becomes readily apparent. For example, he dismisses passive-positives as "well adapted to certain nonpolitical roles, but they lack the experience and flexibility to perform well as political leaders."[97] They are so wrapped up in a search for affection that although they "feel the problem," they are "too easily diverted by the sham and sentimentality of politics to do much about it."[98] He faults active-negatives for compulsively pouring energy into their work, but without appropriate direction. He finds their "energy distorted from within."[99]

By contrast, Barber finds that active-positive presidents excel in having "well-defined personal goals,"[100] and the ability to "move [America] on to the future our children deserve."[101] Active-positive presidents, he says, give "expression in a believable way to convictions momentarily buried in fear and mistrust."[102] They get past the gap of "what people see governments doing and what they hear politicians saying."[103] Importantly, "their approach is experimental rather than deductive. . . . Flexibility in style and a world view containing a variety of probabilities are congruent with a character ready for trial and error, and furnish the imagination with a wide range of alternatives."[104] They have "energetic, optimistic realism," says Barber.[105] *"Active positive Presidents want to achieve results."*[106] Their strength is that they show "orientation toward productiveness as a value, and an ability to use styles flexibly, adaptively, *suiting the dance to the music."*[107] And so it is that Barber brings us back to Greenstein and Goleman's emotionally intelligent man.

The Presidential Superman (Or Whatever You Want to Call Him!)

Goleman's emotionally intelligent person chooses "leadership styles like a pro—using the right one at just the right time and in the right measure."[108] Barber's suits the dance to the music, whereas Greenstein's "channels his emotions to constructive purposes, rather than being at their mercy," much like Barber's picks the right dance steps for the rhythm and Goleman's picks the appropriate club to make a corresponding shot.[109]

Immediately after associating the modern presidents with their fathers' occupations, Greenstein ends his introduction to *The Presidential Difference* by stating that the presidency, although "often described as an office that places superhuman demands on its incumbent" is in fact "a job for flesh-and-blood human beings, who will be better equipped for their responsibilities if they and those who select them do not begin with a blank slate."[110] If the presidency is indeed a job for "flesh-and blood human beings," why does Greenstein not only accept Goleman's theory of emotional intelligence, but also argue that without it, "all else may turn to ashes"?[111]

All Flesh Cries Out for the Living God

Now you may rightly ask: Why spend so much time on emotional intelligence? The answer is straightforward: Emotional intelligence is a contemporary sound for an age-old cry; we want an exceptional person as president. We want a hero, who, in the words of the pop song "never wonders what is right or wrong, he just knew, he just knew . . . "[112] We've always wanted that. We want a person who, outnumbered six to one in a forest thicket, kills all six in a series of six fluid moves. We've always wanted that. We want a leader who, when in need of a golf club, has an "automatic" response . . . who "senses the challenge . . . swiftly pulls out the right tool, and elegantly puts it to work."[113] We've always wanted that.

From the presidency's inception, Americans have sought a person who can serve as a strong leader and yet be a servant of the people: not a tyrant, but strong enough to stand as the figurehead for all America. Throughout presidential history, we have wanted a person who not only has all the qualities on our checklist but also the ability to employ the right one at the right time. This is nothing new. "We require him over and over again to prove himself to us, to be 'all things to all men."[114] We expect him to be "a man for all seasons," as Kellerman writes, one who "must be an expert on everything from clean air to neutron bombs; he must be skilled as a backslapper and military tactician; he must have moral fiber, vision, ambition, energy, brains, craftiness, and decency."[115] He must be, as Laski gets at throughout his work, "an exceptional man."[116] We want an exceptional man, and we've begun to demand one.

All theories call for—some blatantly and some more narrow and inconspicuously—this exceptional person; this prevalent approach has, however, run America head-on into a significant problem: though Americans demand one, there is no exceptional person. There never has been, and there never will be. He simply does not exist. Arguably, theorists have given the public reason to believe that he does. In their extensive lists of what a president must be, theorists on presidential leadership have published an age-old human longing. As their theories become publicized, people have begun to think that the "exceptional man" must be possible, he must be out there. "If such conditions cannot be met, why would experts on Presidential leadership make them?" they ask, perhaps subconsciously. And so it is that many justify their demands for a Presidential superman: theorists have called for one . . . so *why can't we*? Americans laden a burden so heavy that it cannot be carried on the shoulders of one man, and yet they try to lay it there; the rationale of this action is in theories that project the exceptional man.

Putting a Square Peg in the Square Hole

Rather than directing blame for this havoc upon the theories themselves, however, if our premise holds water, the finger should be pointed not at the theorists, but at the misapplication of their theories. Misapplied theories regarding presidential leadership are harmful to presidents and the public. Taking a theory out of its proper place not only makes it faulty, perverted, and subject to criticism, but also destructive.

If the theories we have examined are an artificial construct for making sense of leadership, they are not stating fact—what factually exists—but, rather, what should exist in a world where things made sense, a world where things were right. The feeling of rightness, then, that Goleman's description of golf-pro leadership evokes in the reader is appropriate. As he writes about effective leadership, he is not addressing the question "What do effective leaders do?" Instead from the beginning, he addresses the question "What *should* leaders do?" As Goleman wraps up his description of a superhuman leader he remarks, "Like parenthood, leadership will never be an exact science. But neither should it be a complete mystery to those who practice it."[117] We must keep readily in mind that even when "what should be" is unveiled, "what should be" remains unattainable in the merely human pursuit. As for whether theorists should seek theories that are closer to reality, the jury is still out. The strength of presidential leadership theories is that they give the American people incentive to resist settling for a leader who cannot lead; the weakness of theorists on presidential leadership is that they do not more clearly insist that their theories are merely theories that cannot be realized in this imperfect world.

A comic strip with the caption "waiting for the perfect husband" has two frames. In the first, a young, beautiful woman sits on a park bench, attentively poised, her hands extended in anticipation and clutching her knees. In the second frame, the same woman in the same dress sits on the same park bench. Her old, withered hands are still extended as she clutches her cane. She is still waiting, although not quite as excitedly. The illustration serves as a good check for young women who write out lists of qualities they hope for in their future husband: whereas the list is helpful in not allowing them to settle short, say, for a man who does little more than sit around watching TV and guzzling beer, never in this imperfect world full of imperfect people will it be perfectly attainable. And so it is, that even a poster on a college women's dormitory wall, jam-packed with a huge range of exceptional qualities, is, in its proper place, a good thing.

HISTORY AND CULTURE

A Theory of History

Stephen Skowronek offers a theory of presidential leadership based on historical constraints, concluding that each president fits within one of four categories in a predictable flow of history.[118] Some presidents, such as Thomas Jefferson, Andrew Jackson, Abraham Lincoln, Franklin Roosevelt, and Ronald Reagan, initiate a new order or a "new orthodoxy" by making major changes in public policy, falling into Skowronek's category of the "Politics of Reconstruction." Their successors must then govern within the constraints of the "new orthodoxy." For example, Franklin Roosevelt's New Deal imposed constraints on how his successors could function and what leadership they could provide.

Gradually, as Skowronek views the flow of history, support wanes for the reconstructed new order or "new orthodoxy," which ultimately sets the stage for another president who will create yet another new order or "new orthodoxy." So, as support for Roosevelt's New Deal waned between Presidents Truman and Carter, along came Ronald Reagan to reconstruct American politics in another way.

Presidents serving between such presidents as Roosevelt and Reagan fall into three categories according to Skowronek. In one category are presidents from the opposing party, who do not adhere completely to the "new orthodoxy." They are what Skowronek refers to as presidents serving in an era of the "Politics of Preemption." Although they may offer new ideas about politics and public policy, the "new orthodoxy" they inherited restricts what they can do. Richard Nixon, for example, did not attempt to undo the New Deal, but he did offer a limited agenda for making some changes in social policy and in decentralizing the federal system. In addition to Richard Nixon, the presidents Skowronek places in the "Politics of Preemption" are John Tyler, Andrew Johnson, and Woodrow Wilson.

In a second category of presidents between the eras of "Politics of Reconstruction" are presidents generally supportive of continuing the "new orthodoxy." Typically of the same party and ideological persuasion as the president who created the "new orthodoxy," they affirm their inheritance by rearticulating it. President Lyndon B. Johnson, a lifelong advocate of the New Deal, offered his proposals for a "Great Society," which he intended as an extension and an expansion of the New Deal. Also falling within Skowronek's "Politics of Articulation" are Presidents James Monroe, James K. Polk, and Theodore Roosevelt.

The "Politics of Disjunction," Skowronek's third category, includes Presidents John Adams, John Quincy Adams, Franklin Pierce, James Buchanan, Herbert Hoover, and Jimmy Carter, who are like the dying orthodoxy's last gasp of breath. In short, they are the stage-setters for the "new orthodoxy": John Adams for Thomas Jefferson, John Quincy Adams for Andrew Jackson, Pierce and Buchanan for Abraham Lincoln, Herbert Hoover for Franklin D. Roosevelt, and Jimmy Carter for Ronald Reagan.

A Theory of Culture

Richard Ellis and Aaron Wildavsky[119] develop a complex leadership theory based on the interaction between three competing political cultures and three divergent leadership styles or predispositions: individualist, egalitarian, and hierarchical. Historically, individualism has dominated American culture with egalitarianism bursting on the scene from time to time, such as during the Civil War era and during the Civil Rights movement of the 1960s. Generally, the hierarchical culture and leadership predisposition have not had much currency in American politics, a fact evidenced by the Constitution, which restricts the exercise of centralized leadership.

- The individualist culture and leadership predisposition emphasizes increased citizen autonomy and decreased authority. Ironically, to expand citizen autonomy may entail changing the economic, political, and social order, thus requiring a president to enlarge his authority to ensure increased citizen autonomy, thereby creating a conflict between the individualist culture and a president's individualist leadership predisposition. President Ronald Reagan, for example, argued for freedom of the individual, but he also expanded the scope of government and his own power to achieve that end.
- The egalitarian culture and leadership predisposition stress reduced inequality among individuals, which of necessity means changing the economic, political, and social order. Again, another irony pits a president's predisposition for egalitarianism against the need to expand his authority. Whereas egalitarianism imbued both Franklin D. Roosevelt and Lyndon B. Johnson, they substantially strengthened their power to achieve that end.
- The hierarchical culture and leadership predisposition presume that authority resides in the position held by the leader and that maintenance of continuity, stability, and harmony in the social order are of very high priority. To achieve success, George Washington's hierarchical leadership predisposition required that he adjust to the dominance of individualism in American culture.

Successful presidential leadership, according to Ellis and Wildavsky, requires that presidents balance their leadership predispositions with the prevailing culture or cultures. They must choose between competing approaches to leadership and culture. Inasmuch as an antihierarchical culture customarily prevails in America, presidents cannot look so much to their position as president for authority and leadership, but, rather, to how they can balance other competing cultures and leadership predispositions to achieve their aims.

THE PARADOXES

"What is it about the American Presidency that defies theoretical precision? Why can't we devise propositions that predict the behavior of Presidents and explain Presidential leadership?" ask Cronin and Genovese, authors of *The*

Paradoxes of the American Presidency.[120] A valid question, as theoretical precision most certainly remains elusive. Theorists examine effective presidential leadership factors in "descending order of importance"—ordering their own lists, trying and retrying to define and defend their "number one." Cronin and Genovese raise an appropriate question, but in the end they, too, run with the rest of the pack in this seemingly endless search.

Who's Number One?

Theorists have faithfully identified various contenders for the number one spot, using a wide array of historical evidence and illustrations.

- Greenstein unabashedly argues that emotional intelligence wins the number one spot.
- Barber also places emotional intelligence first, although he does not explicitly call it that.
- Laski theorizes that the president's ability to be an exceptional man so as to be strong against traditional and contemporary restraints is the most important contributing factor.
- Neustadt reasons that it is the power to persuade that deserves the top spot.
- Closely related, Kellerman argues that knowledge of how to use people to maximize power is the primary source of effective presidential leadership.
- More broadly, Rossiter maintains that the power to influence history is the most important determinant of presidential success.
- Rose argues for a more contemporary number one: the president's ability to influence international affairs.
- Skowronek contends that presidents fit into a predictable flow of historical patterns, which determine the nature and extent of their leadership potential.
- Ellis and Wildavsky believe that presidents find themselves in the cross hairs between their personal leadership predispositions and three competing American political cultures.

All theorists, as they attempt in different ways to define the number one factor, possess a fragment of the whole. The whole, however, is not defined; theoretical precision remains elusive.

Everybody Wins

In their search for the "holy grail" of theoretical precision, the theorists Cronin and Genovese suggest that the answer resides not in the scope of one theory alone. "Rather than seeking one unifying theory of presidential politics that answers all our questions," they write, "we believe that the American presidency might be better understood as a series of paradoxes, clashing expectations and contradictions."[121] Thus, Cronin and Genovese set out to discover theoretical precision, listing nine paradoxes of the presidency—each implying both how a president ought to lead and how Americans evaluate effective presidential leadership.

- Paradox 1: "Americans demand powerful, popular presidential leadership that solves the nation's problems. Yet we are inherently suspicious of strong centralized leadership and the abuse of power. Thus we place significant limits on the President's powers."[122]

This paradox reflects the agony behind the struggle of the Founders at the Constitutional Convention: how to have enough, but not too much, power. The presidency has undergone such huge changes since the time of the Founders that the presidency of today bears little resemblance to the presidency of early America. Now, not only is the presidency divided into traditional and modern eras but also according to some theorists, such as Rose, it has moved into a different era: the postmodern presidency. It has become larger, grown in power, and developed a greater connection to the passions of the people.[123] Yet, although the presidency has undergone significant changes we continue to expect from presidents today what the Founders intended then: "an informed, virtuous statesman whose detached judgment and competence would enable him to work well with Congress and other leaders in making and implementing national public policy."[124] Today, we expect the president to embody our passions and yet stay out of our lives.

- Paradox 2: "We yearn for the democratic 'common person' and also for the uncommon, charismatic, heroic, visionary performance."[125]

As Barber writes, "[s]ometimes people want a hero, sometimes they want a friend."[126] The two seem naturally opposed, and yet we require both. "Part of the public mind always recognizes that the President is only a man, with all of man's vulnerability to moral error; part wants to deny that, to foist on the President a priestliness setting him above the congregation."[127] Perhaps this paradox lies beneath the schizophrenia of Americans regarding Clinton's behavior in the White House. Some approve of his infidelity: if he can do it, so can they. Others want to look up to someone who is better than the weaknesses that tempt so many. Most people want both.

- Paradox 3: "We want a decent, just, caring and compassionate President, yet we also admire a cunning, guileful, and, on occasions that warrant it, even a ruthless, manipulative President."[128]

Greenstein, as mentioned earlier, describes the unique American invention of the presidency as the combination of two roles so different that they "seem almost designed to collide."[129] Although most countries assign the roles of constitutional monarch and prime minister to separate individuals, America requires the same man who serves as the "symbol of unity" to be the aggressive warrior for a prosperous economy, favorable social conditions, and to prevent and prosecute wars.[130] Cronin and Genovese echo Greenstein's report: "Our nation is one of the few in the world that calls on its chief executive to serve as its symbolic, ceremonial head of state *and* as its political head of government."[131] Greenstein reasons that Eisenhower succeeded because he fulfilled both functions. Eisenhower was a quiet leader reflective of his times. He used language carefully, he refused to assault his political opponents with personal attacks, and he gave close private attention to others.[132] And yet Greenstein reveals Eisenhower to be a shrewd politician.

- Paradox 4: "We admire the 'above politics' nonpartisan or bipartisan approach, and yet the presidency is perhaps the most political office in the American system, which requires a creative entrepreneurial master politician."[133]

Eisenhower had an electability that lay largely in his "credible reputation as a nonpolitician."[134] Yet his political skills were so well developed that he was able to hide them. The American people may *think* that they want only one side, but again, we want both. Thus, Greenstein proposes that the success of the much-passed-over Eisenhower presidency is his ability to perform both roles while hiding the fact that he was performing one of them. Eisenhower's strength was executing the "Hidden-Hand Presidency." In his discussion of presidential performance, Rose points out the weakness of emphasizing only one side of this paradox. "Jimmy Carter entered office with the simple belief that policy choices were between doing what was right or wrong, but found that presidential politics is about reconciling competing definitions of what is good."[135] Jimmy Carter is no big presidential success story. We should learn from his mistakes. Barber, too, states the paradox: "a president should be a master politician who is above politics."[136]

- Paradox 5: "We want a president who can unify us, yet the job requires taking firm stands, making unpopular or controversial decisions that necessarily upset and divide us."
- Paradox 6: "We expect our president to provide bold, visionary, innovative, *programmatic* leadership, and at the same time to respond *programmatically* to the will of public opinion majorities. That is to say, we expect presidents to lead and follow, and to exercise 'democratic leadership.'"[137]

Cronin and Genovese point out that the very term "democratic leadership" is paradoxical.[138] However, they argue, it can be realized. Similarly Greenstein writes that "It is not a contradiction in terms to speak of Eisenhower's leadership." Instead, the challenge is to unravel it.[139] Paradoxes 5 and 6 are closely related in that: "We want a president who can unify diverse people and interests; however, the job requires taking firm stands, making unpopular or controversial decisions that necessarily upset and divide."[140] We want a president who can stand so much in the middle that he can rally *all* of America. But we won't vote for a man who doesn't represent our pet issues.

- Paradox 7: "Americans want powerful, self-confident presidential leadership. Yet we are inherently suspicious of leaders who view themselves as infallible and above leadership."[141]

Again, both are right. We do long for a perfect leader, but we also know that any such thing is not humanly possible, so we are rightly suspicious of one who claims to be the impossible. Both are right.

- Paradox 8: "What it takes to become president may not be what is needed to govern the nation."[142]

Rose argues that "[t]he biggest problem of the postmodern President is: what it takes to become president has nothing to do with what it takes to be President."[143] He suggests that "An even more troubling prospect must be faced: what it takes to become president actually makes it more difficult to be a successful postmodern President," for, he points out, "[a] politician who dedicates his time to pressing the flesh on the campaign trail has little or no time to think about what he would do if he won the White House."[144]

- Paradox 9: "The presidency is sometimes too strong yet at other times too weak."[145]

Naturally, this is true, and necessarily so. The Founders ensured this result by how they both granted and limited presidential powers. Moreover, the presidency vacillates between strength and weakness, depending on circumstances and personalities. Then, too, beauty is in the eyes of the beholder. When President George W. Bush prosecuted the wars in Afghanistan and Iraq, some deemed his use of power wise and prudent, whereas others considered it dictatorial and undemocratic. So, again, we encounter the mystery of paradox: it is not black-and-white; it is not "either-or;" it must be "both-and."

"To govern successfully," Cronin and Genovese say at the end of their list of paradoxes that "presidents must manage these paradoxes, and must balance a variety of competing demands and expectations."[146] The nine paradoxes result in an extensive list of expectations—and the call to manage them—that would fit well under the exceptional man category. But it is not the intention of Cronin and Genovese to project an exceptional man. They seek to show a reality, and so to make sense of it.

"The mind searches for answers to the complexities of life."[147] In our search to understand reality, "we often gravitate toward simple explanations for the world's mysteries," write Cronin and Genovese.[148] In this, Cronin and Genovese point to the great "problem" of theories: theories are not all encompassing. Theories miss the big picture. As they focus on one topic, the rest are neglected. Is this a problem? Answering "no," Cronin and Genovese state that they are "a natural way to try and make sense out of a world that seems to defy understanding."[149] The problem is not the insufficiency of the theories themselves so much as it is their misapplication. As artificial frameworks constructed to study an object, theories are a tool for zooming in on *parts* of the whole to gain a greater understanding of the whole. All encompassing they are not. "We are uncomfortable with contradictions, so we reduce reality to understandable simplifications."[150] Rather than being the problem of theories, this is their strength, if they are viewed properly and in their proper place.

Cronin and Genovese seek to make sense of the whole by looking at all of its parts. Theorists on presidential leadership allude to paradoxes frequently as they argue for their fragment to be the contender for the number one spot. Cronin and Genovese have gathered many of these paradoxes and encompassed them in their list of nine broad paradoxes. Although theorists in general try to simplify contradictions into understandable simplifications, Cronin and Genovese make clear that "contradictions and clashing expectations are part of life."[151] Paradoxes are everywhere present. "In many ways paradoxes define the presidential office," write Cronin and Genovese, "and it is the paradoxical nature of this institution that makes the search for a unified theory elusive."[152] The result of the Cronin and Genovese work is not a theory so much as it is an examination of reality. They define paradox as "a sentiment or statement that is seemingly contradictory or opposed to common sense and yet may nonetheless be true."[153] By allowing us to show "both sides of the coin" at once, paradox permits us to "put everything out on the table" . . . to understand reality by looking at both sides of it at once.

CONCLUSION

All theories of presidential leadership allude to, if they do not clearly state, the presence of paradoxes and their influence on presidential leadership. If Americans understood all of the contrary demands on presidents, they might exercise greater understanding in their judgment of them. If presidents always understood the paradoxes, they could more effectively lead the nation, distinguishing the possible from the unattainable and educating the public accordingly. In short, understanding the paradoxes of presidential leadership can help both the populace and presidents understand reality.[154]

Theories point to the big picture of presidential leadership, but they are not the picture itself. They provide better understanding of selective parts of presidential leadership, but they do not make sense of reality as a whole. To the extent that theories instruct us about the paradoxes of presidential leadership, they help to unveil the big picture.

Notes

[1]Ida P. Rolf, *Rolfing: The Integration of Human Structures* (New York: Harper & Row, 1977): Preface.

[2]Richard Rose, *The Postmodern President*, 2nd ed. (Chatham, NJ: Chatham House Publishers, 1991): 33.

[3]Richard E. Neustadt, *Presidential Power: The Politics of Leadership* (New York: John Wiley, 1960): 2.

[4]Ibid., 43.

[5]Ibid., 10.

[6]Ibid., 34.

[7]Ibid., 36, 37.

[8]Ibid., 43.

[9]Ibid., 46.

[10]Clinton Rossiter, *The American Presidency*, rev. ed. (New York: Harcourt, Brace and World, 1960): 15–38.

[11]Ibid., 18.

[12]Ibid., 19.

[13]Ibid.

[14]Ibid., 24.

[15]Ibid.

[16]Ibid., 26.

[17]Ibid., 27.

[18]Ibid., 28.

[19]Ibid.

[20]Ibid., 31.

[21]Ibid., 32.

[22]Ibid., 33.

[23]Ibid., 34.

[24]Ibid., 35.

[25]Ibid., 37.

[26]Ibid., 40.

[27]Ibid., 40, 41.

[28]Ibid.

[29]Ibid., 46.

[30]Ibid., 49.

[31]Ibid., 49–68.

[32]Barbara Kellerman, *The Political Presidency: Practice of Leadership* (New York: Oxford University Press, 1984): 16.

[33]Ibid.

[34]Ibid., 19.

[35]Ibid., 21.

[36]Ibid., 35–37.

[37]Ibid., 256.

[38]Harold J. Laski, *The American Presidency* (New York: Grosset and Dunlap, 1940): 17.

[39]Ibid., 13.

[40]Ibid., 14.

[41]Ibid., 16.

[42]Ibid., 22.

[43]Ibid., 24, 25.

[44]Ibid., 259.

[45]Rose, 17.

[46]James David Barber, *The Presidential Character* (Englewood Cliffs, NJ: Prentice Hall, 1992): 485.

[47]Ibid.

[48]Ibid., 486.

[49]Ibid.

[50]Grove City College, Mary Ethel Pew Dormitory, November 25, 2000.

[51]Rossiter, 179–181.

[52]Thomas A. Bailey, *Presidential Greatness: The Image and the Man from George Washington to the Present* (New York: Appleton-Century, 1966): 24.

[53]Charles W. Dunn, Lectures on The American Presidency, Grove City College, January 26, 2000.

[54]Laski, 28, 29.

[55]Ibid.

[56]Ibid., 42.

[57]Ibid.

[58]Ibid., 34.

[59]Ibid., 28–37.

[60]Neustadt, viii.

[61]Kellerman, 13.

[62]Fred I. Greenstein, *The Hidden-Hand Presidency* (New York: Basic Books, 1982): 5.

[63]Ibid., 5, 234.

[64]Fred I. Greenstein, *The Presidential Difference* (New York: The Free Press, 2000): 5, 6.

[65]Fred I. Greenstein, "What Makes for a Good President?" *Wall Street Journal*, October 12, 2000: 20.

[66]Richard Koonce, "Emotional IQ: A New Secret of Success?" *Training and Development*, February 1996: 19.

[67]Paul W. Thayer, "Book Reviews," *Personnel Psychology*, Spring 1997: 222.

[68]Koonce.

[69]Greenstein, *The Presidential Difference*: 6, 200.

[70]Daniel Goleman, "Leadership That Gets Results," *Harvard Business Review*, March–April 2000: 80–86.

[71]Ibid., 80.

[72]Ibid., 83.

[73]Ibid., 84.

[74]Ibid., 87.

[75]Ibid., 86.

[76]Ibid., 85.

[77]Ibid., 80.

[78]Ibid.

[79]Phil Collins, 1993.

[80]Goleman, 90.

[81]Ibid., 88.

[82]Greenstein, *The Presidential Difference*: 8.

[83]Greenstein, "What Makes for a Good President?"

[84]Barber, 2.

[85]Ibid., 3.

[86]Ibid., 5.

[87]Ibid (emphasis supplied).

[88]Ibid.

[89]Ibid.

[90]Ibid., 2–5.

[91]Ibid., 7.

[92]Ibid., 7, 8.

[93]Ibid., 8.

[94]Ibid.

[95]Ibid.

[96]Ibid., 141–143, 227, 387–388, 297, 485–490.

[97]Ibid., 10.

[98]Ibid., 488.

[99]Ibid., 9.

[100]Ibid.

[101]Ibid., 490.

[102]Ibid.

[103]Ibid.

[104]Ibid.

[105]Ibid.

[106]Ibid., 10.

[107]Ibid., 9.

[108]Goleman, 90.

[109]Greenstein, *The Presidential Difference*.

[110]Ibid., 9.

[111]Ibid., 5, 200.

[112]Phil Collins, "Hero."

[113]Goleman, 80.

[114]Kellerman, 13.

[115]Ibid.

[116]Laski, 41.

[117]Goleman, 78, 80.

[118]Stephen Skowronek, *The Politics Presidents Make: Leadership from John Adams to George Bush* (Boston: Harvard University Press, 1993).

[119]Richard Ellis and Aaron Wildavsky, *Dilemmas of Presidential Leadership: From Washington Through Lincoln* (New Brunswick, NJ: Transaction Publishers, 1989).

[120]Cronin and Genovese, *The Paradoxes of the American Presidency* (New York: Oxford University Press, 1998): viii.

[121]Ibid., 2.

[122]Ibid., 4.

[123]Ibid.

[124]Ibid., 5.

[125]Ibid., 6.

[126]Barber, 486.

[127]Ibid., 488.

[128]Cronin and Genovese, 9.

[129]Greenstein, *The Hidden-Hand Presidency*.

[130]Ibid.

[131]Cronin and Genovese, 15.

[132]Greenstein, *The Hidden-Hand Presidency*, 234.

[133]Cronin and Genovese, 12.

[134]Greenstein, *The Hidden-Hand Presidency*, 124.

[135]Rose, 7.

[136]Barber, 6.

[137]Cronin and Genovese, 17.

[138]Ibid., 105.

[139]Greenstein, *The Hidden-Hand Presidency*, 7.

[140]Cronin and Genovese, 15.

[141]Ibid., 21.

[142]Ibid., 23.

[143]Rose, 6.

[144]Ibid.

[145]Cronin and Genovese, 26.

[146]Ibid., 4.

[147]Ibid., 2.

[148]Ibid., 1.

[149]Ibid., 2.

[150]Ibid.

[151]Ibid.

[152]Ibid., vii.

[153]Ibid.

[154]Ibid., 28.

Chapter Four

The Law of Culture

Unanticipated Consequences

History is replete with proofs, from Cato the Elder to Kennedy the Younger, that if you scratch a statesman you will find an actor, but it is becoming harder and harder in our day, to tell government from show business.[1]

—James Thurber

INTRODUCTION TO THE LAW OF CULTURE

> If good leadership requires good acting, then to succeed presidents must rely upon drama, especially in a culture greatly influenced by such institutions as the electronic media and public opinion polling. Although the electronic media and public opinion polling enable presidents to communicate more effectively with the public, they also produce unintended consequences, which may harm democracy.

According to James Thurber's reasoning, good acting is a prerequisite for effective presidential leadership, which raises important questions for American democracy. If style trumps substance, can the nation enjoy reasoned debate about serious ideas and issues? Have television and other electronic media unduly enlarged the importance of style over substance in presidential leadership? Does public opinion polling cause presidential candidates and presidents to play to the poll numbers rather than to follow their conscience and conviction on issues? On the one hand, the electronic media and public opinion polling should enhance democracy by building better bridges of communication and understanding between leaders and followers. But, on the other hand, they may subvert democracy by causing presidents and presidential candidates to emphasize their style of presentation over the substance of their ideas.

Scott Joplin, one of America's most famous ragtime composers, rose to fame through lively pieces such as "The Maple Leaf Rag," but the ice cream man has immortalized him for countless children through "The Entertainer," the musical logo for so many in the ice cream man's trade. Although "The Entertainer" may have primary application to the trade of ice cream men, it could—tongue-in-cheek—rival "Hail to the Chief" as the musical logo of the President of the United States of America. Public discourse in the national media, especially television, has shifted its emphasis from substance to style, making entertainment much more a part of American culture, so that entertainer in chief is now an important presidential role.

Americans once recognized their leaders through their writings, including copies of their speeches,[2] but today's leaders find their images more important than their ideas. For example, in 1992 President Clinton captured the support of many young adults by appearing on MTV. What do we remember from that interview? His substantive answers to substantive questions? No. We remember his preference in underwear and his playing the saxophone with sunglasses on, which gave young people the impression that he was one of them. In 2000, Vice President Gore's poll numbers skyrocketed after "the kiss" of his wife at the Democratic National Convention. Obviously, this had nothing to do with the substance of his ideas or his vision for the United States, but it did portray him as a passionate family man, an appearance that boosted his image. Days later, on the "Oprah Winfrey Show" when George W. Bush's poll numbers had declined, he gave her a "kiss" and then saw his poll numbers rise. Again, the "Bush kiss" had nothing to do with substance, but everything to do with image and entertainment. Today, in the words of Ronald Reagan, "Politics is show business."[3]

Keys to understanding the president's role as entertainer in chief are the impact of two phenomena on presidential leadership: (1) the emergence of style over substance in American culture, and (2) the role of television and public opinion polls.

SUBSTANCE AND STYLE

From the Founding to the Civil War, how did most Americans learn about their presidents? Neil Postman answers that:

> It is quite likely that most of the first fifteen presidents of the United States would not have been recognized had they passed the average citizen in the street. . . . To think about those men was to think about what they had written, to judge them by their public positions, their arguments, their knowledge as codified in the printed word.[4]

But from the Civil War to the early 21st century, the means of learning about current events changed gradually and dramatically. Earlier in American history, not only did most Americans learn about current events through reading, but they also had high literacy rates. According to Postman:

> Although literacy rates are notoriously difficult to assess, there is sufficient evidence (mostly drawn from signatures) that between 1640 and 1700, the literacy rate for men in Massachusetts and Connecticut was somewhere between 89 and 95 percent, quite probably the highest concentration of literate males to be found anywhere in the world at this time. (The literacy rate for women in those colonies is estimated to have run as high as 62 percent in the years 1681–1697.)[5]

In addition to their dependence on reading for information and their high literacy rates, they were "skillful readers whose religious sensibilities, political ideas, and social life were embedded in the medium of typography."[6] Average Americans today find the *Federalist Papers* difficult to read, but when Alexander Hamilton, John Jay, and James Madison wrote them in defense of the proposed Constitution in 1787, average Americans read them throughout all parts of the nation.[7] Statistics document that early Americans were avid readers of more than just the Bible, the book most commonly found in their homes, and also the *Bay Psalm Book*.[8]

> In fact, between 1682 and 1685, Boston's leading bookseller imported 3,421 books from *one* English dealer. . . . The meaning of this fact may be appreciated when one adds that these books were intended for consumption by approximately 75,000 people then living in the northern colonies. The modern equivalent would be ten million books.[9]

When Noah Webster published his *American Spelling Book*, it "sold more than twenty-four million copies between 1783 and 1843."[10] Within three months, Thomas Paine's *Common Sense* sold 100,000 copies, equivalent to selling eight million copies in the same interval today.[11] Howard Fast points out that:

> No one knows just how many copies (of *Common Sense*) were actually printed. The most conservative sources place the figure at something over 300,000 copies. Others place it just under half a million. Taking a figure of 400,000 in a population of 3,000,000, a book published today would have to sell 24,000,000 copies to do as well.[12]

Decades later, Harriet Beecher Stowe's *Uncle Tom's Cabin* sold 305,000 copies in the first year, the equivalent of four million copies today.[13] All of these statistics underscore the passion Americans once had for reading challenging literature.

Culture and Presidential Leadership

Commentators on American culture confirm the influence that reading had on early American society. In 1772, Jacob Duche wrote that:

> The poorest labourer upon the shore of the Delaware thinks himself entitled to deliver his sentiment in matters of religions or politics with as much freedom as the gentleman or scholar. . . . Such is the prevailing taste for books of every kind, that almost every man is a reader.[14]

Samuel Goodrich commented on the American reaction to Walter Scott's novels, saying that: "The appearance of a new novel from his pen caused a greater sensation in the United States than did some of the battles of Napoleon. . . . Everybody reads these books; everybody—the refined and the simple."[15] When authors such as Charles Dickens visited America, they were greeted with the wild enthusiasm now reserved for rock stars, television celebrities, and athletes.[16] Complaining to a Frenchman that the English were stealing an American invention, the technique for making the outer portion of the wheel with one piece of wood, Thomas Jefferson "speculated that Jersey farmers learned how to do this from their reading of Homer, who described the process clearly. The English must have copied the procedure from Americans, Jefferson wrote, 'because ours are the only farmers who can read Homer.' "[17]

Many foreign observers not only noticed a high level of literacy but also its influence on other means of communication. For example, Alexis de Tocqueville observed that Americans always spoke as if they were addressing an audience.[18] Postman argues that: "This odd practice is less a reflection of an American's obstinacy than of his modeling his conversational style on the structure of the printed word."[19]

In large measure reading was so universal because it was the source of information. Substance and ideas rather than style and image were the focus of this reading-saturated society, which had no televisions, telegraphs, or even photographs. People learned about the events of the day primarily through reading.[20] So the public formed their judgments about presidents and presidential candidates chiefly through their writings, not their pictures and images.

The mental and physical requirements of a reading-saturated society help to produce a substance-oriented culture. Readers must sit still and pay attention to a book, newspaper or magazine for an extended period of time, which improves their attention span.[21] They also must have what Bertrand Russell calls an "immunity to eloquence," the ability to differentiate between the style and logic of authors. In other words, readers must distinguish between substance and style.[22] Postman notes that:

> In judging the quality of an argument, you must be able to do several things at once, including delaying a verdict until the entire argument is finished, holding in mind questions until you have determined where, when, or if the text answers them, and bringing to bear on the text all of your relevant experience as a counter-argument to what is being proposed.[23]

Later, he states that reading strengthens such things as conceptual, deductive, and sequential thought; an appreciation for logical thought; a sense of objectivity; and the ability to delay one's response.[24] "In a culture dominated by print, public discourse tends to be characterized by a coherent, orderly arrangement of facts and ideas."[25]

However, this is very different from American society today. Reading no longer functions as the main gateway to information for many, if not most, Americans. In contrast to the near universal literacy in early America, illiteracy is a growing problem. A survey by the U.S. Department of Education notes that: "only 10 to 13 percent of adults with high school diplomas reach the two highest levels [of literacy]."[26] Forty-seven percent of the nation's 191 million adults "do not have the literacy skills they need to function in our increasingly complex economic system."[27] So people no longer rely on reading to gain information about the world and current events. Instead, they rely on television and the Internet. The statistician George Barna has noted that "93% of all adults own a VCR," and "73% of Americans subscribe to cable TV."[28] Apparently watching television now ranks third in the average American's daily routine, behind working and sleeping.[29] Since 1963, television and the Internet have replaced newspapers as the dominant source of news in America. Then television led newspapers by 2 percent, but now by more than 30 percent.[30] As a result, many of the works once read by common people, such as the *Federalist Papers* and Homer, now gather dust on library shelves.

In today's American culture, as television and the Internet have replaced reading as the gateway to information about current events, so, too, has style and image become more important than substance and ideas. Presidents and presidential candidates must now pay more attention to how they say something than to what they say. Perception has become the mother of reality in presidential leadership.

Debates and Presidential Leadership

Presidential debates have changed dramatically, illustrating the shift from substance to style. The classic Lincoln-Douglas debates in 1858 were all-day events. In the first debate, Douglas spoke for an hour, and then Lincoln had one-and-one-half hours for a response. Afterward, Douglas had one-half hour to rebut Lincoln's statements. In another debate about two months later, Douglas started with a three-hour speech. Lincoln realized his response would take about the same amount of time. Because it was already 5:00 P.M., he proposed that everyone dismiss for dinner and then reconvene. The people followed his suggestion, and after dinner there were four more hours of debate.[31] Apparently this was not unusual, as stump speeches during that time often lasted two or three hours.[32] The format and length of these debates allowed the people to thoroughly understand both the issues at stake and the candidates' positions and enabled the candidates to debate the merits of their respective positions rather than merely setting them forth.

The format of these debates also reveals something about the audiences. To listen for three to seven hours to a political debate, people needed very long attention spans.[33] Although these events were also key events on the social calendar, the debate served as the main attraction.[34] The complex substance of the debates required that audiences listen carefully to understand very complicated sentences by ear.[35] Lincoln and Douglas, for example, used intricate and subtle language, something they would have omitted if the people were not able to follow it.[36]

> [W]hile both speakers employed some of the more simple-minded weapons of argumentative language (e.g. name-calling and bombastic generalities), they consistently drew upon more complex rhetorical resources—sarcasm, irony, paradox, elaborated metaphors, fine distinctions, and the exposure of contradiction, none of which would have advanced their respective causes unless the audience was fully aware of the means being employed.[37]

These debates demonstrate the public's detailed grasp of the issues debated. In the writing and delivery of their speeches, the candidates assumed the public's familiarity with the *Dred Scott* decision, political quarrels between the White House and Capitol Hill, controversies within the Democratic Party, and Lincoln's "House Divided" speech.[38] The debates could not have occurred outside of a reading-dominated culture. Before the rise of television, "[T]he use of language as a means of complex argument was an important, pleasurable, and common form of discourse in almost every public arena."[39] Accustomed to reading, the people had built up their habits of critical thinking. This willingness to think critically permitted debates like those of Lincoln and Douglas.

But today a television-dominated culture shapes presidential debates. The famous Kennedy-Nixon debate of 1960 highlights the transition from a reading-dominated to a television-dominated culture. Those who listened to the debate over the radio thought that Nixon won, but those who saw it on television thought Kennedy won. Why? In large measure because Kennedy, who looked more youthful and healthy, used makeup, whereas Nixon, who had just recovered from the flu, did not. Nixon looked "sickly" on television.[40] In 1984, when Reagan debated Mondale, each candidate had just five minutes to answer a question, and his opponent had a one-minute rebuttal.[41] Given these time constraints, image became more important than substance. "Post-debate commentary largely avoided any evaluation of the candidates' ideas, since there were none to evaluate."[42] Instead, theatrics, such as the candidates' gaze, smile, or one-liners, became the basis for determining the victor. The same could be said for the Bush-Gore debates of 2000. Analysts and journalists spent more time evaluating the mood, aggressiveness, stage presence, and confidence of each candidate than the substance of their statements and rebuttals. Bluntly put, style defeated substance and image conquered ideas. As stated by one authority:

> It is easy for the purveyors of personality to become overly absorbed in individual matters of small moment and events of smaller political consequence. Candidate debates have become increasingly trivialized as the reporting, analysis, and commentary revolve around assigning a clear victor or assessing image-oriented concerns such as appearance and style of delivery.[43]

Television and Presidential Leadership

Why has television contributed so much to the shift from substance to style? Four reasons stand out: (1) Television's Superficiality; (2) Television's Visual Nature; (3) Television's Immediate Emphasis; and (4) Television's Audience.

Television's Superficiality. News organizations, especially television, have to move quickly from story to story in order to cover them all. Where radio stations dedicate about three minutes to news every hour, the major television networks devote about 22 minutes once each evening.[44] Television's average news story runs between 30 and 45 seconds,[45] which leaves little time for in-depth thought or analysis. Even Dan Rather has said: "You simply cannot be a well-informed citizen by just watching the news on television."[46] In order to hold their viewers' attention, newscasters must offer a fast-paced, simplified version of the news. Quick changes in camera angles help to create the image of movement in newscasts.[47] Unlike the printed media, viewers cannot reread newscasts, which television newsrooms refer to as "shows." Dramatic pictures with their emphasis on symbols and personalities dominate television news, simplifying even the most complex issues.[48] The media also simplifies the news by creating themes, and then they present each individual story as fulfilling a part of that theme.[49] Although this makes the news easier to follow, it may not accurately represent reality as news producers simplify the stories to fit their thematic molds.[50]

The superficiality of television also affects other media outlets. For example, the chief White House correspondent for *Newsweek* said that:

> Part of our problem is we are a mass circulation magazine and we tailor ourselves to a mass audience, and sometimes more deserving stories go down the tube for that reason. . . . You can't afford to be boring, but some of the most boring stories are the best stories. That is a problem. . . . The stories with the most news value are cabinet changes or scandal. The best stories are frequently without conflict or controversy.[51]

So now news stories, even in magazines, must be chosen for their entertainment value. Television's fast pace has made people accustomed to short stories, and thus, magazines like *Newsweek* must accommodate. "[M]any newspapers have tried to be more visually interesting by changing their makeup, using larger headlines, and photographs, more white space and fewer columns (meaning fewer words per page), and more dramatic language."[52] One major example of this is *USA Today*, which quickly outsold other papers, such as the *Wall Street Journal*.[53] "The success and influence of a newspaper like *USA Today* demonstrate the broad appeal of relying more on the visual display of information."[54]

Television's Visual Nature. As a visual medium, television tends to focus on the flashy, exciting events rather than more substantive issues.[55]

> Coverage is given to dramatic and colorful events such as ceremonies, parades, disasters, and acts of violence more than it is to "talking heads" discussing ideas. Events are tangible, and thus more amenable to film coverage than are ideas. They involve action, and thus are more entertaining.[56]

To make matters worse, the press tends to focus on the most dramatic portion of the events. So if there are hecklers in a rally or there is violence at a march, they will garner the attention of the press to the omission of the rest of the event.[57] Hence, entertainment is more important than content. Postman offers another reason why this is true: the act of thinking does not look good on the screen.

> Thinking does not play well on television, a fact that television directors discovered long ago. There is not much to *see* in it. It is, in a phrase, not a performing art. But television demands a performing art. . . .[58]

Politicians also understand that "engaging visuals carry their own meaning, frequently quite distinct from the words we might hear."[59] During the 1984 presidential race, Leslie Stahl compiled a six-minute story that tried to expose the differences between Reagan's image and his policies, which overjoyed Reagan's campaign according to one aide:

> We're in the middle of a campaign and you gave us four and a half minutes of great pictures of Ronald Reagan. And that's all the American people see. . . . They don't listen to you if you're contradicting great pictures. They don't hear what you are saying if the pictures are saying something different.[60]

Newscasters have also commented on television's visual emphasis. A long-time White House correspondent for ABC, Sam Donaldson, said: "A clip of a convalescent Reagan waving from his window at some circus elephants is going to push an analytical piece about tax cuts off the air every time."[61] The same holds true for print media as well, according to Michael Grossman and Martha Kumar in *Portraying the President*, which cites a prominent White House correspondent:

> [I]t's a lot easier for me to get [my stories] into several newspapers in the chain with a story about Amy [President Carter's daughter] than with a story about an important policy decision. If they use both, the Amy story is likely to get in page one, while the policy story will be buried on page 29.[62]

Television's Immediacy. Television focuses on events of the moment rather than how and why these events occurred. Because past events are old news, television moves on to new stories to keep up with the competition. One of President Ford's staff explained that the White House bombards Washington reporters with the President's views on an issue, knowing that the press quickly tires of reporting on the same subject.[63] Focusing on the present, according to Carl Schorske, makes history irrelevant to most people.[64] Television's Bill Moyers says we live in "an anxious age of agitated amnesiacs. . . . We Americans seem to know everything about the last twenty-four hours but very little of the last sixty centuries or the last sixty years."[65]

Validating Moyers's concerns is the "Education for Democracy Project," which concludes that: "Many students are unaware of prominent people and seminal ideas and events that have shaped our past and created our present."[66] Reinforcing this extensive study, former U.S. Secretary of Education Bill Bennett found that "[m]ore than two thirds of them [17-year-olds] did not know when the Civil War occurred while three fourths of them could not say within twenty years when Abraham Lincoln was president."[67] Bennett writes that:

> More than one-fifth of the students could not identify George Washington as the commander of the colonial forces during the Revolution. Almost one in three did not know Lincoln was the author of the Emancipation Proclamation. And nearly half failed to recognize Patrick Henry as the man who said, "Give me liberty or give me death." . . . Half the students did not know the meaning of the Monroe doctrine. . . . Almost 70 percent did not understand what Jim Crow laws were designed to do.[68]

Yet another study surveyed 609 adults on their governmental and political knowledge, such as the length of a presidential term and the name of the first 10 constitutional amendments. During a 40-year span, the study recorded a 3 percent improvement in knowledge of these subjects. Only 25 percent of these adults could name both of their senators.[69] Although education certainly plays a critical role in these figures, television reinforces this historical apathy and ignorance. As people spend more time watching television, history matters less and less to them, causing them to respond almost exclusively to television's nearly exclusive emphasis on the present.

Television's Audience. George Edwards argues that the nature of television's viewing audience strengthens the shortcomings of television. The public's short attention span causes them to devote less attention to the news media,[70] which generates a self-fulfilling prophecy. Television fosters a short attention span with the very techniques it has used to try to maintain the viewers' attention. Viewers grow accustomed to, and even bored with, the 45-second story. Robert MacNeil of the long-running *MacNeil-Lehrer News Hour* on Public Television states that: "The idea 'is to keep everything brief, not to strain the attention of anyone but instead to provide constant stimulation through variety, novelty, action, and movement. You are required . . . to pay attention to no concept, no character, and no problem for more that a few seconds at a time.'"[71] He also says that new programs assume that "bite-sized is best, that complexity must be avoided, that nuances are dispensable, that qualifications impede the simple message, that visual stimulation is a substitute for thought, that verbal precision is an anachronism."[72] So, to say that short attention spans limit television's impact, one must first admit that television has influenced American culture.

Edwards also notes that the American people's low reading ability limits the effect of the press.[73] Although this limits people's exposure to newspapers and magazines, it makes them more reliant on television. However, television contributes to this supposed limit as well by making it less necessary for people to learn to read. Reading was so universal in early America because it was the only way to learn about current events.[74] Today, however, if people cannot read, they can simply turn on the television to "learn" current events. So, again, in order to argue that this is a limit on the press, one has to admit that television has had a tremendous impact on the culture.

Public Opinion Polls and Presidential Leadership

Public opinion polls also have contributed to the cultural shift from a substance-oriented to a style-oriented society. Indeed, the modern presidency chronicles the rise of these polls as a cultural force. In 1936 the *Literary Digest* infamously predicted that Alf Landon would upset Franklin Roosevelt, but the poll surveyed people with phone numbers or automobiles, which wealthier people had, and not a cross section of society.[75] In 1948 the *Chicago Tribune* proclaimed "DEWEY WINS!" based on Gallup Poll results, which did not measure the surge of support for President Truman during the waning days of the campaign.[76] Since then, the number of polls has blossomed, and their accuracy has improved. A majority of national news organizations, including television and newspapers, now conduct or sponsor polls, which usually come within the statistical margin of error.[77]

Modern presidents have used polls in various ways, but most important as thermometers to tell them about conditions outside the White House.

Roosevelt. Franklin Roosevelt used polls to determine what he needed to do to gain the public's support. When his pollster informed him that the public did not understand the Lend-Lease policy, Roosevelt explained it more clearly in a public address to Congress.[78] "According to his pollster, however, Roosevelt never altered his goals because public opinion was against him or uninformed."[79]

Truman. Truman, who disliked polls, stated: "I wonder how far Moses would have gone if he'd taken a poll in Egypt? What would Jesus Christ have preached if he'd taken a poll in Israel?. . . . It isn't polls or public opinion of the moment that counts. It is right and wrong and leadership . . . that makes epochs in the history of the world."[80] However, his disdain for polls may have hurt him politically. His popularity plummeted at the end of his term, especially after he fired the popular General Douglas MacArthur as Commander of American forces in Korea.

Kennedy and Johnson. Neither Kennedy nor Johnson relied on the polls to establish their sense of direction.[81] Johnson used them in much the same way as Roosevelt, but he also used them (when they were high) to convince undecided members of Congress to support him.[82] Kennedy's short time in office does not allow for a complete assessment of his use of polls.

Ford. Ford followed Truman's example in pardoning Nixon, a move that cost him his initial popularity and likely later cost him the election in 1976 against Jimmy Carter. In the public's eyes, Ford never recovered from the pardon, which now stands out as a profile-in-courage.

Carter. Carter continued Roosevelt's trend of using polls to determine the effectiveness of his communication. Gerald Rafshoon, President Carter's media adviser, recalled that: "If we ever went into the president's office and said, 'We think you ought to do this or that to increase your standing in the polls,' he'd throw us out."[83] Later, Carter's pollster, Patrick Caddell, confirmed this approach:

> This White House uses polls as a kind of a guidepost to determine the direction and distance the President has to go in terms of getting the public to move in favor of positions which he feels are necessary for the country. They are a sounding board for that kind of movement. And they are obviously an indicator of political successes or problems that the President has.[84]

Reagan. Reagan used polls and analyses of public opinion more than any other administration before him; however, his pollster said that "their most important function is to determine when the nation's mood is amenable to the president's proposals."[85] White House aide David Gergen recalls that:

> It was said of Reagan that he never had to take the pulse of the country; he *was* the pulse. He had a fingertip feel for the mood of the country that was as good as anyone we've had in the presidency, including Clinton. That's not to say polls were unimportant to him. He looked forward to his strategy sessions with Dick Wirthlin, who reviewed the latest numbers and offered political counsel. But he relied upon polls less for policy-making than for double-checking his instincts and sharpening his arguments.[86]

Reagan also used Wirthlin's information and techniques to help frame his rhetoric. Wirthlin's "techniques included a 'speech pulse,' by which people holding special computerized dials could test-market presidential speeches. The dials not only tapped positive and negative reactions, but also measured very specific things, such as responses to the speaker's credibility. . . . The results could identify . . . the lines and tones most effective in altering feelings."[87] Wirthlin claimed that his system allowed the president's advisors to determine "what themes we can play after the speech, what phrases we can use again."[88] So although President Reagan was not captive to the polls, he did use them to shape his rhetoric. Since Reagan, however, presidents have begun using polls not only as thermometers but also as thermostats. That is, they now use them to determine their course of action and how to express that action.[89]

Bush. During the 1988 presidential campaign, the Campaign Manager for George Bush Sr., Lee Atwater, used focus groups to determine what issues and what approaches the campaign should use in television advertising. The famous Willy Horton commercial, which now ranks as one of the most widely criticized, but also one of the most effective, campaign commercials in presidential campaign history, resulted from these focus groups. Despite the fact that President Bush Sr. said, "I don't live by the polls," in March 1990,[90] "those closest to Bush said he was 'obsessed' with the polls.' "[91] For example, before Desert Storm he received polls regarding America's reaction to the crisis in the Middle East, but it is not clear how these polls were used.[92] At a minimum, however, "[a]dministration spokespersons could then if they wished, shift the emphasis of their various announcements to reflect these opinions."[93]

Clinton. President Clinton magnified this trend, becoming one of the first politicians to rely on focus-group information in preparing his policies. While commenting on the permanent campaign atmosphere in Clinton's White House, David Gergen points out that:

> There were three prongs to his permanent campaign. One was reliance upon constant polling. All modern presidents have polled heavily . . . but no one before Clinton had taken a poll to determine whether he should tell the truth publicly (the Lewinsky case) or to use American ground troops (Kosovo). The *Wall Street Journal* has reported that President Bush in his first two years spent $216,000 on polls; President Clinton in his first year alone spent $1,986,410, nearly ten times as much.[94]

Bush. Although President Bush Jr. is no exception to the rule of emphasizing polls, he has at least in some instances acted more like Presidents Truman and Ford, taking positions that the public may not support, but then convincing the public that his positions merit their support. His narrow election victory in 2000, losing the popular vote, but winning the electoral vote, did not give him a mandate for bold initiatives. Boldness, however, on many fronts has characterized his leadership on such issues as tax policy, education reform and international affairs. Not, however, until he leaves office will we have a fair and balanced account of Bush's use of polls.

So, whereas most presidents have used polls as thermometers, the growing trend is for presidents to use them as thermostats, shaping policies and key decisions in addition to perfecting rhetoric.

IMPACT ON PRESIDENTIAL LEADERSHIP

How has the cultural shift from substance to style affected presidential leadership? An examination of this shift reveals several unintended consequences. Although television and public opinion polling appear to offer great potential for dramatically strengthening presidential leadership, reality paints a picture colored by irony and paradox. Both assets and liabilities emerge from the impact of television and public opinion polling on presidential leadership.

- **Irony One: Television both increases and decreases the ability of presidents to educate the public.**

Although television may enable presidents to obtain saturation exposure for their ideas and policies, it also limits their ability to educate the public. Television's time constraints and competitive environment make explaining complex issues more difficult. Since networks and stations compete to hold the attention of their audiences and to increase their market share in the ratings, they devise fast-paced news programs with only a brief treatment of each news story. Presidents may sidestep these news programs by giving nationally televised speeches, but they cannot afford to do that too often lest their speeches become commonplace and the public ignores them.[95]

So, most of the time presidents and their staffs must bow to the evening news programs to get their messages out,[96] which requires the boiling down of presidential messages to fit television's demands. During the 1968 presidential campaign, the average sound bite lasted 42.3 seconds, but now the average is well under 10 seconds.[97] Precious little education can fit into today's single sound bite. In 1952, presidential candidates bought 30-minute blocks of time; in 1956, they changed to five-minute speeches; then during the 1970s, the five-minute speech gave way to the 60-second commercial; and now, their commercials usually run 30 seconds or less.[98] Of these statistics, Lloyd Cutler, White House counsel during the second half of Carter's administration, says that:

> TV is quintessentially a medium that transmits simple surface impressions, while national policy issues are infinitely complex and many sided. The ugliness of military combat or economic deprivation can be graphically conveyed in a few pictures and sounds; the policy considerations that usually lie behind a decision to risk these consequences are much more difficult to explain.[99]

Compounding the task of compressing presidential messages on television is what George Edwards calls the "body watch." "[Reporters] are interested in what the president is going to do, how his actions will affect others, how he views policies and individuals, how he presents himself, and whose stars are rising and falling, rather than in the substance of policies or the fundamental processes operating in the executive branch."[100] What a task! Satisfy reporters and at the same time set forth your views on a critical issue. Of this task, Edwards says that: "Major presidential addresses are often reported in terms of how the president looked, how he spoke, and the number of times he received applause as much as in terms of what he had to say."[101] For example, Gerald Ford's speeches were either ignored or covered extremely briefly because the press was more interested in his latest apparent blunder. President Carter became so frustrated with his inability to discuss substance on the air that he once told some reporters, "I would really like for you all as people who relay Washington events to the world to take a look at the substantive questions I have to face as president and quit dealing almost exclusively with personalities."[102] In 1922, Walter Lippman noted that the press had a growing "preference for the curious trivial as against the dull important, and the hunger for sideshows and three-legged calves."[103] This fascination has only grown since his time, making the president's job only harder.

Television also forces presidents to express their messages in very simple language. Postman argues that people accustomed to television commercials do not trust complex language.[104] The press compounds this problem (1) by ignoring the qualifying and cautionary statements presidents make in discussing their positions on issues,[105] and (2) by reporting preliminary findings or hedged statements as absolute fact.[106] President Ford was particularly upset with the willingness of the press to overlook these qualifiers. For example, the *New York Daily News* summarized Ford's speech regarding New York's financial plight, which lasted 45 minutes, with the headline: "FORD TO NY: DROP DEAD."[107] The president must remember a key lesson:

> Brevity is the cardinal principle of television. To receive coverage, especially on the most heavily watched evening newscasts, a public figure has to deliver a message in a sentence or two. Detailed discussions of complex issues are boiled down to simplistic slogans or clever quips as public discourse devolves into unilluminating battles of one-liners.[108]

President Reagan understood this and always had a "line of the day" that he would incorporate into his statements or actions.[109] Bush learned from Reagan and "used unnuanced, tough sounding one-liners for television reports."[110] Of this, Samuel Kernell points out that:

> Getting out "the line for the day" is, in fact, one of the principal activities of the contemporary White House staff; by one estimate more than a quarter of the staff is dedicated in some way to producing the president's public activities.[111]

Reducing complex issues into a "line for the day" causes the public to look for quick and easy solutions. Thus, when a problem arises that does not have a simple solution, such as a recession or a protracted military conflict, the public becomes frustrated with presidential leadership.

- **Irony Two: Television increases the ability of presidents to address issues of immediate concern, but decreases their ability to position those issues in the context of history.**

Television enables presidents to speak quickly and forcefully on issues, but limits their ability to relate their ideas and positions to the flow of history. By removing the opportunity to place a position in its historical context, presidential actions appear like disconnected events.[112] If the president has to make a controversial decision, he will be making it in light of past events. However, as Edwards has noted, the press is very reticent to repeat a story for the benefit of its viewers.[113] To the reporters, it is old news regardless of whether the people understand the topic or not. Thus, the public may not understand the president's action since television tends to ignore the past, even the recent past.

This lack of historical context also makes it easier for presidents to tread on the truth. Without any historical context, even lasting only a few days, the president can obfuscate at will. If people forget (or the press ignores) what he said two days ago, then he is free to contradict himself as much as he pleases. Postman argues that "we are by now so thoroughly adjusted to the 'Now . . . this' world of news—a world of fragments, where events stand alone, stripped of any connection to the past, or to the future, or to other events—that all assumptions of coherence have vanished. And so, perforce, has contradiction."[114] When referring to presidential lies, he states, "The public has adjusted to incoherence and been amused into indifference."[115]

- **Irony Three: The visual nature of television increases the ability of presidents to craft a favorable personal image, but decreases their ability to address ideas and issues and may limit the pool of presidential candidates.**

Camera appeal reduces content appeal. Although television may enhance the ability of presidents to fashion favorable personal images, it reduces their ability to convey the content of their ideas. And, in doing so, it may well limit the pool of presidential candidates. For example, in today's presidential campaigns, who could imagine the nomination and election of the 300-pound William Howard Taft?[116] As Richard Nixon put it:

> Television today has transformed the ways in which national leadership is exercised and has substantially changed the kind of person who can hope to

be elected to a position of leadership. Abraham Lincoln, with his homely features and high-pitched voice, would never have made it on television. Nor would his speaking style, with its long rambling anecdotes, have worked on the tube. The premium today is on snappy one-liners, not lengthy parables.[117]

Later, when Senator Edward Kennedy ran for national office, Nixon advised him to lose 20 pounds.[118] These characteristics have nothing to do with one's ability to govern, integrity, or vision for the country, yet the demands of the television screen mandate them. Postman writes, "We may have reached the point where cosmetics has replaced ideology as the field of expertise over which a politician must have competent control."[119] Just to become president, one must look good on television. Hubert Humphrey, who lost to Nixon in 1968, stated that: "The biggest mistake in my political life was not to learn how to use television."[120]

Moreover, even after their election, presidents must cater to the camera. Harry Truman, the first president to face television cameras, impaired his presidential image, because he would not change his television delivery as his advisers wanted.[121] Many presidents, including Eisenhower, Nixon, and Ford, hired consultants to help improve their image.[122] Ford even hired a comedian to help with his speeches.[123] Johnson, who "projected an image of feigned propriety, dullness, and dishonesty"[124] according to one of his biographers, changed to contact lenses, used makeup, and tried different prompting devices, but to no avail.[125] Nixon, who lost the 1960 presidential in large measure to his poor television image, did not make the same mistake twice in 1968. One of his senior advisors, Ray Price, stated emphatically that:

> *We have to be very clear on this point: that the response is to the image, not to the man,* since 99 percent of the voters have no contact with the man. It's not what's *there* that counts, it's what's projected—and carrying that one step further, it's not what *he* projects but rather what the voter receives. It's not the man we have to change, but rather the *received impression.* And this impression often depends more on the medium [television] and its use than it does on the candidate himself.[126] [Emphasis in original]

After winning the 1968 election, Nixon altered the format of press conferences to counteract the image of an "imperial presidency" aloof from the press and the people. Rather than standing behind a large podium, dominated by a large presidential seal and many media microphones, he addressed the press behind only a single-stand microphone with neither podium nor presidential seal.[127] After Watergate, Ford removed the blue curtains that had served as a backdrop for press conferences because of their theater-like appearance. Instead, he stood in front of two open doors to show that the siege mentality of Nixon was over. But his image as a clumsy and stumbling person constantly haunted him.[128]

In contrast to each of these presidents, Reagan had an innate understanding of his image on television, which his Hollywood acting career had honed.[129] Carefully cultivating the image of an active, vigorous president, one that could motivate and inspire the nation, he insisted on walking into the hospital after being shot, he had daily workouts, including photo opportunities for the press, and he insisted on wearing shirt and tie while working.[130] His manner also reinforced his position as commander in chief. Gergen recalls that: "From day one in the White House, every step was as commander in chief, shoulders thrown back, back ramrod straight, purposeful."[131] He understood just how important his television image was in order to lead the nation.

Is there a danger in television becoming the primary concern of presidents? They need to get coverage in order to gain the nation's support, but their policy statements often get buried by visual images.[132] Could not presidents and their staff, knowing the absolute imperative of getting coverage, begin to look at everything as a television event? Nixon waited in Alaska for nine hours so that he could return to Washington from China during prime time. His entire trip to China involved more than 100 television personnel and three cargo planes of equipment.[133] When he met the French president in Iceland the next year, television was again his main focus. One foreign-service officer complained that:

> All they cared about was how things would look on television. White House aides fussed about the lighting, about who would stand where, what the background would be, and the furniture. The entire time I was assigned to the detail, no one asked me a substantive question. I'm sure they didn't care. All they seemed to care about was television.[134]

Ford followed this trend of selecting events for the sole purpose of enhancing the president's image. He held a briefing on the budget to show he was "competent" in that area.[135] His deputy press secretary said, "Whenever possible, everything was done to take into account the need for coverage. After all, most of the events are done for coverage. Why else are you doing them?"[136] The Reagan White House scheduled events that showed the president in active leadership roles to combat the general impression of his being aloof and passive.[137] Television's impact has increased to the point that presidents and their staff devote a substantial portion of every day to enhancing the presidential image.

Television as a visual medium magnifies presidential blunders. When Richard Nixon accidentally referred to the guilt of Charles Manson even though the trial remained in progress, the press converted his gaffe into a big blunder, even though it was of little or no consequence. Later the press questioned his mental state after he shoved his press secretary.[138] But Gerald Ford suffered more from his blunders than any other president. Edwards notes that:

> Coverage of trivial shortcomings, such as his skiing and golfing mishaps, his awkwardness on plane steps, his saying "Ohio State" instead of "Iowa State" in a speech, and his wearing ill-fitting pants when meeting Emperor Hirohito, regularly appeared on the front pages of America's newspapers and on its television screens.[139]

Later, Ford commented on this matter:

> [E]very time I stumbled or bumped my head or fell in the snow, reporters zeroed in on that to the exclusion of almost everything else. The news coverage was harmful, but even more damaging was the fact that Johnny Carson and Chevy Chase used my "missteps" for their jokes. Their antics— and I'll admit that I laughed at them myself—helped create the public perception of me as a stumbler. And that wasn't funny.[140]

Immediately after his debate with Carter, 44 percent of the people thought Ford had won, whereas 43 percent preferred Carter. A day later, after the press publicized Ford's error in saying that the Soviet Union did not dominate Eastern Europe, Carter was the overwhelming victor by a margin of 62 percent to 17 percent.[141] In 1992, the press magnified Bush's glance at his watch during a presidential debate, making him appear disinterested and desirous of ending it, and they also dumped on Dan Quayle because he misspelled *potato*. These gaffes are more interesting, more entertaining, and more visual than most substantive issues, and thus, they get much more attention than they deserve.

- **Irony Four: Public opinion polls may increase the ability of presidents to know what's on the public's mind but decrease their ability to lead.**

Public opinion polls are like yo-yos, going up and down as they subject presidents to the vicissitudes of public opinion. Although presidents win four-year terms, their leadership faces the constant threats of unfavorable public opinion polls. For example, "Lyndon Johnson and Richard Nixon, reelected by landslide margins in 1964 and 1972, respectively, found their power—that is their claim to be the voice of the people—undercut when polls showed they had lost substantial support."[142] Public opinion polls threaten two-term presidents even more by compounding their weakened status as lame ducks, who cannot succeed themselves. When polls cause presidents to lose their political footing during their second terms, as they usually do, they have few options to regain their footing.[143] Typically, second-term presidents achieve significantly less than during their first terms. Opponents and those who aspire to the presidency have little incentive to follow the leadership of incumbent presidents.

To what extent should presidents heed public opinion polls? Do polls, which represent the views of followers, limit the leadership potential of presidents? Do Americans want a president who simply follows the polls? Do polls create a paradox between leading and following? Ironically, the people elect their presidents to lead, but polls may tie them to the leash of public opinion, which restricts their movement as leaders. If presidents put an ambitious agenda before the people, can or should they ignore the polls about their proposals?[144] Some evidence suggests that Americans do not always prefer that presidents follow the polls.

> In fact some of our greatest presidents have been those willing to disregard the opinion of the moment to do what they thought was right. Truman, ranked highest by historians of modern presidents, had the lowest poll ratings. Paradoxically part of Truman's stature appears to be precisely that he did not care about the polls and took every opportunity to show it.[145]

If presidents govern according to the polls, then they may find their leadership unduly and unwisely constricted.

First, although polls measure public opinion, they do not measure how intensely people hold their opinions.[146] The public holds almost universally intense views, pro and con, on the issue of abortion, but far less intense views on issues pertaining to the Mississippi River. Intensely held views among a substantial portion of the population may limit a president's leadership options, but when the public cares much less about an issue, presidents typically have far more leadership latitude.

Second, as most polls simply ask questions in a yes/no format, they do not reflect the complexity of presidential decisions.[147] "The president must make decisions that may determine a policy's success or failure in being passed by Congress or in meeting its goals. Yet such details do not lend themselves to mass polling because they require specialized knowledge that few Americans possess."[148]

Third, presidents must realize that the wording of a question affects poll results.[149] For example, attitudes toward the Vietnam War in the polls varied according to whether the questions portrayed the war as a patriotic act or as an example of Western imperialism.[150] The same phenomenon happened in 1981, when almost 40 percent of the people supported turning "welfare" over to the states, but a few months later only 15 percent supported turning over federal "aid for the needy."[151]

Fourth, presidents cannot control the timing of the polls, which the White House itself does not conduct. Poll results taken one day can quickly change the next day, if a significant intervening event occurs. During the Iraq War, President George W. Bush found his popularity and leadership subjected to the roller coaster of poll results. A poll taken after a significant success in the War showed increased popular support for the president, whereas another poll taken after a set back lowered his standing.

Fifth, unless polls occur at appropriate intervals, they cannot adequately track changes in public opinion.[152]

Sixth, presidents must understand that their poll numbers will fluctuate according to a normal pattern. Presidents generally lose support after their "honeymoon," and their poll numbers usually continue to fall until they reach a low point in the third year of their terms.[153] In their second terms, presidents lose support in the polls even faster than in their first.[154] Of this, Paul Brace and Barbara Hinckley write:

> It is important to see that this decay occurs independently of all other influences. The decay over time takes place irrespective of the economy, the president, or outside events. All presidents, it seems, must contend with this decay of support, caused by public expectations and the boundaries of a four-year term.[155]

Seventh, polls often reflect popular ignorance of political issues. Ford echoed this when he said:

> I do not think a President should run the country on the basis of polls. The public in so many cases does not have a full comprehension of a problem. A President ought to listen to the people, but he cannot make hard decisions just by reading polls once a week. It just does not work, and what the President ought to do is make the hard decisions and then go out and educate the people on why a decision that was necessarily unpopular was made.[156]

But this is obviously easier said than done:

> [i]f just over half of the people know merely basic information about our political system, one wonders the extent to which those in public life should use survey research to influence what they do. What is actually being measured? Is it genuine political opinion, or is it more akin to collective guesswork, spur-of-the-moment reaction to a series of multiple-choice questions.[157]

Although television and political polls pose some inherent dangers, much still depends on the character of the man in the Oval Office. Michael Novak believes:

> There is a critical difference between public relations image making and genuine symbolic engagement. The one is manipulation from the outside

in; the other is expression from the inside out. The one tries to execute a prior construct or design; the other tries to allow what is inside to manifest itself. The one tries to guide the reactions of observers; the other tries to make contact with them, so as to liberate energies within them.[158]

Ronald Reagan provides an excellent example of someone who avoided many of the dangers of both polls and television.[159] He used both to accent his message without allowing either to manipulate him. Gergen recalls that: "If a speech had an emotional close, his voice would crack, an eye might mist—not because he was acting, but because as an actor, he had learned to let himself go. His emotions were close to the surface, and he wasn't afraid to show them."[160] This is a major reason for President Bush's success in his leadership after September 11, 2001.

In order to govern today, presidents must be able to use television, even though it can hamper them in many ways. "Without some stagecraft that captures and holds the citizenry-audience, effective statecraft that receives the consent of the governed and can stand the test of long-term public good is not possible."[161] However, presidents with good character will remember that television and the polls are merely tools to help them serve the country.

CONCLUSION

The electronic media and public opinion polls would appear to benefit presidential leadership by enabling presidents to communicate more effectively with the public and to learn what the public thinks. These two laudable democratic objectives suffer, however, from unintended consequences. The electronic media and public opinion polling strengthen the bridge of communication between presidents and the public through a democratic dialogue about issues and ideas, but they also weaken the bridge by emphasizing the images of presidents more than their ideas. As style has trumped substance, presidents have had to turn to more imaginative and entertaining ways of gaining public support.

Notes

[1] Robert Schmuhl, *Statecraft and Stagecraft: American Political Life in the Age of Personality* (Notre Dame, IN: University of Notre Dame Press, 1990): vii.

[2] Neil Postman, *Amusing Ourselves to Death: Public Discourse in the Age of Show Business* (New York: Viking Penguin, 1985): 60–61.

[3] Elizabeth Drew, *Portrait of an Election: The 1980 Presidential Campaign* (New York: Simon and Schuster, 1981): 263.

[4] Postman: 60–61.

[5] Ibid., 33.

[6] Ibid., 31.

[7] Ibid., 38.

[8] Ibid., 32.

[9]Ibid.

[10]Ibid., 37.

[11]James D. Hart, *The Popular Book: A History of America's Literary Taste* (New York: Oxford University Press, 1950): 45.

[12]Howard Fast, Introduction to *Rights of Man* by Thomas Paine (New York: Heritage Press, 1961): x.

[13]Postman: 39.

[14]Hart: 39

[15]Ibid., 74.

[16]Postman: 39.

[17]Ibid., 168.

[18]Alexis de Tocqueville, *Democracy in America* (New York: Vintage Books, 1954): 260.

[19]Postman: 42.

[20]Ibid., 41.

[21]Ibid., 25.

[22]Ibid., 26.

[23]Ibid.

[24]Ibid., 63.

[25]Ibid., 51.

[26]Carol Innerst, "America's Illiteracy Increasing," *Washington Times*, September 9, 1993, as quoted in Christopher Klicka and Greg Harris, *The Right Choice: The Incredible Failure of Public Education and the Rising Hope of Home Schooling* (Gresham, OR: Nobel Publishing, 1995): 37.

[27]"Nearly Half of Adults Read Poorly," *The Milwaukee Sentinel,* September 9, 1993: 1A.

[28]George Barna, "Media and Technology," Available online http://www.barNa.org/FlexPage.aspx?Page=Topic&TopicID=27 Printed on December 22, 2000.

[29]Schmuhl: 56.

[30]Ibid., 76.

[31]Postman: 44.

[32]Ibid., 45.

[33]Ibid.

[34]Ibid., 47.

[35]Ibid., 45.

[36]Ibid., 46.

[37]Ibid., 47.

[38]Ibid., 46.

[39]Ibid., 47.

[40]Richard M. Pious, *The Presidency* (Needham Heights, MA: Allyn & Bacon, 1996): 146.

[41]Postman: 97.

[42]Ibid.

[43]Schmuhl: 12.

[44]George C. Edwards, III, *The Public Presidency: The Pursuit of Popular Support* (New York: St. Martin's Press, 1983): 146.

[45]Charles W. Dunn, "Is the Most Mass of All Least of All?" Public Lecture, Grove City College, Grove City, PA, March 1, 2000. See also: Edwards: 146, and Postman: 103.

[46]Edwards: 146.

[47]Ibid., 147.

[48]Ibid.

[49]Ibid.

[50]Ibid., 169.

[51]Michael Baruch Grossman and Martha Joynt Kumar, *Portraying the President: The White House and the Media* (Baltimore, MD: Johns Hopkins University Press, 1981): 65.

[52]Edwards: 148.

[53]Postman: 111.

[54]Schmuhl: 61.

[55]Postman: 92.

[56]Edwards: 147.

[57]Ibid.

[58]Postman: 91.

[59]Schmuhl: 32.

[60]Martin Schram, *The Great American Video Game: Presidential Politics in the Television Age* (New York: Simon and Schuster, 1987): 181–182.

[61]"Washington Press Corps," *Newsweek*, May 25, 1981: 90.

[62]Grossman and Kumar: 231.

[63]Ibid., 90.

[64]Postman: 137.

[65]Bill Moyers, Speech delivered at the Jewish Museum in New York City during a conference of the National Jewish Archive of Broadcasting, March 27, 1984, as quoted in Postman: 137.

[66]William Bennett, "American Education: Making It Work," U.S. Department of Education, April 26, 1988: 13, as quoted in Klicka and Harris: 23.

[67]Ibid., 24.

[68]Ibid.

[69]Schmuhl: 53.

[70]Edwards: 164.

[71]Robert MacNeil, "Is Television Shortening Our Attention Span?" *New York University Education Quarterly*, Winter 1983: 2.

[72]MacNeil: 3.

[73]Edwards: 164.

[74]Postman: 41.

[75]Sheldon R. Gawiser and G. Evans Witt, *A Journalist's Guide to Public Opinion Polls* (Westport, CT: Praeger Publishing, 1994): 18–19.

[76]Ibid., 20–22.

[77]Thomas E. Mann and Gary R. Orren, eds., *Media Polls in American Politics* (Washington, DC: Brookings Institution, 1992): 20–21.

[78]Edwards: 17.

[79]Hadley Cantril, *The Human Dimension: Experience in Policy Research* (New Brunswick, NJ: Rutgers University Press, 1967): 41–42, 71–73.

[80]Robert H. Ferrell, ed., *Off the Record: The Private Papers of Harry S. Truman* (New York: Harper & Row, 1980): 30, as quoted in Paul Brace and Barbara Hinckley, *Follow the Leader: Opinion Polls and the Modern Presidents* (New York: Basic Books, 1992): 19.

[81]Louis Harris, *The Anguish of Change* (New York: Norton, 1973): 23, 26.

[82]Edwards: 17.

[83]Dom Bonafede, "Rafshoon and Caddell—When the President Is the Client," *National Journal*, May 28, 1977: 816.

[84]Bonafede, "Carter and the Polls—If You Live By Them, You May Die By Them," *National Journal*, August 19, 1978: 1312–1313.

[85]Bonafede, "As Pollster to the President, Wirthlin Is Where the Action Is," *National Journal*, December 12, 1981: 2184–2188.

[86]David Gergen, *Eyewitness to Power: The Essence of Leadership, Nixon to Clinton* (New York: Simon & Schuster, 2000): 200.

[87]Jane Mayer and Doyle McManus, *Landslide: The Unmaking of the President 1984–1988* (Boston: Houghton Mifflin, 1988): 43–44.

[88]Ibid.

[89]See Lawrence R. Jacobs and Robert Y. Shapiro, *Politicians Don't Pander: Political Manipulation and the Loss of Democratic Responsiveness* (Chicago: University of Chicago Press); and Diane J. Heith, *Polling to Govern: Public Opinion and Presidential Leadership* (Stanford: Stanford University Press, 2003).

[90]George H. Bush, Informal News Conference, March, 13, 1990, in *The Public Papers of the Presidents* (Washington, DC: U.S. Government Printing Office, 1990), as quoted in Brace and Hinckley: 3.

[91]*New York Times*, October 9, 1990: A21.

[92]Brace and Hinckley: 143.

[93]Ibid., 150.

[94]Gergen: 331.

[95]Edwards: 41.

[96]Schmuhl: 48.

[97]Kiku Adatto, "TV Tidbits Starve Democracy," *New York Times*, December 10, 1989: Section 4, 23, as quoted in Schmuhl: 56.

[98]Kathleen Hall Jamieson, *Eloquence in an Electronic Age: The Transformation of Political Speechmaking* (New York: Oxford University Press, 1988): 10.

[99]Lloyd N. Cutler, "Foreign Policy on Deadline," *Foreign Policy* 56 (1984): 114.

[100]Edwards: 151. See also Grossman and Kumar: 35, 43–45, 168–169, 179; Stephen Hess, *The Washington Reporters* (Washington, DC: Brookings Institution, 1981): 15–16, 60; Grossman and Kumar, "Carter, Reagan, and the Media: Have the Rules Really Changed on the Poles of the Spectrum of Success?" Paper presented at the Annual Meeting of the American Political Science Association, New York, September 1981: 11; Henry Kissinger, *White House Years* (Boston: Little, Brown, 1979): 159, 1053; and Kissinger, *Years of Upheaval* (Boston: Little, Brown, 1981): 160, 1021.

[101]Edwards: 151.

[102]Quoted in Grossman and Kumar, "Carter, Reagan, and the Media," p. 8, and in Edwards: 152.

[103]Schmuhl: 22.

[104]Postman: 131.

[105]Edwards: 151.

[106]Ibid., 160.

[107]Ibid., 151.

[108]Schmuhl: 56.

[109]Ibid., 31.

[110]Ibid., 43.

[111]Samuel Kernell, *Going Public* (Washington, DC: CQ Press, 1997): 94.

[112]Edwards: 147; Postman: 136.

[113]Edwards: 152.

[114]Postman: 110.

[115]Ibid., 110–111.

[116]Ibid., 7.

[117]Nixon, *Leaders*: 342.

[118]Postman: 7.

[119]Ibid., 4.

[120]Schmuhl: 6.

[121]Newton Minow, John B. Martin, and Lee M. Mitchell, *Presidential Television* (New York: Basic Books, 1973): 33.

[122]Edwards: 39–40.

[123]Gerald R. Ford, *A Time to Heal* (New York: Harper & Row, 1979): 303.

[124]Doris Kearns, *Lyndon Johnson and the American Dream* (New York: Harper & Row, 1976): 303.

[125]Minow: 47.

[126]Joe McGinnis, *The Selling of the President 1968* (New York: Trident Press, 1969): 193–194.

[127]Charles W. Dunn, Public Lecture at Grove City College, Grove City, PA, January 28, 2000. See also Edwards: 118.

[128]Edwards: 159.

[129]Gergen: 245.

[130]Ibid., 172, 202, 245.

[131]Ibid., 245.

[132]Postman: 92; Edwards: 147.

[133]Minow: 66–67. See also, Kissinger, *White House Years*: 757, 761, 1054–1055.

[134]Grossman and Kumar, *Portraying the President*: 236.

[135]Ibid., 234.

[136]Ibid., 29, 45–46.

[137]Gergen: 245; Schmuhl: 31.

[138]Edwards: 152.

[139]Ibid., 151.

[140]Ford: 289, 343–344.

[141]Schmuhl: 82–83.

[142]Brace and Hinckley: 18.

[143]Ibid., 1.

[144]Ibid., 7.

[145]Ibid., 6, 7.

[146]Edwards: 12.

[147]Ibid., 12

[148]Ibid.

[149]Ibid., 12, 13.

[150]Ibid., 13.

[151]Ibid.

[152]Ibid.

[153]Brace and Hinckley: 32.

[154]Ibid., 41.

[155]Ibid., 32.

[156]Edwards: 31.

[157]Schmuhl: 54.

[158]Michael Novak, *Choosing Our King: Powerful Symbols in Presidential Politics* (New York: Macmillan, 1974): 251.

[159]Schmuhl: 34.

[160]Gergen: 244–245.

[161]Schmuhl: 48.

Chapter Five

The Law of Morality

Kaleidoscopic Uncertainty

The Presidency is preeminently a place of moral leadership.

—Franklin D. Roosevelt

INTRODUCTION TO THE LAW OF MORALITY

Successful presidential leadership requires that presidents function effectively in a culture of moral diversity and uncertainty. Not only do presidents bring their own personal morality to bear on their decisions, but they also confront division and dissent about what is morally acceptable in public policy. Both personal and public policy morality are now less clearly defined than in earlier generations.

Generally acknowledged as one of America's greatest presidents, Franklin D. Roosevelt placed morality on the center stage of presidential leadership. Roosevelt understood that moral storm clouds hang over every major presidential decision. As people and groups fight to define what is moral and right for the family, art, education, law, domestic politics, economics, and foreign policy, presidents daily confront division and discontent about definitions of the morally acceptable.

Before the invention of computers, global positioning systems, or even accurate maps, sailors used the stars, particularly the North Star, to plot their course. With clear and certain guiding lights, they could find their way across stormy waters on dark nights. But presidents of the United States often navigate stormy political waters without clear and certain guiding lights, especially on moral matters. In short, they often find themselves without a moral North Star.

In their personal lives presidents also face differences about morality. Is a president's private morality a proper subject for public debate? Is there a relationship between a president's private morality and public policy? Should presidents lie if that would help them pursue a greater good for the American public? Some argue that a president's private morality should always remain private; others vehemently disagree. Some argue that the public interest always outweighs and overrides questions of personal morality; others believe the opposite.

Perceiving an inherent moral quandary for presidents, Thomas Jefferson said: "I know well that no man will ever bring out of that office the reputation which carries him into it." On the canvas of presidential history, moral issues have painted a broad-brush stroke over presidents and presidential leadership. Inevitably all presidents, whether moral or immoral, face charges of moral corruption. Where their portraits hang in the museum of presidential greatness often depends on how well they handled moral issues.

Regarding the moral order in America, James Q. Wilson writes that: "Many Americans worry that the moral order that once held the nation together has become unraveled."[1] American morality has become kaleidoscopic, reflecting an increasing variety of competing ideas about morals and religion, blurring the lines separating right and wrong. Although total agreement about American morality never existed, basic agreement was once more common. The directions of American morality have shifted from uniformity to diversity, from simplicity to complexity, and from singular to plural.

Kaleidoscopic morality makes presidential leadership more difficult. Presidents can no longer count on widely accepted moral standards to guide their actions. They must defuse moral land mines by trying to accommodate, appease, and appeal to differing moral interests.

MORAL ISSUES IN THE MODERN PRESIDENCY

Although sex scandals hover like dark clouds over the presidencies of John F. Kennedy and Bill Clinton, modern presidents have faced a range of allegations about moral issues. Among these not-necessarily-true accusations are:

- Franklin Roosevelt's complicity in handing over Central and Eastern Europe to the Soviet Union after World War II,

- Truman's defense of scandal among his advisors and his decision to drop the atomic bomb on Japan,
- Eisenhower's lying about the U-2 Spy Plane incident and his apparent laxness in standing up to Senator Joe McCarthy,
- Kennedy's abortive Bay of Pigs decision, his links to the Mafia, and his affairs with several women,
- Johnson's lying about the Vietnam War,
- Nixon's order of illegal military incursions into Cambodia and his Watergate cover-up,
- Ford's pardon of Richard Nixon,
- Carter's misleading use of religious language,
- Reagan's involvement in the Iranian hostage scandal to gain an electoral advantage against Jimmy Carter,
- George Herbert Walker Bush's reversal of his "read my lips" pledge against no tax increases,
- Clinton's Whitewater scandal, cover-up of various sexual indiscretions, and exchanging atomic secrets for campaign contributions with the Chinese, and
- George W. Bush's misleading of the American public about weapons of mass destruction in Iraq and failure to perform his duties as a member of the National Guard.

Although moral issues of a sexual nature may excite great interest and wound presidential reputations, other moral issues may sound the death knell for presidents as they did for Presidents Johnson and Nixon, when issues totally unrelated to sex decapitated their presidencies. Johnson lied when he told Americans he would not send American boys to fight a war that Asian boys should fight. He sent some 550,000 troops to Vietnam where more than 58,000 gave their lives. Facing the possibility that his own party would not renominate him in 1968, he withdrew from the race. Nixon covered up the Watergate burglary and then denied that he had. Legal and constitutional questions caused the U.S. House of Representatives to begin impeachment proceedings against him. Realizing he lacked the votes in the U.S. Senate to stop it from convicting him on those charges, he resigned from office.

Johnson and Nixon entered office on the heels of two of history's greatest landslide victories. Moral issues, however, short-circuited their grand visions for America and the world, lowered the public's esteem for them, and left a legacy of popular distrust of government and the presidency.

TYPES OF MORAL ISSUES

Presidents face many moral issues, not all of their making, but all of which may alter their reputations. All of the moral issues facing presidents fall into at least one of six categories: (1) Personal, (2) Constitutional, (3) Financial, (4) Political, (5) Tangential, and (6) Procedural and Substantial.

1. **Personal.** Behavior before and during the presidency can significantly alter the reputations of presidents. President Clinton's alleged inappropriate relationships with a variety of women—Jennifer Flowers, Paula Jones, Juanita Broadrick, Julie Hyatt Steele, Kathleen Willey, and Monica Lewinsky—not only raised serious questions about his personal morality but also required considerable expenditure of time and financial resources to defend him.

2. **Constitutional.** President Nixon's behavior in the Watergate scandal produced a constitutional scandal of great moment, not only causing the U.S. Supreme Court to order the release of presidential tape recordings as evidence in a criminal case against him, but also leading to his premature departure from office. As the presidential race heated in 2004, critics charged that President George W. Bush had misled the American people regarding intelligence reports, which he had used to justify American involvement in the Iraqi War. In response, President Bush named an independent commission to examine the matter.

3. **Financial.** Sometimes presidents, especially before their presidency, have financial ties that raise questions about their morality. In his famous Checkers speech in 1952, vice presidential nominee Richard M. Nixon had to defend himself against charges of having either an illegal or unethical political fund. In like manner, President Clinton's pre-presidency participation in the Whitewater land deal raised the moral ire of many.

4. **Political.** Early in 2004 charges surfaced that President George W. Bush may have failed to meet his service obligations in the National Guard some 30 years earlier. Daily media accounts over several weeks forced the President to release his entire military record to demonstrate that he had fulfilled his obligations and had received an honorable discharge. Even then, however, the press and the political opposition persisted in raising questions about his service and whether he had obtained favors through political pressure from his father or others. During the Clinton-Gore administration, political fundraising appearances by Vice President Gore at a Buddhist Temple and the solicitation of campaign contributions from foreign financiers in Indonesia and China tarnished their moral credibility.

5. **Tangential.** Even "squeaky-clean" Jimmy Carter, who campaigned on the theme, "You can trust me," confronted moral scandals. His Director of the Office of Management and Budget, Bert Lance, a trusted friend and long-time political confidant, lost his position early in the Carter administration due to his involvement in a Georgia banking scandal. Although not personally involved in the scandal, Carter felt the effects of his friend's moral turpitude.

6. **Procedural and Substantial.** The public, press, and politicians put presidential policies under a moral microscope, looking for flaws in their procedural implementation and in their substantive results. In the modern era from Franklin D. Roosevelt through George W. Bush, every president has faced charges about their policies. Most recently, critics charged George W. Bush with favoring the rich in his tax policies and with failing to work appropriately with the international community in the Iraqi War.

PERSPECTIVES ON PRESIDENTIAL MORALITY

Many presidents have had high personal moral standards, which helped them weather the storms of moral charges and ultimately to gain national acclaim and praise. But other intensely moral men have had their careers ruined when they displayed high moral standards. Further complicating the picture are those presidents with few or no moral yardsticks at all that have received accolades for their leadership.

Is there a moral North Star for the office of the presidency? Although perhaps disconcerting to think not, an honest examination of history reveals that morality does not always lead to political success. Yet at other times, morality stands out as the only stabilizing force in a nation on the brink. Why the seeming inconsistency? Understanding morality and the presidency requires knowing that presidents do not serve their country in a vacuum. Numerous influences determine how presidents serve, and how the public perceives their service. To understand how morality has affected the presidency, and in turn, how presidential morality has affected the nation calls for an examination of how three primary factors have colored presidential and national history.

1. **The Presidential Perspective**

   - What situation placed a president under the moral microscope?
   - How did a president handle the situation?
   - How did a president's handling of the situation affect his reputation?

2. **The Event Perspective**

   - What events affected the situation?
   - How did these events salvage or sabotage a president's image?

3. **The Media Perspective**

   - How did the president treat the media?
   - Did he court or condemn them?
   - Did they coddle or consume him?

PRESIDENTIAL MORALITY HISTORICALLY EXAMINED

An examination of these three perspectives in a cross section of presidencies—George Washington, Thomas Jefferson, Abraham Lincoln, Andrew Johnson, Woodrow Wilson, Warren Harding, Herbert Hoover, Franklin Roosevelt, John Kennedy, Richard Nixon, and Jimmy Carter—illustrates the many different aspects of morality and the presidency.

George Washington

Having fought a war against the excesses of executive power in the hands of King George III, yet knowing that the weak executive in the Articles of Confederation would not serve the nation's interests, the American Founders cautiously, suspiciously, and warily scrutinized the untested office of the presidency. Thus, any person occupying the post would face intense scrutiny, George Washington being no exception.

On the personal front, many contemporaries considered him a man with little intellect, whereas others spread rumors that he had fathered illegitimate children.[2] But those charges failed to capture popular attention. Instead, his vision for America as the first president captured the imagination of the American people, which ultimately placed him in the pantheon of America's greatest presidents.

Studiously concerned about setting proper precedents for the presidential office, Washington carefully considered his actions. But his careful judgments about establishing proper precedents frightened many, sometimes causing controversy about the most mundane subjects. People even complained about his schedule. Rather than balking at the absurdity of the charge, Washington asked his advisors to determine appropriate scheduling policies and procedures. Accepting their recommendation, he set aside two times each week for interested persons to speak with him. Although that failed to placate some complainers, this example demonstrated his rational and visionary approach for handling problems.[3]

Not only did Washington recognize the importance of setting proper precedents, but he also knew the significance of avoiding scandal, which could undermine his efforts to place the presidency on a sound footing. In this regard, he followed the same levelheaded and visionary approach: "He was concerned less with his appointees' expertise than with their reputation for good character."[4]

Typical of presidents, George Washington loathed the media's treatment of him,[5] especially allegations of marital infidelity and intellectual inadequacies, but he was hardly a media punching bag when compared to later presidents.

On June 20, 1791, *The Connecticut Courant* made Washington the measuring rod for presidents: "Many a private man might make a great president, but will there ever be a president who will make so great a man as Washington?"[6] Journalists followed Washington's every move, detailing his every action. When arriving in new places, groups often greeted him with songs of adoration. In one tribute a church choir sang:

He comes! He comes! The hero comes!

Sound, sound your trumpets, beat your drums

From port to port, Let canons roar

His welcome to our friendly shore.

So, for the most part, the media acknowledged Washington's upstanding morality, and joined the nation in cheering him.

In summation, Washington as "the first president sought to win the trust of Congress and the people so that he and future presidents would be able to exercise power forcefully when it seemed most appropriate."[7] Although scandals emerged, he took extraordinary measures to prove them unfounded. By projecting a pure personal morality, he could project a clear vision for America. He removed the possibility of a damaging focus on his personal morality, so that his vision could become a guiding compass for America.

Thomas Jefferson

Long before he became president in 1801, Thomas Jefferson confronted many rumors of immorality, but during his first term, the rumors exploded. In a series of newspaper articles, a muckraking journalist, James Callender, accused Jefferson of fathering an illegitimate son with Jefferson's slave, Sally Hemmings.[8] Although a 1998 DNA test tentatively verified a link between Jefferson and the alleged son, any male relative of Jefferson could have fathered him.[9] And so, the debate has raged for over two centuries.

But then in response to the flurry of controversy, which Jefferson appeared to ignore, he dispersed surrogates to respond to the charges, while he himself never directly denied them. The historian Dumas Malone states: "There seems to be no record of his ever having referred specifically even in private to the story connecting him with his slave Sally Hemmings."[10] Several explanations surround his silence. Perhaps he remained silent so as not admit any wrongdoing or to avoid lying to the public by denying the charges or simply to let his surrogates indirectly state his innocence.

Whether guilty or not guilty of the accusations is in some ways less relevant than how he dealt with them and how those charges affected the public's perception of his presidency. A mock trial in 1994, convened by the Bar Association of the City of New York, ruled on whether Jefferson's alleged hypocrisy outweighed his contributions to America. The jury overwhelmingly agreed that the good outweighed the bad,[11] concluding ". . . that the trial was not about whether Jefferson was prone to hypocrisy, which seems to be a given. The question of the evening was, 'are we willing to forgive him for it?' "[12]

Although not Washingtonian in stature, Jefferson continues to rank among the greatest of America's great presidents. Allegations of moral impropriety hardly constitute a spot of dirt on a breathtaking painting of Jefferson's presidential success.

Abraham Lincoln

Abraham Lincoln's early life in a log cabin has stimulated many a childhood dream of glory and grandeur along the pathway from rags to riches, but would Lincoln himself have willingly suggested that schoolchildren dream of becoming president? This shy backwoodsman, brought to the presidency more by an electoral fluke than by a popular mandate, found himself leading a disruptive and divisive country. Little wonder that political adversaries plagued his presidency with gross insinuations and innuendos about his morality.

Lincoln responded to the South's Secession from the Union by launching the Civil War without congressional approval. Then during the War, he suspended the writ of habeas corpus, imposed a naval blockade, and established martial law in many areas. Many wondered if these were the actions of a dictator or a president. But this alleged "dictator," who faced almost certain defeat in 1864, insisted that the election be held. He "accepted a risk and permitted his power to be threatened in a way that no dictator, constitutional or not, would have allowed."[13]

To properly understand Lincoln's administration requires an examination of its surrounding circumstances. As Sidney Milkis and Michael Nelson note, "Absent the Civil War, Abraham Lincoln's ability to lead the nation would have been severely constrained."[14] The circumstances that bred the moral charges against him depended almost entirely on the War's existence.

Accusations of moral impropriety against Lincoln centered in the charge that he had created a constitutional dictatorship. Believing that his Oath of Office compelled him to use extraordinary measures to uphold the Constitution. Lincoln reasoned that "It was senseless . . . to obey legal niceties while the foundation of the law itself—the preservation of the Union—was threatened."[15]

Premising his difficult decisions on these grounds, he issued several controversial orders. For example, Lincoln ordered a naval blockade of the Confederacy before Congress had declared war, an action he hoped would quickly end the Southern insurrection. When this matter came before the U.S. Supreme Court in 1863, the shipping industry argued that as only Congress could legally declare war, the blockade was unconstitutional. The Court, however, upheld Lincoln's order, concluding that desperate times called for desperate measures.[16]

Lincoln made many controversial decisions, which detractors regarded as immoral, but which admirers considered as good for the nation. Lincoln's admirers say he did not act to increase his power as president, but to increase the strength of a struggling nation. Understanding that the morality of his presidency was about much more than his personal reputation, he believed that the presidency as an institution was larger and more important than the president himself.

Andrew Johnson

Sometimes when politics and politicians cry out for blood, they sacrifice presidents on the altar of morality. Such was the case with Andrew Johnson, whose ascension to the presidency in the wake of Abraham Lincoln's assassination thrilled the radicals. Desiring to impose harsh punishment on the South for its rebellion, the radicals looked askance at Lincoln's lenient reconstruction policies. But they saw Johnson as one of them. After all Johnson himself had said: "I say the traitor has ceased to be a citizen in joining the rebellion and has become a public enemy."[17] Shortly after Lincoln's assassination, a leading radical, Senator Benjamin Wade, said to Johnson: "Johnson, we have faith in you. By the gods, there will be no trouble now in running the government."[18] But these same radicals, who once welcomed his presidency with open arms, later charged him with High Crimes and Misdemeanors, impeaching him in the U.S. House of Representatives and trying him in the U.S. Senate, where they fell one vote short of removing him from office.

What prompted this dramatic shift of opinion? According to Kenneth M. Stampp, it "resulted in part from subsequent modifications of his ideas about Reconstruction, in part from his own limitations as a politician, and in part from the utter failure of the radicals to understand him."[19] On entering the office, Johnson and the radicals agreed that the North must suppress the Southern rebellion to preserve the Union; that the 13th Amendment warranted enforcement; and that Southern planter aristocrats had engaged in repulsive behavior.[20] Stampp points out that Johnson's beliefs stemmed from his background of poverty: "His humble origin and the scorn the planter class had heaped upon him made him bitter, pugnacious, and self-assertive. He had no ease, no grace, no self-confidence."[21]

But the longer Johnson served as president, the more his views about reconstruction became like Lincoln's, who believed that a more magnanimous program of reconstruction would heal the wounds of War more quickly and satisfactorily. Furiously reacting to Johnson's change of heart and mind, the radicals posted 11 articles of impeachment against him, including the 10th article, which charged that Johnson had engaged in "intemperate, inflammatory, and scandalous harangues."[22] Ultimately Johnson's impeachment "resembled less a trial to determine if Johnson had committed high Crimes and Misdemeanors, than a convention of the Radical Republican Party to run Johnson out of office."[23]

Woodrow Wilson

Sometimes presidents with strong moral foundations can lose sight of where they are leading the nation. Although a moral stalwart, Woodrow Wilson's impeccable morality ironically contributed to his downfall. As an admirably strong leader, he showed incredible strength in his ability to unite and lead Congress in various causes, such as World War I, which he called "A War to Make the World Safe for Democracy." Wilson firmly believed that his duty required him to articulate a vision and convince the nation to follow.[24] During the first part of his presidency, he did precisely that while justifying American participation in World War I.

> It is a fearful thing to lead this great people into war, into the most terrible and disastrous of all wars. *But the right is more precious than peace*, and we shall fight for a universal dominion of right by such a concert of free peoples as shall bring peace and safety to all nations and make the world itself at last free.[25]

Wilson's moral vision for the nation, or rather the world, was clear. He must lead all people toward that which was right. And he had the ability to inspire and lead as noted by *The New York Times* in 1913: "President Wilson probably has no equal in this country as an effective speaker."[26] The nation responded to his eloquent rhetoric by joining in his causes.

But failure tarnished Woodrow Wilson's sterling record, beginning with the 1918 mid-term elections. Wilson's morality caused him to believe that the achievement of his goals depended on the presence of a Democratic majority in Congress. So fervently did he campaign for a Democratic majority in Congress that he faced a sharp backlash for implying that only Democrats had enabled him to succeed.[27] When Republicans captured control of both the

House and Senate, Wilson's strong leadership began to ebb. Suddenly Congress became his enemy in his moral fight for truth and justice. When the United States Senate challenged his League of Nations proposal, Wilson's resolute personal morality allowed for no compromise.

The tide had turned. No longer did the nation adore Wilson for his moral leadership and vision for America. Instead they began to abhor him for his immovable and inflexible personal and subjective morality. The presidency became less a symbol of democracy and more a portrait of a president intent on getting his way. Wilson's stubborn morality cost him the trust and admiration of the American people.

Warren G. Harding

Because personal moral scandals swirled like a tornado around the life and presidency of Warren G. Harding, historians might agree with his self-assessment: "I'm not fit for the office, and should never have been here."[28] Affairs with several women, wild White House parties, and allegations of his wife's connivance in his mysterious death soiled his reputation.[29] What some might consider as moral insensitivity to the plight of the unemployed also haunted Harding. Arriving in the White House during an economic slump, he failed to act sympathetically to their troubles, stating that "There has been vast unemployment before, and there will be again."[30]

Why did Harding, given these failings, have one of the longest "honeymoons" in presidential history? His lasted for over a year, but not by accident. Harding courted the press, holding biweekly press meetings, which he seemed to enjoy. His technique was simple: Take journalists into his confidence and trust them to act discretely.[31] In appraising Harding's presidency, Andrew Sinclair reveals the strengths and weaknesses of his approach.

> During Harding's life, he was praised for his humanity. After his death, he was blamed for his indiscretion. His intimacy with journalists provided each of them with a personal story of Harding's failings. Thus by successfully wooing the press during his life, Harding invited damnation by the press after his death.[32]

Herbert Hoover

Like Andrew Johnson, Herbert Hoover went into the presidency on the wings of great hope and expectation. He had political experience, serving as the Food Administrator for the Wilson administration and as Secretary of Commerce under Warren Harding and Calvin Coolidge. But, also like Johnson, personal foibles and current events contributed to his undoing. In the end, like Johnson, a cloud of disappointment hovered over the head of his departure from office.

As a conservative president, he believed that the presidency garnered its power primarily from the Constitution and not from extraconstitutional sources. According to Eugene Lyons, Hoover considered his position the principled or morally correct interpretation of the Constitution.

> In the first year of depression, he faced a headstrong Congress, in the rest of his term, a brutally hostile Congress. But out of devotion to the principle of separation of legislative and executive power, he used none of the available tricks for circumventing Capitol Hill.[33]

When the stock market crashed on October 24, 1929, leading to the greatest era of depression Americans had ever known, Hoover thought that as president he should encourage private institutions to support and fund relief efforts. As a believer "in the so-called trickle-down theory of economic prosperity, he wanted economic recovery to occur through rejuvenated business and not through government handouts."[34] Congress proposed many public works projects, but Hoover vetoed them, believing that they were constitutionally indefensible.[35] In a radio address on the anniversary of Abraham Lincoln's birthday, Hoover said:

> I have the feeling that if you could sit in the middle of the government and see the tools with which we have to work and the disasters which confront us at all times in the use of these human tools, you would not want us to extend the area of government but rather to keep the government as nearly as we can in its greatest function—the safeguarding of human rights.[36]

Hoover did not simply sit back and do nothing during his tenure in office. Repeatedly he encouraged businessmen to pursue more just business practices. However, the same philosophy that prevented him from expanding the federal government to feed the nation also prevented him from expanding his presidency to promote the benefits of his ideas. Unwilling to aggressively advance his own philosophy, while still vetoing efforts to ease the pain of the nation, Hoover became known as cold-hearted and uncaring. What he saw as morally principled action, the people saw as morally cruel disregard for their plight.

Franklin Delano Roosevelt

Current events created a political undertow, which drowned the presidencies of Andrew Johnson and Herbert Hoover. Lacking the ability to swim against the undertow of hostile political currents, they left office in political disgrace.

Franklin Roosevelt was quite the opposite. Recent historical surveys rank Roosevelt as the second greatest president, surpassed only by Abraham Lincoln.[37] In fact, the very circumstances that led to the political death of Herbert Hoover boosted the popularity of Roosevelt. For example, "Legions of experts on the government payrolls were engaged in selling the New Deal, which inevitably meant unselling the old."[38] Roosevelt turned negative circumstances into a positive gain, namely the longest presidential reign in American history. How big of a turnaround was it? "In 1931, men and woman all over the world were seriously contemplating and frankly discussing the possibility that the western system of society might break down and cease to exist."[39]

Although Hoover's morality kept him from expanding the powers of government, Roosevelt's morality would not allow otherwise. Because the nation suffered, he used the lever of government to relieve suffering. Roosevelt believed he should experiment with government programs until he found those that worked. And so he brought about the largest peacetime expansion of government in American history.

Whereas Roosevelt's political morality benefited him, his personal immorality slightly shrouded his greatness. For example, he had a long-standing affair with his wife's secretary, Lucy Mercer, which ended in 1918 after his wife, Eleanor, demanded that it stop. This affair, however, resumed near the end of his life. He died in the presence of his mistress, not his wife, who was several hundred miles away.[40] Roosevelt also hid from the public his paralysis from the waist down.[41] Although some argue that the nation had no need to know this information, others contend that he was less than morally forthright.

On the one hand, Roosevelt was a man of great strength, who powerfully led the nation through a disastrous time by restoring pride to thousands of people previously out of work. On the other hand, he had an affair with his wife's secretary and covered up his paralysis. Despite his moral contradictions, the public elected him four times. To his adoring public, the events of the time combined with his vision for the future far outweighed his moral shortcomings.

John F. Kennedy

Few presidents rank as high on the scale of immortality as does John F. Kennedy, but equally few rank as high on the scale of immorality. To his admirers, Kennedy stands out as one of America's most inspirational presidents. Carl Brauer said: "Kennedy was inspirational in a way few presidents have been,"[42] and *New York Post* columnist Murray Kempton wrote: "I have never known a politician who seemed to me quite so privately engaging."[43]

But his detractors allege that the Mafia helped to finance Kennedy's presidential campaign, that he had an affair with an ex-girlfriend of a Mafia boss while Mrs. Kennedy was expecting the birth of their child and that he revealed security secrets to Marilyn Monroe.[44] Despite the controversy about his public record and personal life, Kennedy continues to rank high as one of America's most inspiring presidents.[45]

In 1960 during one of America's closest presidential elections, Kennedy used the emerging medium of television to exude confidence, excitement, and charm. Before the first debate with Richard Nixon, Kennedy trailed Nixon in public opinion polls. Ironically among those who watched the first debate with Richard Nixon on television, Kennedy won, but among those who listened on radio, he lost. On television, Nixon looked haggard, whereas Kennedy appeared poised and self-assured, but on radio Nixon's arguments carried more weight with the listening audience than Kennedy's.[46] The Kennedy-Nixon debates turned the tide of public opinion to Kennedy and unveiled television as the most important modern medium of political communication.

His campaign themes of "The New Frontier" and "Let's Get America Moving Again" inspired and excited the nation, which knew little or nothing about allegations concerning his personal immorality. Kennedy served in an era when the media did not report on the moral failings of presidents. One reporter, James Bacon, who had knowledge of the affair between John Kennedy and Marilyn Monroe, refused to report it, saying:

> Before Watergate, reporters just didn't go into that sort of thing. I'd have had to have been under the bed in order to put it on the wire for the AP. There was no pact. It was just a matter of judgment on the part of the reporters.[47]

Richard M. Nixon

During a close race for the presidency in 1968, Nixon promised to end the unpopular Vietnam War, which he did, but several years later. Four years later in 1972, while on the road to winning one of history's biggest landslide victories, Nixon benefited from his policy of gradual deescalation of American involvement in Vietnam. Unknown to the public, however, Nixon had ordered unconstitutional military incursions into Cambodia on behalf of his Vietnam policy and had also approved of an illegal raid on Democratic Party headquarters in Washington's Watergate complex. When these events became public, Nixon fell from grace. His top aide, H. R. Haldeman, understood the significance of the Vietnam War when he said: "I firmly believe that without the Vietnam War, there would have been no Watergate."[48]

In a period of national turmoil and distrust surrounding the Vietnam War, Nixon committed immoral acts. Ironically, he did not need either the Cambodian incursions or the Watergate break-in to win the 1972 election. So Nixon fell on a sword of his own making and transformed public identification of the highly unpopular Vietnam War from President Lyndon B. Johnson and the Democratic Party to himself and the Republican Party.

Large antiwar marches deeply bothered President Nixon.[49] To continue his efforts to deescalate the War and hopefully to leave Vietnam honorably, Nixon needed a firm base of American public support, which public protests eroded. Determining "not to be destroyed by the war, (Nixon) proceeded on a path of leak plugging, wire tapping, and criminal acts."[50] Also along the way press paranoia overcame him. Unlike Harding, who looked on reporters as allies, and Kennedy, who saw them as a group to be charmed, Nixon distrusted them and desperately distanced himself from them. In his own words: "My public standing had been driven so low that I do not think there was any allegation about me—no matter how horrendous or base that would not have been believed if published."[51]

Ironically, his percentage of newspaper endorsements in the 1960, 1968, and 1972 presidential campaigns totaled 54, 60, and 71, respectively,[52] hardly the numbers of a person despised by the press. Certainly the "press had an increasingly important role in shifting public opinion against the president,"[53] but only after Nixon had given them reason to report facts against him. Because Nixon failed to see the media as a tool he could use, he saw them as his enemy.

When confronted with Nixon's immoral acts, the media had no reason not to print them. He had lied to them, and they believed the nation deserved to know. As a result Nixon had no pillow of affection or admiration to rest on. The media, seeing nothing in Nixon to inspire the nation, had no reason or desire to protect him.

Jimmy Carter

Sadly, the impeccably moral Jimmy Carter has never risen above average on the scale of presidential greatness. According to Richard G. Hutcheson, Carter's morality contributed to his average standing: "In certain identifiable ways, Carter's presidency was probably handicapped or weakened by his deep religious faith."[54] Kenneth Morris explains in *Jimmy Carter: American Moralist* that: "Whereas moral leadership articulates a vision that others are inspired to realize, moral character merely displays a trait that others find laudable."[55] Carter never managed to extend his morality into a moral vision for America. He viewed every problem that confronted him as one with either a right or a wrong solution, but many times right and wrong do not exist, only effective or ineffective.

Appearing like a flawless figure of self-righteousness, Carter isolated himself from others. Had he faced a Nixon-like scandal, his self-righteousness would likely have made his fate the same. Nixon and Carter could neither laugh at themselves nor respond to criticism graciously. And like Nixon, Carter never befriended the media, though he tried.

To appear more humble and less distant from the people, President Carter walked up Pennsylvania Avenue to the Capitol during his Inauguration, banned playing "Hail to the Chief" at presidential appearances, often carried his own luggage, conducted Town Hall meetings and wore a cardigan on national television.[56] Calculated to make him closer to the people, a little more like their friend than their president, these and other similar moves ultimately backfired, because they made him seem less presidential. The public wanted a president they could look up to.

Carter's self-righteousness and efforts to lessen the distance between the public and him drew the ire of the media. In one instance, an Associated Press reporter taped a poster of Carter drawn to resemble Jesus behind Carter as he spoke. The poster's caption read, "JC can save America." Then in another instance of trying to identify with the American people, he gave an interview to *Playboy*, which the press ridiculed, because he described his sin of "lust in the heart."[57] Also in his campaign, he declared to the public: "I'll never lie to you."[58]

The Carter presidency was about Carter and his morality. When Carter tried to draw closer to the people by removing the "unnecessary" prestige and props of the presidency, ridicule followed. Carter never understood that the presidency was bigger than he was. Air Force One, the putting green on the White House lawn, these things were not there for Jimmy Carter, but for the President of the United States, the chief symbol of the nation. What Carter saw as humbling himself, the nation saw as humiliating the presidency.

Carter inspired neither the press nor the people. His personal morality did not help him produce a moral vision for the nation that the media could write about or that the public could grasp. His speechwriter, James Fallows, put it this way: "I came to think that Carter believed fifty things, but no one thing."[59]

Conclusion

Consider again the ship sailing at night. Whether the ship reaches its intended destination largely depends upon the captain knowing and applying the laws of astronomy. Presidents are no different. Both their personal morality and moral vision for America can significantly influence the destiny of their leadership and their place in history.

PRESIDENTIAL MORALITY AND THE MORAL KALEIDOSCOPE

But presidential morality is like a ship on the high seas facing stiff cross-currents, created by the nature of American society, politics, and government. These cross-currents include: (1) cultural conflict in an adversarial society, (2) the intersection of moral character and moral issues, (3) the press and presidential scandal, (4) presidential strategies during moral crises, (5) ideology's moral spawning ground, (6) religion's moral lens, (7) constitutional cultivation of moral issues, (8) historical revisionism and presidential greatness, (9) national debate about moral decline, (10) public policy's moral cloak, (11) public expectations of presidential behavior, and (12) personal versus public policy morality.

Cultural Conflict in an Adversarial Society

Some argue that America is in a state of cultural collapse, rendering traditional moral issues much less important. According to this argument, most Americans no longer view historic Judeo-Christian standards as controlling influences in American life. Quickly cited as evidence is the public's seeming willingness to brush off allegations about President Clinton's moral offenses and the advancing acceptance of homosexuality, including homosexual marriages. According to this line of thinking, America is in the midst of a great culture war between a fading culture of moral certainty and an emerging culture of moral relativism. The former emphasizes absolute standards of right and wrong, whereas the latter deemphasizes them.

Others argue that any president, Democrat or Republican, conservative or liberal, now faces intense moral scrutiny unlike previous presidents, making governance more difficult. Presidents and candidates for the office know the lens of high-powered cameras will photograph skeletons in their closets. Nothing is off limits or outside camera shot. Their lives become the targets of both fact and fiction. The laserlike focus on presidential morality can blind, debilitate, paralyze, and evict presidents. As the White House becomes a firestorm of moral controversy, it appears like a giant foxhole in a war zone. The president can hardly poke his head out of the foxhole without facing fire.

Which view is correct? Perhaps both. As the argument goes, Americans look at moral character through the lens of economic self-interest. Clinton survived in part because of a strong economy, but a weak economy contributed to Nixon's demise.

Each view offers sound arguments and illuminates our understanding of moral scandals. Truth, however, may rest somewhere between the lines of the respective arguments. In short, no simple explanation explains the relationship between morality and the modern presidency.

The Intersection of Moral Character and Moral Issues

Presidents confront the constraints of moral issues as Abraham Lincoln did during the Civil War and as Franklin Roosevelt did during World War II. Lincoln met the moral dimensions of slavery and the abolitionist movement. Roosevelt encountered the moral imperative of opposing the evils of Nazism. Moral issues present both challenges and opportunities to presidents. How they handle them significantly influences their standing in history. Lincoln and Roosevelt rank high on the scales of presidential greatness because of how well they dealt with major moral issues. Failing to deal appropriately with moral issues usually mars a president's record. Presidents paint a self-portrait of their leadership as their moral character interacts with the moral issues facing them.

The Press and Presidential Morality

An industry of moralists and moralizers has emerged in the press, looking for the latest headline grab and lead story. Sometimes they turn opinion into fact and a thin thread of evidence into a compelling case against a president. Reporters and commentators on the far left harass conservative and Republican presidents, while those on the far right irritate liberal and Democratic presidents. Conspiracy theories abound. *Who, what, when, why,* and *how*? These small words spark big questions and a litany of charges and countercharges. Nixon apologists and Nixon himself thought they did him in, and that was also a major part of President Clinton's defense. Hillary Rodham Clinton and other Clinton defenders took to the airwaves to condemn right-wing conspiracy theorists.

Beginning in the late 1960s, the American press corps gradually became more adversarial to government and public officials and more willing to inquire into areas once considered off-limits. They turned a blind eye and a deaf ear to John F. Kennedy's immorality during the early 1960s, but thoroughly exposed Clinton's during the 1990s. During the Watergate and Whitewater scandals, the press became like a pack of hounds on the trail, each racing to get out front with the latest titillating revelation.

Presidents today can continue to govern effectively if attacks on their morality only come from reporters and commentators outside the mainstream. The mainstream press usually does not get into the fray until an event sparks their interest. Nixon's cover-up of Watergate and Clinton's verbal squirming about Monica Lewinsky attracted their interest. These actions lent credibility to the charges of immorality originally brought by reporters and commentators outside the mainstream.

Presidential Strategies during Moral Crises

Presidents caught in the midst of moral crises can pursue several strategies. They can admit error, alter policies, change personnel, offer to cooperate with authorities investigating their administrations, and blame previous administrations. For example, when charged with complicity in the Chinese espionage scandal in 1999, Clinton immediately welcomed new policies and procedures; at the same time, he argued that the Bush and Reagan administrations had also permitted such incidents. President Reagan dismissed Secretary of Interior James Watt to remove the sting of a brewing scandal, and he also required his administration to cooperate fully with the Iran-Contra investigation. The combination of these illustrations reveals six strategies presidents can pursue when facing moral crises, especially those of a personal nature.

1. **Delay.** During the moral crises facing Presidents Nixon and Clinton, they stonewalled. Nixon refused to hand over subpoenaed documents until the U.S. Supreme Court ordered him to. Clinton filed many lawsuits and appeals, losing almost every one, to delay cooperating with the investigations against him. Nixon and Clinton fought for time, hoping that the public and the press would shift their interest to something else.

2. **Deny.** Occupying the most powerful and prestigious office in the world, presidents can use the moral authority of the office to forcefully deny charges of moral impropriety. Nixon denied knowledge of the Watergate break-in, and Clinton denied having an affair with Monica Lewinsky until discovery of his DNA on her infamous dress.

3. **Discredit.** Using the presidential bully pulpit, Presidents Nixon and Clinton and their allies trashed the character of the opposition, calling them names, charging them with lying, and attempting to link them with conspiracies against the president. Nixon and his supporters charged that Archibald Cox, the independent prosecutor, was part of a liberal Democratic conspiracy to get him. Clinton, his wife, and his supporters railed against an alleged vast right-wing conspiracy that wanted to evict him from the White House.

4. **Deflect.** Presidents can deflect attention from moral crises by taking the offensive on other issues, announcing new plans and policies that appeal to

key groups in American society, and traveling extensively. Their image handlers make them appear at work on behalf of the American people. Presidents Nixon and Clinton also pursued this strategy.

5. **Diminish.** When President Clinton finally admitted to an affair with Monica Lewinsky, he merely confessed to "inappropriate" behavior, not wrong, harmful, damaging or sinful conduct. His choice of words diminished the seriousness of the affair. Nixon attempted to play down the importance of charges against him by insisting that his actions were either in the public interest or outside his knowledge and purview. Supporters of both argued that what they did was essentially no different from what other presidents had done.

6. **Divulge.** Critics have suggested that if Presidents Nixon and Clinton had made early and full admissions of guilt, they would have bolstered their public support and negated the need for congressional and judicial investigations. When charged with failing to perform his duty in the National Guard, President George W. Bush sought to let the air out of a ballooning crisis by releasing his entire military record. During the 1992 presidential campaign, President and Mrs. Clinton divulged their marital problems before the press and critics had an opportunity to expose them.

Ideology's Moral Spawning Ground

Ideology is a natural spawning ground of questions about moral character. Conservatism and liberalism, right and left, in America, offer conflicting explanations of America's origins and competing visions of America's future. For example, conservatives usually advocate limited government and lower taxes, while liberals often advance causes associated with enlarged government and increased taxes. Taking their explanations and visions very seriously, the respective sides fight for advantage. Questions about moral character can deeply wound the opposition and limit the advancement of its cause. Conservatives and liberals advance conspiracy theories about their opponent's motives as both Nixon and Clinton apologists did in defending their leaders. Conservatives argue that a liberal bias in the mainstream media of network television and the nation's major newspapers gives liberals a distinct advantage in presenting the liberal case to the public. Liberals contend that conservative dominance of radio talk shows enables conservatives to foment opposition to liberals and their agenda.

Religion's Moral Lens

America's unique religious heritage causes many people to see morality through the eyes of religion. To them only religion offers a 20–20 lens for accurately viewing American morality. Put another way, they believe that religion is the touchstone of morality. The religious impulse in America leads to rapier-like thrusts about morality, including presidential character and behavior. Just as ideology divides Americans, so too does religion. Persons of conservative religious persuasion normally identify with and defend ideologically conservative presidents, whereas the liberally inclined do the opposite. Members of the Christian Coalition are in the vanguard of conservative and Republican politics, whereas members of the National Council of Churches identify more with liberal and Democratic Party politics.

Symbolically, presidents use religious symbols to capture the moral high ground and to identify with important groups.

- President Clinton went to church, Bible in hand, during the height of revelations about his alleged affair with Monica Lewinsky. On the Sunday he allegedly met with her and suggested how she could cover up their affair, he waved his Bible to the crowd as he left church. He and his family also had the Reverend Jesse Jackson in the White House for prayer and counsel during this time. To help him overcome personal problems, he chose three Protestant ministers to guide him.
- President Ford, seeking a larger slice of the Southern Baptist vote, attended church Sunday before the Tuesday election at the prestigious First Baptist Church of Dallas, Texas, where he had a photo-op with the then best-known Southern Baptist preacher, W. A. Criswell.
- President Nixon had Sunday services in the White House, featuring Jewish, Protestant, and Roman Catholic clergy.
- Almost every president from Kennedy through Clinton has used Evangelist Billy Graham for Inaugural prayers, and White House photo-ops. President Nixon even attended one of Graham's crusades.
- On becoming president, George W. Bush began to meet regularly with evangelical Protestants and conservative Roman Catholics.

Rhetorically, presidents invoke religious language to put a moral gloss on their positions, policies, and campaigns.

- President Carter proclaimed that he was "born again," a not-so-subtle appeal to evangelical Protestant voters.
- President Johnson, in defense of his Voting Rights Act of 1965, said to Congress: "For with a country as with a person, 'What is a man profited, if he shall gain the whole world, and lose his own soul?' Above the pyramid on the great seal of the United States it says in Latin, 'God has favored our undertaking.' God will not favor everything we do. It is rather our duty to divine His will. I cannot help but believe that He truly understands and that He really favors the undertaking that we begin here tonight."

- President Clinton used the Biblical term *covenant* during his 1992 acceptance speech at the Democratic National Convention and later in his campaign.
- President George W. Bush spoke frequently of faith-based initiatives in public policy.

Analytically, writers about the presidency often turn to religious and moral language to capture their views of the institution.

- The Roman Catholic scholar Michael Novak said: "Americans treat America as a religion. Hatred for political opponents waxes theological. Like separate islands, the political religions of the land are connected through a single office. The president is the one pontiff bridging all."[60]
- The political scientist Clinton Rossiter referred to Abraham Lincoln as "the martyred Christ of democracy's passion play."[61]
- The *New York Times* journalist James Reston said: "The White House is the pulpit of the nation and the president is its chaplain."[62]

The presidency and presidents, encased in a cocoon of religious symbols and rhetoric, invite intense attention to moral questions.

Constitutional Cultivation of Moral Issues

American government and politics include structures and principles that cultivate questions about moral behavior. The Constitution's First Amendment guarantee of freedom of the press gives a broad grant of authority and immunity to reporters and columnists to pursue moral questions. They can win Pulitzer Prizes, promotions, and book contracts by reporting tantalizing tales about presidential morality. Rush Limbaugh makes a fortune by his attacks on liberals and Democrats. Questions about Bill Clinton's morality became cannon fodder for his radio talk show. During the Nixon presidency, then little-known *Washington Post* reporters Bob Woodward and Carl Bernstein became internationally famous with their titillating front-page stories and Pulitzer Prize about "Deep Throat" and the Nixon character.

America's two-party system with its emphasis on winning the grand prize, the presidency, ensures that each party explores and exposes moral weaknesses in the candidates and office holders of the other party. In their zeal for victory, candidates, campaigns, and parties sometimes cross the line between legal and illegal activities. President Clinton's campaign apparently engaged in substantial fund-raising efforts outside the color of law, notably foreign fund-raising through several East Asian conduits. President Nixon's Watergate scandal broke when a night watchman discovered a break-in at the Democratic Party's headquarters.

Separation of powers, especially when Democrats and Republicans divide control of the Congress and the White House, ensures the airing of dirty linen through prolonged committee investigations. The Senate Watergate Committee did that with Richard Nixon. Both House and Senate Committees turned the searchlight on Bill Clinton.

The American judiciary is not an innocent bystander as the storm clouds of morality hover over the White House. Independent prosecutors Leon Jaworski and Kenneth Starr became household names through their investigations of Nixon and Clinton, respectively. Jaworski obtained a unanimous decision from the U.S. Supreme Court in *U.S. v. Nixon* (1973), which held that the doctrine of executive privilege does not allow a president to withhold evidence that is material to a criminal trial. Starr obtained guilty pleas and convictions of more than a dozen of President Clinton's political associates in the Whitewater case. Lesser-known independent prosecutors also surfaced in other administrations to investigate such issues as the Iran-Contra affair in the Reagan-Bush years. Lawrence Walsh, the best known of the other independent prosecutors, investigated the Reagan-Bush administrations, but had little success. U.S. Attorney General Janet Reno named a record number of independent prosecutors, seven, during the administration of President Clinton.

Historical Revisionism and Presidential Greatness

A treasure trove of archives in presidential libraries and elsewhere enables historians, journalists, and political scientists to subject presidential legacies to the pen of criticism and correction. President Truman left office with one of history's lowest popularity ratings. Now, however, he occupies a much higher ranking on the scales of presidential greatness. Most historians, journalists, and political scientists finally concluded that President Truman successfully made more courageous foreign policy decisions than perhaps any other president. These decisions included dropping the atomic bomb on Japan to end World War II, helping Europe recover from the War through the Truman Doctrine and Marshall Plan, and assisting in the defense of Europe through the creation of NATO (North Atlantic Treaty Organization). Fred Greenstein's *Hidden-Hand Presidency*[63] put a new gloss on President Eisenhower. Charged with moral weakness in failing to publicly challenge Senator Joe McCarthy, Eisenhower's reputation suffered until Greenstein revealed that he had a successful hidden-hand or behind-the-scenes strategy of challenging McCarthy.

Moral character is a critical measuring rod of presidential greatness. Both Franklin Roosevelt and John F. Kennedy have had their presidential legacies reviewed and revised. In Kennedy's case, moral revisionism took the bloom off the rose of Camelot. He no longer occupies as high a position on the scale of presidential greatness.[64] Although Franklin Roosevelt remains an icon on the shelf of presidents, a layer of dust now covers his once bright image.[65]

Roosevelt and Kennedy served when the press avoided reporting on the moral foibles of presidents; however, political earthquakes high on the Richter Scale during the 1960s and 1970s changed that. Vietnam and Watergate put presidents under high-powered moral microscopes. President Clinton's personal life, a taboo subject in earlier decades, became ripe for public consumption, most likely lowering his ultimate ranking on the scale of presidential greatness.

National Debate about Moral Decline

Intense national debate now centers on the state of morality in America. Many analysts believe that America is in a state of moral decline, arguing that America is like a nation at sea without a moral anchor.

- The Editor-in-Chief of *U.S. News and World Report*, Mortimer B. Zuckerman, concludes: "There is a great yearning in the country to provide our national life and institutions with a larger moral dimension."[66]
- Former U.S. Secretary of Education William J. Bennett argues: "The real answer to the perils of our time is that we simply must become more civilized. We must pay attention to something that every civilized society has given preeminent importance: instilling in our children certain fundamental traits of character—traits like honesty, compassion, courage, perseverance, altruism, and the fidelity to one's commitments."[67]
- Dr. Benjamin Spock stated: "This century has seen a progressive relaxation of many of our standards of behavior and the souring of many commonly held beliefs. Taken one by one, most are of little importance. Taken together, I believe they show that we have lost our way."[68]

Because presidents occupy a unique position as the only nationally elected leader, they more than anyone else can serve as a moral anchor. Little wonder then that presidents become embroiled in debate about America's moral condition. Critics and pundits often expect them to act as a bulwark against moral decline.

According to this analysis, moral scandal in the White House tears at the fabric of society by shredding our belief in heroes. Because people depend on presidents for moral guidance and leadership, they are like stars in the sky, providing moral direction and light. When presidents no longer cast light along the moral pathway, Americans stumble and fall in the moral darkness.

Public Policy's Moral Cloak

Presidents frequently wrap a moral cloak around their policy initiatives, placing the opposition in a morally defensive position.

- President Eisenhower wrapped the moral cloak of national defense around several of his initiatives. He promoted the interstate highway system as the National Defense Highway Act, and enlarged federal contributions to higher education through the National Defense Education Act. In that era with its great fear of communist expansion, national defense was a moral symbol and slogan used to package new policies.
- President Kennedy, inheriting Eisenhower's drably titled Public Law 480, renamed it "Food for Peace" and greatly expanded its scope. He called his Latin American policy initiatives, "Alliance for Progress," and his best-known international policy initiative, "The Peace Corps." Moral gloss made his programs more appealing.
- President Johnson used titles such as "War on Poverty," "Safe Streets," "Head Start," and "Model Cities" to put the opposition on the defensive. Opposing these policies on their merits was difficult because of the compelling titles.
- The presidential candidates Barry Goldwater and George McGovern in 1964 and 1972, respectively, went so far as to claim: "In your heart, you know he's right," and "Right from the start." Even the successful presidential campaign slogans, such as the New Deal, Fair Deal, New Frontier, and Great Society, created a moral tone of right versus wrong, posing a disadvantage for opponents.

The moral cloak of slogans and symbols dresses up presidential policy initiatives, sometimes covering up serious policy defects. Opponents must not only debate the substantive merits of policy proposals, they also must undress them.

Public Expectations of Presidential Behavior

Critics marvel at how well and how long Bill Clinton survived the high winds of moral hurricanes, whereas George Bush Sr. could not weather the light wind of adversity from his "read my lips" reversal. The word *expectation* may explain why. Apparently the public expected more of George Bush and less of Bill Clinton. Bush offered a highly moral persona to the American public, but Bill Clinton issued several confessions even while campaigning for president. He confessed, for example, to using marijuana and to causing "pain" in his marriage. Going back to Jimmy Carter, he faced a problem similar to George Bush's when he stated in his 1976 campaign: "You can trust me." Early in his administration, however, his closest and most trusted advisor, Bert Lance, then the Director of the Office of Management and Budget, got caught in a banking scandal, which rocked public confidence in President Carter. The public apparently expected more of Bush and Carter and less of Clinton.

Personal versus Public Policy Morality

Apologists for Presidents Nixon and Clinton staunchly defend their moral integrity, decrying the immorality of political foes. Central to their defense is this argument: Americans should judge these presidents, not by their personal morality, but by how well they led the country. Did their public policies benefit Americans at home and abroad? What is good for America then becomes the measure of morality, not the president's personal behavior. The Democratic Party's 1984 vice presidential candidate, Geraldine Ferraro, put it this way in her 1998 defense of President Clinton: "Morality is how you deal with the problems of the country."[69]

Nixon apologists argue that he (1) got America out of the Vietnam War, (2) successfully defined a new American foreign policy that led to diplomatic relationships with China, and (3) began the needed rebalancing of government power, shifting more responsibility to the states and away from the national government. Clinton advocates consistently point to his high public approval ratings and the strength of the American economy. His private life, they argued, is not our business.

Countering the moral morass of the Nixon era, Jimmy Carter campaigned in 1976 on this theme, "You can trust me." This not-so-subtle indictment of Nixon's personal immorality helped pave the way for defeating President Gerald Ford, who pardoned Nixon. Just before pardoning him, President Ford's approval rating was higher than any president's at a comparable time, but just after, his approval rating plummeted, giving Jimmy Carter an opening to win the 1976 election.

Attacking the moral quagmire of the Clinton administration, critics demonstrated links between personal morality and public policy. They pointed out that President Clinton's defense against charges of personal immorality engulfed him and his staff. The time and resources necessary to defend the president, they argued, kept him from effectively leading the

Congress and the nation. President Clinton, like President Nixon, won a major reelection victory, but charges about his personal immorality torpedoed his opportunity for significant public policy leadership. He lacked the personal moral standing necessary to fight for major changes in public policy. Ironically, the public approved of his job performance, but not his personal character. They distinguished between Clinton the president and Clinton the person.

CONCLUSION

The presidency is a place of moral leadership, conditioned by personal moral character, the constraints and pressures that mold the nation's moral condition, and moral issues themselves. Together they shape the exercise of presidential leadership. History records how well a president's moral character intersects and interacts with the nation's moral condition and moral issues. On that may hinge the political lifespan and legacy of presidents.

Morality, like beauty, is in the eyes of the beholder. Americans see morality through many lens, including politics, religion, ideology, and language. They are the cut and shape of the moral kaleidoscope, the guiding lights of morality, because they define direction and purpose. American morality has become kaleidoscopic precisely because there is increasingly less agreement on the definition of morality, which makes presidential leadership more complex.

As the cut and shape of America's moral kaleidoscope have changed, voices have become more shrill and strident, speaking with greater assurance about the morality of their respective causes. Believing that their ideas occupy the moral high ground, people press their views on presidents, making their ability to achieve compromise in the interest of national unity more difficult.

Notes

[1] James Q. Wilson, *Moral Judgment* (New York: Basic Books, 1997): 1.

[2] Charles W. Dunn, *The Scarlet Thread of Scandal: Morality and the American Presidency* (Lanham, MD: Rowman & Littlefield, 2000): 42.

[3] Sidney M. Milkis, and Michael Nelson, *The American Presidency: Origins and Development* (Washington, DC: CQ Press, 1999): 70.

[4] Ibid., 73.

[5] Dunn, 42.

[6] Richard Norton Smith, *Patriarch George Washington and the New American Nation* (Boston: Houghton Mifflin, 1993): 117.

[7] Milkis and Nelson: 74.

[8] Annette Gordon-Reed, *Thomas Jefferson and Sally Hemmings: An American Controversy* (London: University of Virginia Press, 1998): 1.

[9] Dunn, 45.

[10] Gordon-Reed, 140.

[11]Ibid., 105.

[12]Ibid., 106.

[13]Milkis and Nelson, 157.

[14]Ibid., 158.

[15]Ibid., 150.

[16]Ibid., 151.

[17]Kenneth M. Stampp, *The Era of Reconstruction, 1865–1877* (New York: Vintage Books, 1965): 51.

[18]Milkis and Nelson, 164.

[19]Stampp, 53.

[20]Ibid.

[21]Ibid., 60.

[22]Milkis and Nelson, 168.

[23]Ibid., 169.

[24]Ibid., 225.

[25]As quoted in Milkis and Nelson, 233.

[26]Milkis and Nelson, 227.

[27]Ibid., 237.

[28]Dunn, 72.

[29]May Dixon Thacker, *The Strange Death of President Harding* (New York: Guild Publishing, 1930): 114, and Dunn, 73.

[30]Andrew Sinclair, *The Available Man: Warren Gamaliel Harding* (New York: Macmillan, 1965): 201.

[31]Ibid., 219.

[32]Ibid., 220.

[33]Eugene Lyons, *Our Unknown Ex-President: A Portrait of Herbert Hoover* (New York: Doubleday and Co., 1948): 260.

[34]Dunn, 77.

[35]Ibid.

[36]Lyons, 260.

[37]Milkis and Nelson, 263.

[38]Lyons, 1.

[39]Milkis and Nelson, 263.

[40]Joseph Alsop, *FDR 1882–1945: A Century Remembrance* (New York: Viking Press, 1982): 55; Dunn, 83–93.

[41]William D. Hassett, *Off the Record with FDR, 1942–45* (Rutgers, NJ: University Press of New Brunswick, 1958): x.

[42]Milkis, 301.

[43]Victor Lasky, *JFK: The Man and the Myth* (New York: Macmillan, 1963): 4.

[44]Dunn, 118–119.

[45]Ibid., 115.

[46]Ibid., 115–122.

[47]Ibid., 119.

[48]Michael A. Genovese, *The Watergate Crisis* (Westport, CT: Greenwood Press, 1999): 9.

[49]Ibid., 9.

[50]Ibid., 5.

[51]Richard M. Nixon, *In the Arena: A Memoir of Victory, Defeat and Renewal* (Norwalk, CT: Easton Press, 1990): 21.

[52]Genovese, 98.

[53]Ibid., 45.

[54]Richard G. Hutcheson, *God in the White House: How Religion Has Changed the Modern Presidency* (New York: Macmillan, 1988): 235.

[55]Kenneth E. Morris, *Jimmy Carter: American Moralist* (Athens: University of Georgia Press, 1996).

[56]Milkis and Nelson, 331.

[57]Dunn, 147.

[58]Morris, 214.

[59]Ibid., 334.

[60]Michael Novak, *Choosing Our King* (New York: Macmillan, 1974): xv.

[61]Clinton Rossiter, *The American Presidency* (New York: New American Library, 1960): 239.

[62]As cited in Thomas E. Cronin, "The Textbook Presidency and Political Science," *The Congressional Record* (October 5, 1970): S17–106.

[63]Fred Greenstein, *The Hidden-Hand Presidency* (New York: Basic Books, 1982).

[64]Richard Reeves, *A Question of Character* (New York: Free Press, 1991).

[65]Dunn, 83–93.

[66]Mortimer B. Zuckerman, "Where Have Our Values Gone?" *U.S. News and World Report* (August 8, 1994): 88.

[67]William J. Bennett, "How to Teach Values," *Ladies Home Journal* (September 1994): 142.

[68]Benjamin M. Spock, *A Better World for Our Children: Rebuilding American Family Values* (Bethesda, MD: National Press Books, 1984): 93.

[69]As stated by Geraldine Ferraro on "Larry King Live," CNN, July 27, 1998.

Chapter Six

The Law of Politics

Steadiness and Strategic Thinking

*"Surely, I'm the quickest one around," he boasted to the other animals. "Of
course, we all know Tortoise is the slowest."*

*Tortoise had heard this speech many times and was more than a little
tired of it. "But you've never proved yourself, Hare," said Tortoise. "I'll challenge you to a race. Then we'll see who is quicker."*

*"You're the slowest one around," laughed Hare. "But if you're serious
about this silly race, fine with me."*

"I may be slow, but I'm always steady," whispered Tortoise.

—Aesop's Fables

INTRODUCTION TO THE LAW OF POLITICS

Long and sustained public careers together with stable political and public policy
strategies usually mark successful presidential candidates and presidents. Thus,
presidents have customarily had their personal abilities, character, and policy
inclinations tested along the way. The political system customarily filters out candidates with policy ideas outside the mainstream of American politics, making
"centrist" candidates and presidents the norm.

In the famous fable of *The Tortoise and the Hare*, Tortoise personifies the law of presidential politics. Despite being slow, Tortoise won the race, defeating his faster and quicker opponent, Hare. Tortoise won with a simple strategy: remain steady and stay on course. Successful presidential candidates and presidents, like Tortoise, keep their eyes focused on the goal, winning election and reelection. They steadfastly avoid rabbit trails, which would slow them down and take them off course, and while bumps and potholes may slow them down, they continue their forward progress.

The law of politics requires that successful presidential candidates and presidents (1) present an appropriate personal and political background; (2) offer public policy stability; (3) pursue a sound campaign strategy; (4) understand the dynamics of presidential elections; and (5) follow a steady administrative strategy.

PERSONAL AND POLITICAL BACKGROUNDS

In the personal and political backgrounds of successful presidents, four factors stand out. They sustain long public careers, grasp the political dynamics of presidential backgrounds, function effectively within a changing political system, and stay on the offense politically.

Sustain a Public Career

Successful presidential candidates sustain long public careers. Using the modern presidents from Franklin D. Roosevelt through George W. Bush as illustrations:

- Franklin D. Roosevelt served in the president's Cabinet and as Governor of New York;
- Harry S. Truman held the offices of U.S. Senator and Vice President;
- Dwight D. Eisenhower had a very public career as one of history's most notable generals and as President of Columbia University;
- John F. Kennedy won election to both the U.S. House and Senate;
- Lyndon Johnson did the same but also had a stint as Vice President;
- Richard M. Nixon not only served in both houses but also as Vice President and as a losing presidential candidate;
- Gerald R. Ford held office in the U.S. House of Representatives from 1946 until replacing President Nixon in 1974;
- Jimmy Carter had a long career in Georgia politics as both a State Senator and Governor;
- Ronald Reagan not only had a public career as an actor but also as Governor of California;

- George H. W. Bush held numerous offices, including membership in the U.S. House of Representatives, Director of the Central Intelligence Agency, and Envoy to China;
- William Jefferson Clinton served as both Attorney General and Governor of Arkansas; and
- George W. Bush was a two-term Governor of Texas.

The same holds true for earlier presidents. Abraham Lincoln, for example, ran for office, winning and losing, over several decades, and Theodore Roosevelt served as both governor of New York and as vice president. But candidates who do not sustain a long public career, such as Wendell Wilkie, the Republican Party's 1940 standard-bearer, usually come up short, failing to demonstrate to key leaders in politics, the media, and interest groups as well as to the public at-large that they have the desire, dedication, intellect, organizational skill, and wisdom, among other things, to stay the course and go the distance. In 2004 U.S. Senator John Edwards (D, NC), who had served less than one term in the U.S. Senate, ran a credible campaign for the Democratic Party's nomination, but lacked the nationwide breadth and depth of political and financial contacts to challenge U.S. Senator John Kerry's (D, MA) superior resources, which he had built over a much longer political career. The complexities of America—political, economic, social, religious, geographic, and cultural—make the race for the White House a marathon run and not a 100-yard dash.

Grasp the Political Dynamics of Presidential Backgrounds

The electoral power of the "Big Ten States," that is, the nation's most populous, opens the door to understanding the types of candidates who win the White House. Of the 19 occupants of the White House from William McKinley through George W. Bush:

- 14 have hailed from "Big Ten States,"
- 18 have identified with a mainstream Protestant denomination, and
- 13 have graduated from our nation's most prestigious colleges and universities.

Interestingly, in 1952 General Eisenhower, who had no religious affiliation, became a Presbyterian, and his opponent, Adlai E. Stevenson, a Unitarian, became a Presbyterian, which is more within the comfort zone of mainstream Protestantism. Change, however, is on the horizon. Roman Catholics, whose population has greatly increased, especially in the "Big Ten

States," now play a greater role in presidential politics. Likewise, African Americans have increased their influence in presidential politics along with Hispanics. Again, both of these groups have sizeable populations in the "Big Ten States." The South and Sun-Belt South have produced four of our five most recent presidents, two from Texas, one from Georgia, and one from Arkansas. As population has shifted from northern industrial states, sometimes called the Rust Belt, to the Sun Belt, Southern strength in the Electoral College has increased. Among the "Big Ten States" are three from the South and the Sun-Belt South, Florida, North Carolina, and Texas. As shown in Table 6.1, prestigious colleges and universities stand out among presidents elected between 1896 and 2004. They include Harvard (3), Yale (3), Princeton (1), Stanford (1), Michigan (1), Amherst (1), West Point (1), Naval Academy (1), and Georgetown (1).

Function Effectively within a Changing Political System

In Shakespeare's *Julius Caesar*, these words from Mark Antony's funeral oration capture what sometimes happens with presidents: "The evil that men do lives after them; The good is oft interred with their bones." All too often,

Table 6.1

PRESIDENTIAL BACKGROUNDS: 1896–2004

President	State	Religious Affiliation	College/ University
McKinley (R)	Ohio	Methodist	Allegheny
Roosevelt (R)	New York	Dutch Reformed	Harvard
Taft (R)	Ohio	Unitarian	Yale
Wilson (D)	New Jersey	Presbyterian	Princeton
Harding (R)	Ohio	Baptist	Ohio Central
Coolidge (R)	Massachusetts	Congregational	Amherst
Hoover (R)	California	Quaker	Stanford
Roosevelt (D)	New York	Episcopal	Harvard
Truman (D)	Missouri	Baptist	
Eisenhower (R)	New York	Presbyterian	West Point
Kennedy (D)	Massachusetts	Roman Catholic	Harvard
Johnson (D)	Texas	Disciples of Christ	San Marcos State
Nixon (R)	New York	Quaker	Whittier
Ford (R)	Michigan	Episcopal	Michigan
Carter (D)	Georgia	Baptist	Naval Academy
Reagan (R)	California	Presbyterian	Eureka
Bush (R)	Texas	Episcopal	Yale
Clinton (D)	Arkansas	Baptist	Georgetown
Bush (R)	Texas	Methodist	Yale

Americans know the defects and defeats of presidents but not their successes in improving American government.

Successful presidents, whether great or not, use their energy, initiative, and prerogatives to meet the nation's changing needs. President William McKinley occupies an all-but-forgotten place in the annals of presidential history as the assassinated predecessor of the swashbuckling Theodore Roosevelt, but McKinley put into place most of the elements of the modern presidency. Most Americans remember President Warren G. Harding for his elicit affairs and the Teapot Dome scandal, but they do not remember his modernization of government through the Budget and Accounting Act of 1921 or his naming of three of the most outstanding Cabinet secretaries in American history.[1] Neither McKinley nor Harding ranks high on the scales of presidential greatness, but they made important contributions to the presidency, which greatly benefited such "great" presidents as Franklin D. Roosevelt and Ronald Reagan.

Trust in others stands out as perhaps the most fundamental change in presidential leadership. Spiraling growth in government, increasing complexity in American society and government and continuing expansion of executive power combine to cause presidents to place more trust in other people and institutions. In response, many presidents have contributed to the president's expanded trust in others. For example, Franklin D. Roosevelt created the Executive Office of the President (1939) to help presidents govern the growing bureaucracy. Harry Truman created the Council of Economic Advisors (1947) to help presidents provide sound economic leadership. Dwight D. Eisenhower highlighted the importance of staff assistance in the White House by naming the first Chief of Staff (1953). Richard M. Nixon created the Office of Policy Development (1970) to help presidents provide better leadership on a variety of issues.

These represent but a few presidential initiatives that reflect the increasing measure of trust that presidents must place in others. But both successes and problems result from this trust. On the success side, Joseph Califano under Lyndon B. Johnson and Henry Kissinger under Richard M. Nixon played key roles in crafting The Great Society and the New China Policy, respectively. On the problem side, President Johnson's Press Secretary, George Reedy, found that staff clouded the president's view of reality by almost always agreeing with the president rather than giving him sound advice and counsel that differed from the president's views.[2] Richard M. Nixon's Chief of Staff, H. R. Haldeman, also contributed to presidential isolation from reality by closely circumscribing access to the president, which contributed significantly to the Watergate Scandal.

Governing and leadership styles change with each president. The style of leadership that presidents practice reflects in part the measure of trust they place in their staffs. Leaders who motivate, create a mission, and build a culture that include staff in the design of their plans achieve more beneficial results than leaders who demand slavish attention to detail and unquestioning precision in executing assignments.

No single leadership style serves as the best for all presidents; rather, like a good symphony, theme and variation are the keys to success. Presidents must blend various styles to achieve their goals. John F. Kennedy rejected Dwight D. Eisenhower's formal style with its chief of staff as the guardian of presidential access, choosing rather to grant direct access to him by many staff, which enhanced the sense of teamwork in his administration but also created a more chaotic administration.[3] Franklin D. Roosevelt generated creative competition by pitting one staff member against another on the same assignment without either staff member knowing it. Ronald Reagan achieved considerable success by functioning more in the mold of Eisenhower's administrative style.

Stay on Offense

Presidents Bill Clinton and George Bush Jr. determined not only to stay on offense but also to run motion offenses. Believing that the best defense is a good offense, they kept their candidacies and administrations in a constant state of motion, knowing that a moving target is more difficult to hit than a motionless object. First, political opponents have greater difficulty hitting a moving target. Just as opponents would begin to rally to the point of attack against them, Presidents Clinton and Bush would already have moved on, traveling widely and advocating new programs. Second, a motion offense reinforces in the public mind that their president is doing something about their problems. In any given week of the Clinton and Bush presidencies, they advocated several new ideas and policies on behalf of the people. Third, emergencies provide an excellent venue for staying on offense. If a natural disaster occurs, such as a hurricane or a tornado, presidents can fly to the scene to inspect the damage, console people about their losses and announce the release of federal funds to help out. International emergencies also enable presidents to act decisively. President Jimmy Carter's failure to act decisively during the hostage crisis at the end of his administration gave his challenger, Ronald Reagan, an opening to challenge his leadership. In effect, Carter began to play defense, while Reagan played offense, which helped him win the 1980 election. When President Bush failed to act immediately in response to the Tsunami and Katrina disasters, criticism quickly mounted within 24 to 48 hours, but he then responded with major relief initiatives. From World War II until now, presidents have faced increasing numbers of international crises, which have enabled them to act decisively on the international stage. Their decisions in the short run always bolstered their standing in the polls when they acted decisively, but in protracted conflicts, such as Vietnam and Iraq, they sometimes lost popular support.

Public Policy Stability

Marking the approaches of successful presidents to public policy are three crucial considerations. They advocate reasonable changes in public policy, appeal to the magnet of the moderate mainstream, and balance the competing interests of elitism, pluralism, and populism.

Advocate Reasonable Changes in Public Policy

In 1964 the Republican Party candidate for president, Barry Goldwater, advocated abolition of Social Security while campaigning in St. Petersburg, Florida, and elimination of the Tennessee Valley Authority on a campaign trip to Tennessee. Then, in 1972, the Democratic Party candidate, George McGovern, advocated a major shift in tax policy, increasing taxes on middle and upper classes and transferring the revenue to social welfare programs. Whereas other reasons contributed to their defeats in two of history's greatest landslides, the advocacy of radical policy changes contributed significantly to their losses.

Elsewhere in American history, William Jennings Bryan, three times the Democratic presidential candidate (1896, 1900, and 1908), paid dearly for violating this dictum when he advocated "free silver" to replace the American gold standard and delivered one of history's most famous Convention addresses, declaring in 1896 that "You shall not press down upon the brow of labor this crown of thorns, you shall not crucify mankind upon a cross of gold." Several decades later, America went off of the gold standard, but in 1896 his proposal was too radical.

In these three instances, the Republican and Democratic Parties nominated presidential candidates whose views more closely resembled the more extreme positions of third-party candidates, which makes an important point: Whenever a major party nominates a candidate who acts like a third-party candidate, that party will likely suffer an overwhelming defeat. Third parties with an ideological bent, such as the Socialist and Communist Parties, advocate positions far outside the American mainstream. Other third parties, such as the Populist (1892), Progressive (1924), States Rights (1948), and

American Independent (1968), promote positions that may later gain acceptance but, when first introduced, the political system finds them unacceptable.

In America, change comes slowly. Only after protracted debate, often over several decades, does change occur. Successful presidential candidates and presidents advocate changes that the political system is ready to digest.

Appeal to the Magnet of the Moderate Mainstream

Prospective presidential candidates, who often sought the advice of Richard M. Nixon after he left office, heard him say that Republican and Democratic candidates should tack hard right and hard left, respectively, to win their party nominations, but then tack back to the center to win the General Election. The middle, Nixon understood, governs in America, but the center of gravity of power in the Republican and Democratic Parties, respectively, is to the right and left ideologically. Goldwater and McGovern tacked right and left to win their nominations, but they then failed to tack back to the center. In the General Election, they did not adjust their candidacies to the magnet of the moderate mainstream.

Ideologically, Americans are like a bell-shaped curve. Most identify with the center or the moderate mainstream, reflecting the nation's history as a nonideological people. But in the Republican and Democratic Parties the centers tilt right and left, respectively, and even more so because of the Goldwater and McGovern campaigns, which moved the center of gravity of power in their respective parties even farther away from the electoral center. In 1964 and 1972, large numbers of new delegates with a fervent ideological bent participated in the Republican and Democratic National Conventions in San Francisco and Miami Beach. The new Republican delegates booed such traditional party stalwarts as New York's Governor Nelson Rockefeller and New York City Mayor John Lindsey, whom they considered liberal. And in the Democratic Party, the McGovern delegates refused to seat such power brokers as Mayor Richard J. Daley of Chicago and George Meany, president of the AFL-CIO. In the end Goldwater won only six states, and McGovern only two.

Successful candidates, such as Ronald Reagan and the two Bushes in the Republican Party plus William Jefferson Clinton in the Democratic Party, heeded Richard Nixon's point. After appealing to their party's center of gravity of power to win the nomination, they shifted to the middle not only to win the General Election but also to govern. That, of course, created difficulties, and in the instance of President Bush Sr., he lost his campaign for reelection in large measure because of attacks from the right. Conservative television personality Pat Buchanan challenged and wounded him in Republican Primaries in 1992, and Ross Perot ran against him as an Independent. In winning the Republican nomination in 1980, Ronald Reagan advocated abolition of the Department of Education, which appealed to Republican conservatives, but as president he did not follow through, which prompted criticism from some conservatives. William Jefferson Clinton successfully pursued welfare reform and free-trade policies, which alienated many in the liberal wing of the Democratic Party, but had great appeal to the American mainstream. After his State of the Union Address in 2004, President Bush Jr. faced an onslaught of conservative criticism for failing to address the budget deficit and other issues as conservatives would have liked.

Ideology is the seasoning, not the meat and potatoes, of presidential politics. Successful presidential candidates understand that too much seasoning will ruin the flavor of the meat and potatoes. So they must judiciously apply the seasoning, trying to satisfy the ideologically inclined, but without alienating the moderate mainstream. Facing reelection in 2004, George W. Bush delivered a State of the Union Address, which bothered fiscal conservatives, who disliked his plans for new programs and expanded spending. To placate them, the next week his Budget Message to Congress called for significant cutbacks in spending.

Balance the Competing Interests of Elitism, Pluralism, and Populism

These three interests significantly influence presidential campaigns, dictating that successful presidential candidates balance their appeals to them. According to the elitist explanation of American politics, a handful of elites—governmental, corporate, military, and labor—govern as elected leaders in response to elitist interests. Or put another way, the elites are the puppeteers and the elected leaders are puppets, so that to win presidential candidates must successfully appeal to American elites. The pluralist explanation contends that elected leaders make public policy in response to competition among interest groups. As interest groups compete against one another in a game of tug-of-war, the winners attain preeminence in public policy. Thus, as the argument goes, winning presidential candidates will represent the dominant interest groups. Big business versus big labor represents perhaps the oldest and best-known example of interest-group competition. Populism, the third explanation, argues that the ultimate repository of power in American politics—the people—determines winners and losers in public policy. Accordingly, winning presidential candidates will appeal to the interests of the popular majority.

In reality, although all three forces offer legitimate explanations of American politics, none holds the upper hand. Successful presidential candidates and presidents understand the dynamic tension existing among them.

Major economic, political, religious, and social elites supported President Lyndon Johnson's Vietnam War policy. For example, among religious elites, the most influential Roman Catholic Cardinal, Francis Spellman of New York City, and the world's most popular evangelist, Billy Graham, supported the War. But elitist support of the Vietnam War crumbled as interest-group and popular opposition developed. In the end, President Johnson's failure to maintain a cross section of interest group and popular support for his policy caused him not to seek reelection in 1968. Interest groups, new and old, and populist leaders, such as Senator Eugene McCarthy (D, MN), successfully challenged President Johnson's leadership.

Presidential candidates can also place undue emphasis on the support of interest groups. In his 2004 campaign for the Democratic Party's presidential nomination, Richard Gephardt sewed up the support of major labor unions, but he lacked a sufficient populist appeal to rank-and-file voters. Although labor unions play a major role in the Democratic Party, too much reliance on them can lead to defeat.

Regarding populism, many populist candidates have fallen by the wayside, including major, third-party, and independent candidates: Gene McCarthy and George Wallace (1968), John Anderson (1980), and Pat Buchanan and Ross Perot (1992). The Electoral College accounts for one reason why third-party and independent candidates fall by the wayside. Rarely do they win any electoral votes. For example, in 1992 Ross Perot won about 20 percent of the popular vote but no electoral votes. In 1968 George C. Wallace won 13.8 percent of the popular vote but only 8 percent of the Electoral College vote.

Although their populist impulses may make them attractive, they lack sufficient appeal to elites and interest-group leaders to wage successful national campaigns. William Jefferson Clinton (1992, 1996) and George W. Bush (2000) won the presidency by balancing elitist, interest group, and populist interests. For example, recognizing the rising tide of popular discontent with public welfare programs, which many elites and interest groups supported, especially those closely identified with the Democratic Party, Clinton pledged to "end welfare as we know it." And George W. Bush, comprehending popular dissatisfaction with the public schools in 2000, responded with his ideas of "no child left behind" and "compassionate conservatism." In 2004, U.S. Senator John Edwards (D, NC) ran an effective populist campaign, but he lacked sufficient support among elites and interest groups to sustain his campaign in the end.

PRESIDENTIAL CAMPAIGNS

Typically, seven factors stand out among successful presidential candidates in their presidential campaigns. They concentrate on microcosm and swing states; adjust to shifting electoral dynamics; prepare for early or front-loading primaries and caucuses; recognize the assets and liabilities of a long campaign; develop innovative campaign techniques and strategies; make a wise decision concerning public or private campaign finance; and know the psychology of voter behavior.

Concentrate on Microcosm and Swing States

Ten states have more than enough electoral votes to elect the president— California (55), Texas (34), New York (31), Florida (27), Pennsylvania (21), Illinois (21), Ohio (20), Michigan (17), New Jersey (15), and North Carolina (15). Having one more than the magic number of 270 electoral votes necessary to win the presidency, these 10 states generally feature:

- Competitive two-party systems,
- Substantial minority group populations,
- Significant industrial complexes,
- Big labor unions,
- Major agricultural interests,
- Sizeable suburban areas, and
- Large cities and small towns.

In short, they not only serve as excellent cross sections of the United States, but they also represent each major geographic region.

Among the "Big Ten States," several "Swing States"—Florida, Pennsylvania, Ohio, and Michigan—had only a few thousand votes separate Al Gore and George W. Bush in 2000. These states together with other smaller "swing states," such as Missouri and New Hampshire, require that presidential candidates focus sufficient time and resources in appealing to their diverse interests. So the "Big Ten States" and "Swing States" receive much more attention in crafting winning campaign strategies.

But, to win, candidates must campaign nationally, avoiding unduly narrow appeals to geographic regions and to parochial interests. Candidates who attempt to win by narrow appeals lose. In 1888, Grover Cleveland won the popular election by 100,000 votes, piling up large victory margins in the South with parochial appeals to sectional interests, but he lost every other region of the nation and lost the presidency. In 1976, Jimmy Carter recognized that he could not win by narrowly appealing to his native South, so he cultivated a campaign strategy that made him a truly national candidate. For example, as a Southern Baptist in the heart of the "Bible Belt," he granted *Playboy* magazine an exclusive interview, which toned down his parochial past. The electoral force of the "Big Ten States" and "Swing States" helps to ensure that wining presidential candidates have developed a national appeal by responding to a cross section of interests.

All states with the exceptions of Maine and Nebraska use the winner-take-all method of casting their electoral votes, so that the candidate winning either the plurality or majority of a state's popular vote receives all of that state's electoral votes. Historically, the winner-take-all method benefits the presidential candidate with the best cross-sectional or national appeal in that winning candidates almost always receive a higher percentage of electoral votes than they did popular votes. For example, in 1860, Abraham Lincoln received 38.7 percent of the popular vote but 59.4 percent of the Electoral College vote. In 1960, John F. Kennedy narrowly beat Richard M. Nixon in the popular vote by 0.2 percent, 49.7 to 49.5, but his Electoral College margin was 6.7 percent. In 1976, Jimmy Carter won 50.5 percent of the popular vote but 55 percent of the Electoral College vote. President Bush narrowly lost the popular vote in 2000 to Al Gore, but he won a larger cross section of all states, including the District of Columbia, 30 to 21, giving him a 271 to 266 Electoral College majority. Thus, candidates who win the popular vote in the "Big Ten States" and "Swing States," albeit narrowly, usually win by much larger margins in the Electoral College.

While in office, presidents must carefully nurture their relationships with the "Big Ten" and "Swing" states. For example, President Bush, Jr. regularly traveled to Ohio and Pennsylvania to enhance his prospects for winning there in 2004. Additionally, incumbents may dole out large sums of grants and contracts to these states to benefit their reelection campaigns.

Adjust to Shifting Electoral Dynamics

Presidential candidates should have political weathervanes that reveal the shifting winds of American politics. Several questions indicate what their political weathervanes need to reveal. Do the times dictate an active or a passive president? Do changes in American society require a different campaign in style and substance? Do the behavior patterns of the incumbent president necessitate creating a clear contrast?

Between 1932 and 1952, the activist presidencies of Franklin D. Roosevelt and Harry S. Truman featured the New Deal and Fair Deal in response to economic problems, and in response to the expansion of fascism and communism, World War II, the Korean War, creation of NATO (North Atlantic Treaty Organization), and adoption of the Truman Doctrine and the Marshall Plan, which were policies designed to assist countries ravaged by World War II. After this activist 20-year period, the succeeding eight years featured General Dwight David Eisenhower's much more passive style of presidential leadership. Then, in 1960, John F. Kennedy campaigned on the theme of "getting the country moving again," an implicit indictment of President Eisenhower's leadership style. Throughout American history, an ebb and flow between activity and passivity has marked presidential campaigns and administrations. In this regard, the political weathervanes of victorious presidential candidates measure the mood of the electorate, recognizing that presidential campaigns are times of national self-examination.

Political campaigns focus on retrospective and prospective issues and themes. In 1952, General Eisenhower campaigned retrospectively against "Crime, Corruption and Korea," running against the Truman record, which the Democratic presidential candidate, Adlai E. Stevenson, inherited. In 1960, John F. Kennedy campaigned prospectively on his slogan of "The New Frontier." In 1992, Bill Clinton campaigned prospectively, emphasizing a vision for America, suggesting thereby that President Bush Sr. lacked one. He also campaigned retrospectively, suggesting that President Bush was out of touch with the many Americans out of work. In 2004, candidates for the Democratic nomination shot much of their ammunition against President George W. Bush rather than against one another, retrospectively arguing that he misled the people on the Iraq War and had an out-of-control economic policy with skyrocketing budget deficits.

In style and substance, presidential campaigns should adjust in response to technological and other changes in American society. Obviously, television and the Internet stand out among these changes. Without television in 1960 and 1968, John F. Kennedy would not have successfully challenged Richard M. Nixon, and U.S. Senator Eugene McCarthy's campaign would not have ended the presidency of Lyndon B. Johnson. Kennedy and McCarthy understood how to use the new medium of television, wherein candidates with a conversational style will more likely earn the nod of success. Ronald Reagan used his ease with television to good advantage in 1980 and 1984 against Jimmy Carter and Walter Mondale, respectively.

In his race for the 2004 Democratic presidential nomination, Vermont Governor Howard Dean imaginatively used the Internet to raise some $40 million, generally in small donations, and to create a nationwide network of volunteers. Dean's success, which caught the other candidates for the Democratic nomination off-guard, propelled him into first place both in fund-raising and in national polls during the latter half of 2003. Ironically, as television focused more on Dean's flamboyant style just before and after the Iowa Caucuses early in 2004, he lost his lead in the polls. During his Iowa campaign, he ordered a questioner to sit down, hardly a way to influence a national television audience, and in his concession speech just after losing, he literally screamed and waved his arms wildly on television, causing commentators to say he was out of control. So television negated Dean's Internet advantage. Not unmindful of Howard Dean's Internet success in raising money and creating a nationwide network of volunteers, George W. Bush followed suit, even eclipsing Dean's success.

Who would challenge this premise: The mantle of President Clinton's moral malfunction, draping heavily around the neck of Al Gore, cost him the White House in 2000? In a photo finish, Vice President Gore narrowly won the popular vote but lost the Electoral College vote by a hair's breadth. Running on a record of a robust economy, usually considered the most important predictor of electoral success for the party in the White House, Al Gore had good reason to expect victory. But during the campaign, Republican candidate George W. Bush successfully hammered home the theme of restoring dignity and morality to the White House. Certainly other factors may have contributed to the outcome of the 2000 election, but Clinton's moral turpitude surely ranks high among them.

Gradually between the mid-1960s, when liberal economic, political, and social policies were at their zenith, until the early 1980s, liberalism descended and conservatism ascended in America. By the 1980s Republicans began to tag Democrats with the so-called L-Word, *liberalism*. From the mid-1960s forward, many new conservative think tanks emerged to cultivate conservative ideas, which conservatives used to bolster their candidacies. Then, when Republicans won the White House they turned to those conservative think tanks for personnel to run their administrations. Among the many conservative think tanks are the Heritage Foundation and the American Enterprise Institute.

As electoral dynamics shift, candidates and their parties must adjust. Bill Clinton, Al Gore, and other centrist Democrats recognized that they would continue to lose presidential elections if they did not move the Democratic Party back to the center and away from extreme liberalism, which had led to the defeat of such Democratic candidates as Walter Mondale (1984). So in the mid-1980s they organized the Democratic Leadership Council, a centrist organization designed to promote moderate policies and candidates. During the 2004 campaign for the Democratic nomination, Senator Joe Lieberman, a member of the Democratic Leadership Council, attempted to promote his candidacy by staking out a position as the moderate candidate in a field of nine candidates.

Prepare for Early or Front-Loading Primaries and Caucuses

Three small states—Iowa, New Hampshire, and South Carolina—have wielded inordinate power in presidential nominations. Coming in January and early February, these caucuses and primary states illustrate the impact of early or so-called front-loading primaries and caucuses.

Candidates must raise substantial cash and devote extensive time to campaign in these states and those that follow immediately thereafter. In the race for the 2004 Democratic nomination, Governor Howard Dean spent most of his nearly $40 million war chest in Iowa and New Hampshire, leaving him cash-strapped for campaigns in succeeding states. In short order, Iowa comes first, then a week later, New Hampshire, followed shortly thereafter by South Carolina, the gateway to the South, and then a week later onto six other states (Arizona, Delaware, Missouri, Oklahoma, New Mexico, and North Dakota).

Front loading (1) effectively excludes late entries from getting into the nomination race; (2) determines party nominees long before the national conventions, which usually convene in July or August; (3) requires that candidates have substantial sums of money to mount effective campaigns in primaries and caucuses across the nation; and (4) makes the conventions nothing more than rubber stamps of primaries and caucuses. No longer are conventions dramatic spectacles of last-minute fights for the nomination, replete with the possibility of a compromise candidate emerging.

Two reasons account for South Carolina's significance: its large proportion of African-American voters, especially in the Democratic Party, and in its status as the first-in-the-South presidential primary. By winning a major victory there in 2004 Senator John Edwards (D, NC) catapulted himself to the position of principal rival to Senator John Kerry (D, MA), who had won Iowa and New Hampshire. In 2000, then Governor George W. Bush (R, TX) breathed new life into his campaign in South Carolina by beating Senator John McCain (R, AZ), who had beaten him badly in New Hampshire.

Recognize the Assets and Liabilities of a Long Campaign

To the casual observer, American presidential campaigns are excessively long. In some countries, national campaigns last no more than 30 days. But in America, they begin not with the 60- to 90-day, head-to-head race between the major party candidates after the national conventions, which campaigns for delegates in conventions, primaries, and caucuses precede by many months, but they also include several years of serious exploratory efforts by prospective candidates to raise funds and to create campaign organizations. Although prognosticators might have thought that advanced communication technology and greatly improved transportation would reduce the time necessary for campaigns, the reverse has happened. Advances in technology and transportation along with front-loading of caucuses and primaries have combined to lengthen presidential campaigns. In anticipation of 2008, prospective candidates in both parties began to establish exploratory committees and to travel to such key states as Iowa and New Hampshire in 2005.

Critics contend that elongated American presidential campaigns waste substantial sums of money on advertising, travel, media coverage and campaign staff. But these same lengthy campaigns with all of their costs also have benefits by:

- Functioning as the only test of whether candidates have sufficient mental, emotional and physical capabilities and energies to survive the extraordinary rigors of four years in office;
- Providing time for a divided party to unify behind its candidate, especially after divisive primaries and caucuses;
- Allowing time for candidates to try out issues and ideas to determine how well the public responds;
- Testing whether candidates have sufficient administrative skill to organize personnel and to develop coherent policies; and
- Enabling candidates who start out far behind the front-runner, such as Hubert H. Humphrey against Richard M. Nixon in 1968 and Gerald R. Ford against Jimmy Carter in 1976, time to catch up. Significantly in these instances Humphrey and Ford overcame double-digit deficits in public opinion polls and lost by razor-thin margins on election day.

Develop Innovative Campaign Techniques and Strategies

When Vice President George Bush Sr. trailed far behind his 1988 opponent, Massachusetts Governor Michael Dukakis, Bush's campaign manager, Lee Atwater, used a new technique, focus groups, to determine which television advertisements would exploit his opponent's weaknesses. Once these advertisements began running, Bush rose in the polls. Among the advertisements was one of the best-known ever used in a presidential campaign, Willie Horton, which featured a revolving door of criminals walking out of prison in Massachusetts.

In 1968 and 1972 Richard M. Nixon used radio in an unusual way, buying inexpensive and large late-at-night blocks of time, and then airing long policy speeches, which the media then covered at no expense to his campaign. His speeches typically got front-page coverage in newspapers and lead stories on television news.

Without the Internet in 2003–04, Vermont Governor Howard Dean could not have mounted a serious campaign, and without television in 1960, John F. Kennedy would have lost to Richard M. Nixon. Dean's organization and fund-raising depended almost entirely on this new medium as he brought thousands of first-time participants in a presidential campaign. Television, of course, enabled John F. Kennedy to close the deficit between Richard Nixon and himself and to eke out a victory of less than one vote per precinct nationwide. Both in television debates and campaign commercials, Kennedy exploited his energetic strategy of "getting the country moving again."

Photographers snapped one of the most famous pictures in the history of national party conventions during the 1960 Democratic National Convention— campaign manager Robert F. Kennedy walking the convention floor talking on a new medium of communication, a walkie-talkie, to manage the delegate count for his brother, John F. Kennedy.

Direct mail and telephone banks have played interesting roles in campaigns, but not always with the utmost integrity. In the nasty 2000 primary fight between George W. Bush and John McCain, both used direct mail and telephone banks to underscore opponent's weaknesses. Because Bush had spoken at Greenville, South Carolina's Bob Jones University (BJU), which the national press had painted as an "anti-Catholic" institution, McCain used direct mail and telephone calls to Roman Catholic voters in the Michigan primary to remind them of Bush's appearance there. McCain, of course, did not mention that Ronald Reagan and other national leaders had spoken there, along with leading Roman Catholics, such as Pat Buchanan. Bush, by contrast, used direct mail and telephone banks during the South Carolina primary campaign to target voters who revered the Confederate flag and the Old South with a message suggesting that McCain was hostile to their interests.

Decide Between Public and Private Campaign Finance

George W. Bush made a strategically wise decision in 2000 and 2004 to decline public funding of his campaign, which enabled him to raise much more from private sources. Public funding enlarges the potential pool of presidential candidates by initially funding those who otherwise would likely not enter the race. Early in the race for the 2004 Democratic nomination, the party had 10 candidates, all of whom depended on the lifeline of public funding. But first Howard Dean and then John Kerry opted out of public funding when they determined that private funding would benefit them more. Public funding may have at least two benefits: (1) creating more choices in candidates and ideas for the electorate to consider, and (2) perhaps eliminating or at least reducing the ties between candidates and major contributors.

Know the Psychology of Voter Behavior and Public Opinion

The American public is like the wavelength spectrum. Some have longer wavelengths, similar to radio, whereas others have shorter wavelengths, similar to ultraviolet radiation. By analogy candidates and presidents must craft their appeals to varying wavelengths along the spectrum. How is this done?

In American presidential campaigns of recent decades, the portrait of the American electorate that develops from the data is not one of an electorate straitjacketed by social determinants or moved by subconscious urges triggered by devilishly skilled propagandists. It is, rather, one of an electorate moved by concern about central and relevant questions of public policy, of governmental performance, and of executive personality.[4]

According to this picture of the American electorate, issues, job performance, and personal character influence voters more than advertising propaganda and other stimuli. Although debatable, this conclusion directly contrasts with what the Framers of the Constitution presumed: namely, that presidents would have a significant degree of independence from the public, given the high stature and dignity of the office along with its term of four years and the indirect and nonpopular method of presidential selection, the Electoral College. But modern presidents must not only respond to the demands of the public; they must reach out to the public through modern technology and the institution of political parties.

Party identification is at the core of the psychological theory of voting behavior, which holds that psychological predispositions determine voting decisions.[5] These predispositions include education, geographic location, economic status, religion, and race. Between the Great Depression of the 1930s and today, the Democratic Party has lost support among some groups, such as Southern Protestants, Northern Roman Catholics, and military veterans, and the percentage of voters identifying as Democrats and Republicans has declined. These and other changes mean that voters now fall primarily into three relatively equal groups: Democrats, Republicans, and Independents. To win, presidential candidates must solidify their partisan bases of support and then reach out to nonaligned voters. By scheduling their caucuses and primaries early in 2004, Democrats hoped to choose their presidential nominee early, thus allowing that person time to unify the Party and reach out to

Independents. And they also hoped to nominate a presidential and vice presidential ticket that would enable Democrats to compete for blocs of voters whose party loyalty has slipped from their grasp—Southern Protestants, Northern Roman Catholics, and military veterans.

In addition to connecting with the electorate through their political parties, the most dependable and stable connection, candidates connect with voters through such historic means as public meetings, flyers, newspapers, and radio. But now candidates have turned much more to the powerful mass media of television and the Internet, which further weaken political parties by enabling candidates to bypass traditional political party channels of communication and organization and to go directly to the people. Candidates now place considerable emphasis on building their own political and fund-raising organizations to strengthen their ability to appeal to the electorate.

The media play an important role in interpreting candidates and campaigns to the electorate. During the 2003–04 campaign for the Democratic presidential nomination, the media, like a pack of hounds, got on the scent of Howard Dean, who became the all-but-certain nominee. Almost as quickly, however, the media pursued the scent of John Kerry, making him the heir apparent to the nomination. In both instances, favorable media attention increased fund-raising opportunities for the two candidates, but when the media turned away from Howard Dean, his fund-raising potential took a hard hit. As conduits between candidates and the voters, the media play a powerful and sometimes conclusive role in determining winners and losers.

Candidates and presidents creatively craft images in their appeals to the electorate. For example, Richard Darman, an aide to Ronald Reagan, sketched his 1984 campaign strategy against Walter Mondale, which revolved around the president's role as the defender of freedom:

> Paint RR (Ronald Reagan) as the personification of all that is right with or heroized by America. Leave Mondale in a position where an attack on Reagan is tantamount to an attack on America's idealized image of itself.[6]

By using this strategy, Reagan became an unassailable hero. Many candidates and presidents have used the image of the president as a folk hero or defender of freedom to appeal to the electorate, such as Abraham Lincoln's Log Cabin image in 1860.

The now commonplace polls chart the attributes of candidates and presidents, measure the public's concern about various issues, and the degree of success that candidates and presidents have had in penetrating the public's mind with their messages. From Ronald Reagan forward, presidents have extensively polled the public. Although the Reagan White House polled the public once every three or four weeks, the Clinton presidency did so sometimes daily but often weekly. But tailoring decisions to poll results presents problems. President Carter said: "When things go bad you get entirely too much blame. And I have to admit that when things go good, you get entirely too much credit."[7]

Along with polling, focus groups have become important. Composed of carefully chosen people, these small groups interpret how candidates and presidents should present themselves and their positions on issues. In 1996 President Clinton effectively used focus groups in conjunction with advertising to determine which pictures and phrases would have the greatest impact on various constituencies.

PRESIDENTIAL ELECTIONS

Two important factors, not always controlled or necessarily influenced by presidential candidates, influence the outcome of presidential elections: the types of presidential elections and the models for predicting presidential elections.

Types of Presidential Elections

Great epochs in American history—the Civil War and the Great Depression—charted new courses for the Democratic and Republican Parties. After the Civil War, the Democratic Party became the minority party and the Republican Party, the majority party. After the Great Depression, their roles reversed. Although no epoch, certainly none comparable to the Civil War and the Great Depression, has occurred since the 1930s, majority versus minority status has changed for the two parties. As measured by public opinion polls, seats in Congress, state legislative seats won, governorships held and years in the White House, the Democratic Party has gradually lost strength and the Republican Party has gained power. Important for presidential candidates to understand are the five types of presidential elections they may face, based on their parties' majority versus minority status.

1. **Perpetuation elections** arise when the majority party retains the White House as occurred during the presidencies of Franklin D. Roosevelt and Harry S. Truman and the Kennedy-Johnson presidencies between 1960 and 1968;

2. **Deviation elections** occur when the minority party wins the White House as Eisenhower did in 1952 and 1956;

3. **Restoration elections** take place when the majority party regains the White House as Democrats did in 1960;

4. **Transformation elections** happen when the two parties switch majority and minority status;

5. **Aberration elections** emerge when one of the two major parties nominates a candidate on the ideological fringe, such as Republicans did with Goldwater in 1964 and Democrats with McGovern in 1972.

Beginning in the 1970s, identification of the majority and minority parties became more difficult, provoking sharp debates among scholars and between the parties about their majority versus minority status. At least three reasons help to explain the decline and rise of the Democratic and Republican Parties: (1) a rising tide of ideological and religious conservatism, which helped to elect Ronald Reagan twice; (2) the population shift from the urban and industrial North to the Sunbelt states, which gave more electoral votes and seats in the U.S. House of Representatives to conservative states, based upon the decennial census every 10 years; and (3) the so-called social issue, which George C. Wallace identified as a third-party candidate in 1968 and which Richard Nixon and the Republicans captured. Wallace, from Alabama, tapped a growing alarm among Southern voters and blue-collar Northern voters about behavior outside America's historically accepted norms.

Although the major parties remain close in public opinion polls, the Republican Party has emerged as the majority party based on state legislative seats won, governorships held, seats in Congress, and years in the White House. These factors serve as built-in advantages for Republican presidential candidates in organizing their campaigns, raising campaign funds, and developing issues.

Models for Predicting Presidential Elections

Models for predicting presidential elections generally rest on one or more of the following seven premises.[8]

1. **Economic considerations** may buoy prospects for victory by the incumbent party in the White House, if economic growth is up, inflation is down, and disposable income is up.

2. **Candidate optimism**, as measured by optimism in speeches, may enhance the prospects for victory of the candidate who is more optimistic and hopeful about America's future.

3. **Charismatic personality**, as shown in John F. Kennedy's victory over Richard M. Nixon in 1960, suggests that the candidate with more charisma may have an advantage.

4. **Party record** can benefit the incumbent party in the White House, if it has a good performance record on major issues.

Table 6.2

THIRD-PARTY PARTICIPATION IN PRESIDENTIAL ELECTIONS

Election Year	Third-Party Vote (%)	Incumbent Verdict
1848	10.2	Lost
1856	21.6	Won
1860	30.7	Lost
1892	10.9	Lost
1912	35.0	Lost
1924	17.1	Won
1968	13.9	Lost
1992	19.6	Lost

5. **Third-party participation**[9] usually sounds the death knell for the incumbent party in the White House (see Table 6.2). In the eight presidential elections when a third-party candidate has entered the fray, the incumbent party has lost the White House on all but two occasions. Looking at 1912 as an illustration, Theodore Roosevelt's Bull Moose or Progressive Party won enough votes to place second to the Democratic Party's winner, Woodrow Wilson, leaving the Republican incumbent, William Howard Taft in third place. Ironically, either Roosevelt or Taft would have beaten Wilson in a head-to-head race. And as another example, Ross Perot's independent candidacy in 1992 took votes primarily from President Bush Sr., costing him the election.

6. **Intraparty contests** customarily damage the candidacy of the incumbent party in the White House. In 1992 President Bush Sr. not only faced the independent candidacy of Ross Perot but also the insurgent campaign of conservative television commentator Pat Buchanan. In 1980 President Jimmy Carter faced an intraparty challenge from Senator Edward Kennedy (D, MA). Both Bush and Carter lost, in part because of intraparty wounds, which did not heal by the General Election.

7. **Consecutive elections won**[10] also serves as a useful barometer of electoral success. The incumbent party in the White House normally wins reelection after the first term and also has a marginal advantage in an election for a third term as shown in Table 6.3.

ADMINISTRATIVE STRATEGIES

Successful presidents appreciate the possibilities and perplexities of the presidency; use their vice presidents effectively; understand the metamorphosis of presidential administrations; instruct the public about unwarranted expectations; and interact effectively with Congress and the Courts.

Table 6.3

CONSECUTIVE PRESIDENTIAL ELECTIONS WON
BY CANDIDATE AND PARTY: 1860–2004

Consecutive Wins	Number	Year	Winner/Party
1	3	1884	Cleveland (D)
		1892	Cleveland (D)
		1976	Carter (D)
2	6	1912–16	Wilson (D)
		1952–56	Eisenhower (R)
		1960–64	Kennedy (D)
		1968–72	Nixon (R)
		1992–96	Clinton (D)
		2000–04	Bush (R)
3	2	1920–24–28	Harding (R)
			Coolidge (R)
			Hoover (R)
		1980–84–88	Reagan (R)
			Bush (R)
4	1	1896–00–04–08	McKinley (R)
			McKinley (R)
			Roosevelt (R)
			Taft (R)
5	1	1932–36–40–44–48	Roosevelt (D)
			Roosevelt (D)
			Roosevelt (D)
			Roosevelt (D)
			Truman (D)
6	1	1860–64–68–72–76–80	Lincoln (R)
			Lincoln (R)
			Grant (R)
			Grant (R)
			Hayes (R)
			Garfield (R)

Appreciate the Possibilities and Perplexities of the Presidency

"Ask not what your country can do for you, ask what you can do for your country," John F. Kennedy's famous phrase in his 1961 Inaugural Address, inspired many young people to launch public service careers. Although his Inaugural Address illustrates the possibilities of presidential leadership, his presidency demonstrates the perplexities. His narrow victory against Richard M. Nixon and thin Democratic majority in the Congress severely limited what he could accomplish. So, looking back on his three years in office, he inspired the public with his rhetoric, but he left behind a limited legislative legacy.

The office of president is at once an office of extraordinary possibilities and enormous perplexities. The presidency has evolved from the simple office instituted by the Founders to a far-flung bureaucracy that requires cooperation and creativity in leading the world's most powerful nation. Leadership of this institution, vested in one person, the president, receives commendation and criticism as it functions in the atmosphere of a fish bowl. In the end, few presidents succeed in mastering the presidency and earning a place in the pantheon of presidential greatness.[11]

"No office within American government, or for that matter within most other systems, has commanded the attention, stirred the imagination, and generated the emotions that the presidency has."[12] Why is this the case? Executive officials look to the office for direction in policy making; members of Congress, for setting priorities and for presidential influence and help on matters of interest to them, including constituent service; heads of foreign governments, for keys to understanding American foreign policy; and the general public, for strength in solving problems and building public trust.

During the Constitutional Convention in 1787 Pennsylvania Delegate James Wilson argued that the presidency should possess "energy, dispatch, and responsibility."[13] In the end, the Founders gave great responsibility to the president, but at the same time restricted presidential powers, creating a government divided by checks and balances or separation of powers.

Successful presidents have used their energy, initiative, and creativity to unify the government and the nation. Their leadership has nurtured stability either by maintaining the established order or by challenging the established order to accept new ideas.[14] James Monroe, James K. Polk, and Dwight D. Eisenhower are among those who fostered stability largely by maintaining the established order, whereas Thomas Jefferson, Andrew Jackson, Abraham Lincoln, Franklin D. Roosevelt, and Ronald Reagan changed the established order. National crises, such as the Civil War and Great Depression, lend themselves to change-oriented presidential leadership, which establishes new governing coalitions and sets the nation on a significantly different path.[15]

Thomas Jefferson and James Polk illustrate the two contrasting leadership styles. Jefferson brought to the presidency an unprecedented partisan mission that infused his leadership with ideological purposes and that involved him in all aspects of the government.[16] Not only did he succeed in removing Federalists from power, but as one contemporary said, he also had significant influence in Congress through his partisan leadership: "Behind the curtain, [he] directs the measures he wishes to have adopted; while in each house a majority of puppets move as he touches the wires."[17]

By contrast, James Polk, who received the torch of leadership from Andrew Jackson, committed himself to moving forward along the well-marked path of Jacksonian ideas. Ironically, Polk desired to innovate, but his innovation interfered with his leadership inherited from Jackson. Thus, Jefferson changed the nation, whereas Polk continued the nation on the path he inherited.

More recently, William Jefferson Clinton became famous for a third way of leading, a hybrid, often called *triangulation*, which fuses personal ideas with those of others. For example, he sometimes blended Republican ideas with his own to create a different idea or approach, such as on crime control and social welfare, making it difficult for opponents to oppose him. But is that new? After all, Woodrow Wilson had it said of him: "He changes, he moves, he shows another side, or turns completely around."[18]

Character and personality also contribute to the possibilities and perplexities of leadership, which background and upbringing both limit and expand, making a president's past a good predictor of his future behavior.[19] Why did Lyndon B. Johnson, despite his dominating personality and boundless energy, always appear ready to please people and to enact massive new programs to change American society? Could his insecure childhood have created his craving for praise? Could his unhappy mother, who married beneath her social status and alternated between praising her son, on the one hand, and resenting and criticizing him, on the other, have contributed to her son's pursuit of ambitious social policies? Or could the warmth and gratitude of Franklin D. Roosevelt's mother have contributed to his soothing Fireside Chats to the American people during the Great Depression and to the encouragement of his Inaugural Address: "First of all, let me assert my firm belief that the only thing we have to fear is fear itself—nameless, unreasoning, unjustified terror. . . "[20]

Successful presidents understand their time and place in history and what they must do to promote unity and to create stability. Adjustment to changing times and circumstances, including recognition of how the presidency has changed, is a must for successful presidents. Although the Founders gave the president certain responsibilities, such as the administration of the government, the task of carrying out enacted laws, and overseeing the departments that the Congress would create, they would not recognize what their ideas have become in today's presidency.

The Founders, who opposed the creation of political parties and did not anticipate their rise, intended that the Electoral College would actually meet and select the president and vice president from candidates nominated through the popular votes in the states. But that did not work. Instead, the two candidates receiving the most Electoral College votes became president and vice president, respectively. And that did not work either, because presidents and vice presidents were soon elected from different parties. Obviously, the party of the president wanted a vice president who supported the president and his party positions on issues.[21] Since then, the nomination process has become more open, the amount of criticism the eventual candidates have had to endure has risen from opponents and the press, and the promises that the nominees have had to make to win the presidency have increased, creating almost insurmountable burdens and unattainable expectations.

Use the Vice President for Political and Policy Purposes

Once considered the burial ground of politicians and a vestigial organ, the vice presidency now performs useful political and policy functions for the president. Republican leaders, who did not like Theodore Roosevelt, the Governor of New York, decided to bury him in the vice presidential cemetery, but they did not account for the assassination of President William McKinley. John Nance Garner, the first of Franklin D. Roosevelt's four vice presidents, said: "The Vice Presidency is not worth a pitcher of warm spit."[22]

Historically, presidential candidates selected vice presidential candidates to help them win office, emphasizing considerations such as building party unity and reaching out to key voting blocs in the General Election.

1. Geographically some presidential candidates balance their state of residence with that of the vice presidential choice. In 1952 on the Republican ticket, President Eisenhower (New York) chose Richard Nixon (California), whereas on the Democratic ticket, presidential candidate Adlai E. Stevenson (Illinois) chose John Sparkman (Alabama).

2. Ideologically in 1960 the more conservative Richard M. Nixon balanced his ticket by choosing the more liberal Henry Cabot Lodge (Massachusetts).

3. Religiously in 1960 Roman Catholic John F. Kennedy chose a Southern Protestant, Lyndon B. Johnson, as his running mate.

Although these three criteria remain important, two other criteria have emerged as vice presidents have become more important in helping presidents govern and also as they have surfaced as successors to presidents.

4. Ability to help the president govern played a significant role in Bill Clinton's choice of Al Gore as his running mate. Gore, who had extensive experience in both houses of Congress, which Clinton did not have, brought an understanding of Washington politics to the Clinton administration.

5. Ability to succeed the president in the event of a vacancy in the presidency has become more important. In 2000, George W. Bush chose Dick

Cheney, who had served in Congress and also as a Cabinet Secretary and presidential advisor to Presidents Nixon, Ford and Bush Sr.

In each of these instances, Clinton-Gore and Bush-Cheney, a sixth criterion became apparent.

6. Compatibility with and loyalty to the president became obvious as Clinton selected Gore, a fellow southerner, Southern Baptist and member of the centrist Democratic Leadership Council. Immediately after the 1992 Democratic National Convention, Clinton and Gore began a highly successful bus tour, which helped to cement their compatibility in the public mind. Bush chose Cheney, whose compatibility and loyalty became increasingly obvious during the Terrorist crises and the wars in Afghanistan and Iraq.

Because five vice presidents assumed the presidency during the 20th century by filling a vacancy created through presidential assassination or resignation, the criteria of help in governance, potential successorship, and compatibility and loyalty now stand out as exceedingly important. The vice presidents, who assumed the presidency in this manner, were Theodore Roosevelt after William McKinley's assassination, Calvin Coolidge after Warren Harding's death, Harry Truman after Franklin Roosevelt's death, Lyndon Johnson after John F. Kennedy's assassination, and Gerald Ford after Richard Nixon's resignation.

Where once vice presidents routinely never ran for president, now they often appear as the heir apparent. Former vice presidents who won their party's nomination for president since 1900 include Theodore Roosevelt (1904), Calvin Coolidge (1924), Harry Truman (1948), Richard Nixon (1960, 1968), Lyndon Johnson (1964), Hubert Humphrey (1968), Gerald Ford (1976), Walter Mondale (1984), George Bush Sr. (1988), and Al Gore (2000).

The vice presidency has come a long way since Finley Peter Dunne's Mr. Dooley described it this way:

It wasn't a crime exactly. Ye can't be sint to jail f'r it, but it's a kind of disgrace. It's like writing anonymous letters.[23]

Understand the Metamorphosis of Presidential Administrations

The winning presidential candidate must understand the six stages in the metamorphosis of presidential administrations: (1) Transition to Office, (2) Preparation for Midterm Elections, (3) Maturation in Office, (4) Preparation for Reelection, (5) Completion of Mission, and (6) Anticipation of Departure. Beginning with the transition, politics daily confront presidents, regardless of their stage in office either in a first term or a second term.

Even before winning the election, prospective presidents must begin planning for the transition between election in early November and inauguration on January 20. Political potholes and pitfalls confront new presidents in selecting personnel, creating the appropriate image for the new administration, and preparing a legislative agenda. How do new presidents balance the coalition of competing interests, which elected them, and reach out to others, which opposed their election? Although the transition should help new presidents unify the country, the decisions they must make often create division.

Once in office presidents must look down the road to midterm elections only two years away. Ideally presidents should have a good honeymoon during their first year when they obtain widespread congressional approval for their legislative proposals. But, in their second year, they must expect significant opposition to their proposals as the opposing party prepares to increase its numbers in Congress. Economic downturns over which presidents may have little control can seriously jeopardize their party's success during midterm elections. Because the party holding the White House normally loses seats during midterm elections, presidents must plan to diminish the significance of their losses and to develop an offensive game plan for the new Congress.

During the third and fourth years of the first administration, presidents have a much more mature administration, but at least three problems usually face them: confronting a reinvigorated opposition party in the Congress, preparing for reelection, and knowing that many key personnel are already planning their exit from the administration. So at a time when the experience of the first two years should enable presidents and their staffs to act in a more mature manner, they face serious obstacles to achieving success.

Reelection planning requires the development of a solid record of accomplishment legislatively in Congress and in making daily decisions. Because incumbent presidents rarely lose after the first term, they have an advantage, but they can squander their advantage as President Jimmy Carter did in 1980. A somewhat weak legislative record, in part because of his failure to cultivate good working relationships with his own party in Congress, and his failure to act decisively in foreign policy sorely damaged his prospects for reelection. Additionally, he failed during his first term to secure his political base in the South, thereby allowing Ronald Reagan to win several states, which he should have easily won.

Once reelected to a second term, presidents immediately become lame ducks. Although the second term should enable presidents to focus much more on just being a good president rather than on the politics of the presidency, the opposite often occurs. Aspiring presidential candidates who would like to succeed them in four years begin planning their campaigns in earnest, and personnel who would like to use their administrative positions to get better positions elsewhere leave their administrations. These and other problems may limit what presidents can achieve during their twilight years in office.

Finally, as presidents prepare to leave office, they customarily make plans for building their presidential libraries, which entails raising considerable amounts of cash, and deciding what they would like to do in their post-presidential careers. They may focus more on retiring and less on governing.

Instruct the Public about Unwarranted Expectations

Because presidents occupy an exalted position in the American mind, the public sometimes generates unduly high or conflicting expectations. Illustrative of these expectations are the public's desire that presidents:

- Provide strong leadership internationally, but without neglecting leadership domestically;
- Possess an open and a flexible mind, but at the same time make decisive decisions;
- Act like a statesman, but participate in partisan politics;
- Conduct important secret negotiations in foreign affairs, but maintain an open administration;
- Serve as the nation's symbol of unity as Head of State, but divide the people while making policy decisions as Chief Executive.[24]

To diminish the adverse consequences of such expectations, presidents must anticipate problems and instruct the public about the difficulties in solving them. By lowering popular expectations, presidents are less likely to suffer acute drops in their popularity. For example, in the War on Terrorism, President George W. Bush counseled the public about the long, essential and difficult battles the nation would face to win. He acted in the same manner regarding economic difficulties, consistently pointing out the intractable nature of the problems and the patience needed to solve them. In this role, the president is both a teacher and an actor. He teaches the public as in a classroom about the reality of problems the nation faces, and he acts as on a stage to dramatize the difficulties the nation faces.

Interact Effectively with Congress and the Courts

Congress. Communication, collaboration, and compromise stand out as the principal sources of success for presidents in their relationships with Congress. They enable presidents to learn what is happening in Congress and to gain allies for their legislative interests. Often cited as the way not to do it, the administration of President Jimmy Carter performed a comedy of errors in its early days, including having no one in the White House with adequate knowledge of Congress and failing to return phone calls to members of Congress.[25] The Carter administration never completely recovered from these early miscues. In its early days, the administration of President Lyndon B. Johnson illustrates how he used communication, collaboration, and compromise to win passage of his Great Society programs. By bringing Congress, especially key leaders, into the planning of Great Society programs, he coopted their support. President Ronald Reagan, facing a U.S. House of Representatives controlled by Democrats, worked closely with key Southern Democrats to gain their support for his supply-side economic program. Later, some of these members became Republicans. Occasionally, presidents have success by standing up to Congress, such as President Harry S. Truman's campaign charge of the "Do Nothing Congress" in 1948. Or presidents may gain an advantage through vetoing or threatening to veto legislation as President George W. Bush did in 2004 with regard to proposals to repeal the president's tax reductions. In the main, however, presidents have more success through communication, collaboration and compromise.

Negotiation is at the heart of relationships between presidents and Congress. By having a clear set of priorities, presidents set the stage for negotiation with the fractured Congress, which consists of 535 members divided into two parties in two houses, into several hundred committees and subcommittees and into many caucuses of various subgroups. Negotiation requires the president to have clear priorities while in office, so that he can negotiate with the many overlapping and competing interests in Congress.

Presidents with outstanding legislative records practice communication, collaboration and compromise with Congress. They present clear priorities to Congress, which set the stage for successful negotiations.

Courts. Clinton Rossiter said about the Supreme Court: "For most practical purposes, the President may act as if the Supreme Court did not exist."[26] Alexander Hamilton said that the courts do not have force or will, but judgment, and that they depend on the executive for the enforcement of their judgments. Although true in one sense, it is not true in another sense. The courts, notably the Supreme Court, may exercise independent judgment to declare presidential actions and Acts of Congress unconstitutional. For example, when President Harry S. Truman seized the steel mills during the Korean War, the Supreme Court declared his action unconstitutional.[27] The courts may not possess the force of executive power to implement their rulings, but in the American tradition, presidents and others almost always comply with court decisions.

An aide to President Richard M. Nixon, Tom Charles Huston, argues that presidents indirectly influence the courts through their nominations.

> It is necessary to remember that the decision as to who will make the decisions affects what decisions will be made. That is, the role the judiciary will play in different historical eras depends as much on the type of men who become judges as it does on the constitutional rules which appear to [guide them].[28]

President George W. Bush fought to achieve indirect influence over the U.S. Supreme Court through his nominations of Chief Justice John Roberts and Justice Samuel Alito, who have conservative judicial philosophies. But serious problems may line the way of this method of influence. First, judicial nominees may not live up to how presidents may think they will rule on cases. When President George Bush Sr. nominated David Hackett Souter to the U.S. Supreme Court, he thought Souter would help to build a conservative majority on the nine-member court. To the contrary, Justice Souter became one of the more liberal members of the Supreme Court. Second, the U.S. Senate may refuse to confirm presidential nominations as it sometimes did during both the Clinton and Bush administrations. Typically, this occurred not in votes by the full Senate but by senators of one party refusing to allow the full Senate to vote on nominees of the other party. Third, as a price for confirmation, the Senate may extract promises from nominees, as it did with Justice Clarence Thomas, making him promise that he would not draw on natural law in rendering decisions on the bench.

Through the Solicitor General's Office in the U.S. Department of Justice, presidents may determine what cases it will appeal to the U.S. Supreme Court and how it will defend its positions on those cases. Also, the Solicitor General, acting on behalf of the president decides what cases the administration will prosecute in the courts. Again, these methods represent indirect means of influence.

CONCLUSION

In *The Tortoise and the Hare*, the tortoise embodies the law of politics, steadiness, and strategic thinking. While the hare slept, the tortoise walked on by. He won the race, not because of speed or cunning, but because of his motivation and concentration on the goal of winning. Successful presidential candidates and presidents must exhibit the same quality: adhering to a strategy, despite difficulties along the road and temptations to go down rabbit trails. Most often, their careers follow a pattern of serving in elective offices at the state and national levels, which in turn necessitates a long period of time to rise to the stature of a presidential candidate. Both campaign and presidential challenges and responsibilities can overwhelm candidates and presidents, unless they remain focused on a clear and coherent strategy that appeals to the mainstream of the American public.

Notes

[1]Lewis L. Gould, *The Modern Presidency* (Lawrence: University Press of Kansas, 2003).

[2]Charles Funderburk, *Presidents and Politics: The Limits of Power* (Monterey, CA: Brooks/Cole, 1982): 168.

[3]Ibid., 174.

[4]Robert Cantor, *Voting Behavior & Presidential Elections* (Itasca, IL: F.E. Peacock, 1975): 15.

[5]Cantor: 29.

[6]Michael Nelson, et al., ed., *The Presidency and the Political System* (Washington, DC: CQ Press, 2000): 310–311.

[7]Ibid., 100.

[8]*Wall Street Journal*, August 24, 1988: 40A.

[9]*Congressional Quarterly*, July 13, 1996: 1987.

[10]*American Political Science Review*, June 1995: 201–206.

[11]George C. Edwards III and Stephen J. Wayne, *Presidential Leadership: Politics and Policy Making* (New York: St. Martin's Press, 1997): xv.

[12]Ibid., 1.

[13]Ibid., 2.

[14]Stephen Skowronek, *The Politics Presidents Make: Leadership from John Adams to Bill Clinton* (Cambridge, MA: Harvard University Press, 1997): 34.

[15]Ibid., 38–39.

[16]Skowronek: 72

[17]Ibid., 73.

[18]Ibid., 458.

[19]Funderburk: 278.

[20]Ibid., 318.

[21]Edwards and Wayne: 22.

[22]http://www.vicepresidents.com/new_page_2.htm

[23]Peter Finley Dunne, *Mr. Dooley in the Hearts of His Countrymen* (Small, Maynard and Co., 1899).

[24]Nelson: 14.

[25]Funderburk: 221.

[26]Ibid., 299.

[27]*Youngstown Sheet and Tube Co. v. Sawyer* (1952).

[28]Nelson: 507.

Chapter Seven

The Law of Management

Indirection

Because government is so large and complex, the best way for a president to "control" the executive branch is to manage it indirectly.[1]

—Judith E. Michaels

INTRODUCTION TO THE LAW OF MANAGEMENT

Successful presidents must master the complexities of management by indirection through political persuasion. The executive branch, albeit constitutionally accountable and responsible to the president, responds more favorably to indirect managerial methods than to those of command and control. Notwithstanding the lack of direct constitutional control in relationships with the legislative and judicial branches, presidents must still seek to influence those institutions, since the public holds presidents accountable for the implementation of their policies.

Judith E. Michaels understands that administrative appearances are misleading. Constitutionally, presidents appear at the apex of authority in Article II. For example:

- "The executive power shall be vested in a President . . . " (Article II, Section 1);
- "The President shall be Commander in Chief of the Army and Navy of the United States . . . " (Article II, Section 2);
- "[H]e may require the Opinion, in writing, of the principal officer in each of the executive Departments, upon any Subject relating to the Duties of their respective offices . . . " (Article II, Section 2);
- "He shall from time to time give to the Congress Information of the State of the Union, and recommend to their Consideration such Measures as he shall deem necessary and expedient . . . " (Article II, Section 3); and
- "[H]e shall take Care that the Laws be faithfully executed, and shall Commission all the Officers of the United States" (Article II, Section 3).

But appearances are deceiving. Although charged with managing a massive bureaucracy, presidents face serious managerial shortcomings, creating an administrative gap between promise and performance. Although Michaels addresses presidential management of the executive branch, she overlooks the need for presidents to manage relationships with the Congress and Courts. Constitutionally, once again, the president appears to have substantial authority or at least influence. For example, among other things presidents possess the power:

- To veto acts of Congress (Article I, Section 7);
- To nominate Cabinet officers, Ambassadors, and Judges (Article II, Section 2);
- To advise the Congress on the State of the Union (Article II, Section 3); and
- To submit recommendations to Congress (Article II, Section 3).

Whether managing relationships within the executive branch or with the Congress and the Judiciary, presidents confront major obstacles to their authority and influence. Indeed, these obstacles bring into question whether the nation needs a managerial president, who governs by direction, or a political president, who governs by indirection.

MANAGERIAL OR POLITICAL PRESIDENT?

Although theoretically presidents have the ability to direct, demand and decree the carrying out of their decisions by subordinates in the executive branch, practically seven significant features of American politics limit their command and control authority.

Vision and Communication. Presidential campaigns and elections do not stress the managerial skill of candidates but, rather, their ability to

persuasively communicate a vision and direction for America and to successfully organize a winning coalition of voting groups. Even the closest presidential elections do not turn on managerial ability. For example, in 1960 John
F. Kennedy could not lay claim to superior managerial skill in beating
Richard M. Nixon, but he did communicate a superior vision for America in
their head-to-head debates as he hammered home the twin themes of "Let's
get the country moving again" and "The New Frontier."

Presidential Greatness Scales. Neither the rankings of presidential
greatness[2] nor major scholarly studies[3] about presidential leadership stress
managerial skill. Indirectly, these rankings and studies may address the
importance of management but more as a secondary concern. Richard
E. Neustadt's classic work, *Presidential Power: The Politics of Leadership*,
declares that:

> The President of the United States has an extraordinary range of formal
> powers, of authority in statute law and in the Constitution . . . **despite** his
> "powers" he does not obtain results by giving orders—or not, at any rate,
> merely by giving orders . . . **despite** his status he does not get action with-
> out argument. Presidential *power* is the power to persuade.[4] (Emphasis
> added)

The managerial effectiveness of presidents may slightly alter their rankings either up or down on scales of presidential greatness, but in the final
analysis their rankings depend far more on their accomplishments. President
Harry S. Truman, who had no managerial background before becoming president and made some serious managerial blunders as president, gradually rose
on the scales of presidential greatness as scholars and others examined his
successes in ending World War II through ordering the atomic bomb dropped
on Hiroshima and Nagasaki, in rehabilitating Europe through the Marshall
Plan and Truman Doctrine, and in responding to the Cold War through the
North Atlantic Treaty Organization (NATO).

James David Barber in *Presidential Character* places a premium on
active and positive leadership, considering Franklin D. Roosevelt and other
presidents with active policy agendas and positive personalities much better
than those without them.[5] By the standards of proper management, President
Roosevelt managed poorly, creating division, friction, uncertainty, and competition among his subordinates rather than unity and confidence in their relationships with one another and with him. To illustrate, sometimes he gave two
subordinates the same task, but without letting each one know what the other
was doing.

Managerial Resistance. American government hinders and often pre-
cludes presidential success in management. The bureaucracy, whose existence
transcends a president's term, may resist presidential directives. Long-time

FBI Director J. Edgar Hoover survived six presidents, including some who wanted to replace him, but could not by virtue of his bureaucratic strength, interest-group support, and congressional ties. Effective bureaucrats, such as Hoover, can use this "Iron Triangle" of relationships to undercut presidential directives. Not only that, but Congress through its powers of confirmation and investigation can make life miserable for presidents. Congress stifled President William Jefferson Clinton's ability to lead his administration by refusing to confirm his first two choices as Attorney General. Similarly, the Senate, before narrowly confirming John Ashcroft as President George W. Bush's Attorney General, put him through protracted hearings. Then, once in office, such subordinates may face adversarial investigatory hearings by congressional committees.

Republican presidents since the New Deal have confronted an added problem, exponential bureaucratic growth during liberal and Democratic administrations, such as Roosevelt's New Deal, Truman's Fair Deal, Kennedy's New Frontier and Johnson's Great Society. During his first term, Richard Nixon attempted to use traditional means to implement his policy initiatives by making his Cabinet and sub-Cabinet appointments, asking Congress to adopt his policies, and seeking appropriations for his programs. But even with his appointees in place and with congressional support for some of his policies, the bureaucracy resisted his leadership. To overcome bureaucratic resistance during his second term, he began to place his personnel lower in the bureaucracy to achieve greater control over the levers of power in policy implementation. He even placed some of his high-ranking White House staff during his first term down in the bowels of the bureaucracy during his second term. The storm clouds of the Watergate crisis and his subsequent resignation, however, aborted his plan.[6]

The bureaucracy, which has no overarching national vision and is known more for its own vision of self-preservation, needs the vision that only a president can impart. So presidents can give to the bureaucracy what it cannot give to itself, direction. Herein is one of the secrets of presidential success and of higher rankings on the scales of presidential greatness. Typically, both successful presidential candidates and successful presidents convince the public and persuade the bureaucracy that they have a superior vision. Successful presidential leadership, therefore, depends not so much on good management as on convincing and persuading others, including the bureaucracy, to accept a president's vision and policy direction.

Presidential Honeymoon. When is Congress more likely to act favorably on a president's policy initiatives? During the presidential honeymoon. Historically, early in presidential administrations presidents enjoy a grace period when adversaries lay down their political knives in the interest of allowing a newly elected president the opportunity to lead free of partisan and ideological bickering. But what do we know about that time? It's brief. Presidents have not yet put all of their personnel in place, and they have not secured adoption of all of their policies. So, ironically during their honeymoons, when least well prepared to lead, they have the best opportunity to lead. Honeymoons have decreased, however, in length and spirit as division in America has increased. For example, President Dwight D. Eisenhower had all of his Cabinet appointees confirmed within 28 days, but some three decades later President Ronald Reagan had to wait 64 days for the completion of action on his nominees. And now the time is even longer. Presidents Clinton and Bush had to wait several months for the completion of senatorial confirmation of their appointees.

Presidential Preparation. Do Americans elect persons trained in management as presidents? No. From Franklin D. Roosevelt to the present, only George W. Bush received formal management training, an MBA from Harvard, which hardly prepared him to lead the vast federal bureaucracy. Among the others, Dwight D. Eisenhower had military managerial experience, which hones decidedly different leadership skills from that needed in the far-flung executive branch. Although each president worked his way up the political ladder, Nixon and Clinton received their training as lawyers; Reagan, as an actor; Carter, as an engineer; Truman, as a failed businessman; and George Herbert Walker Bush, as an oil entrepreneur. Kennedy, the beneficiary of his father's great wealth, immediately launched a political career in 1946 on leaving the military after World War II.

Separation of Powers. The ingenious design of the Founders divides the power of the national government among three branches, allowing them to check one another. Whereas the Constitution charges presidents, as the chief executive, with managing the executive branch, it does not give them managerial authority over the other branches. Yet presidents depend on the other branches for the implementation of their policies. So in a sense and of necessity the managerial requirements of presidents naturally extend to the legislative and judicial branches, especially as the people have the right to hold presidents accountable for their leadership of the nation and the implementation of their policies.

Public versus Private Management. Successful managers in the private sector effectively supervise production and sales, statistically measurable commodities. But that is far different from the abstract goals of government, such as liberty, equality, and justice, which defy precise numerical measurements. As a result, imprecision marks the measurement of the managerial performance of presidents. Great presidents, such as Abraham Lincoln, Franklin D. Roosevelt, and Ronald Reagan, have achieved success in large measure through rhetorically articulating visions of goals that advance liberty, equality, and justice, not through managerial precision in the administration of the executive branch. In effect, they used political rhetoric to move the nation and thus to manage the achievement of their policies. We remember Lincoln for such great speeches as "The Gettysburg Address," Roosevelt for "The Four Freedoms," and Reagan for "Mr. Gorbachev, take down this wall." Their political rhetoric, much more than their managerial skill, advanced their policies and directed the nation.

The nation needs successful political presidents who indirectly become effective managerial presidents. Herbert Hoover, perhaps the best administrator and manager ever to occupy the White House, failed miserably. But his successor, Franklin D. Roosevelt, who was not a gifted administrator and manager, succeeded remarkably. Hoover lacked the political skills, which Roosevelt had in abundance. Similarly, Jimmy Carter brought the managerial skill of his engineering education to the White House, whereas Ronald Reagan brought the rhetorical skill of his acting experience. Carter bogged down in managerial detail, whereas Reagan moved the nation. What then separates presidents like Hoover and Carter from presidents like Roosevelt and Reagan?

MANAGING THE EXECUTIVE BRANCH

If the nation needs presidents who are successful politicians more than presidents who are successful managers, how can successful politicians manage effectively in the White House, particularly as managerial success in the public sector is more abstract than in the private sector? Four keys unlock the answer: (1) managerial style; (2) successful transition; (3) organizational model; and (4) promotion of ideas and vision.

1. Managerial Style

Presidents should know their administrative style whether it is (1) informal; (2) formal; or (3) rigid. Because each style has its own strengths and weaknesses, presidents need to learn how to compensate for their weaknesses, lest they make major mistakes and miscalculations.

Informal Style. Franklin D. Roosevelt, John F. Kennedy, and William Jefferson Clinton stand out as examples of informal administrators. Because flexibility is their administrative calling card, they use an ad hoc managerial approach, working both inside and outside the formal channels of the bureaucracy. For example, Roosevelt made popular his "kitchen cabinet," a group of informal, unelected advisors, outside of the government. Kennedy used the ad hoc approach in both the Bay of Pigs and Cuban missile crises, establishing working groups as he deemed them necessary. Clinton used his wife, an unelected and unappointed official, along with many persons outside the bureaucracy to forge his healthcare policy recommendations.

In this model, the president serves as the hub of the wheel, which secures his central and usually unchallenged administrative role. But although this style allows for flexibility, it also fosters contention and confusion in that the flip side of flexibility is disorder. Subordinates may have difficulty in knowing what their position is, as decision-making roles frequently change. When Kennedy's informal style failed him during the Bay of Pigs crisis, he turned to a more formal style during the Cuban missile crisis, relying much more on formal channels of authority.

Formal Style. Presidents Eisenhower, Ford, Reagan, and the two Bushes fall in this category. They follow closely the administrative chain-of-command and require that issues and ideas receive a proper and full airing below before coming up the hierarchy to them. President Eisenhower, a five-star general, made the most of the formal model, naming a Chief of Staff through whom all communication came to the president. Before ideas and issues ascended to him, President Eisenhower wanted to have an executive summary of them in a brief memorandum, preferably no more than one page.

Orderliness and confidence rank high among the advantages of this style. Subordinates, knowing their positions in the administrative hierarchy, can have confidence in who they are and how they can influence decisions. Of course, as a principal downside the formal style may limit the diversity of ideas and issues going up to the president who depends primarily on subordinates for advice and counsel. The formal style, to function effectively and successfully, requires a talented and collegial staff that reaches out to make sure that they bring in the best advice and counsel for input along the various levels of the chain of command as information moves upward to the president.

Rigid Style. Among the few presidents in this category, Richard Nixon stands out. Desiring to keep information and ideas "close to the vest," he restricted access to himself and his ideas, trusting only a very few people to know his thoughts on issues. Chief among them was his foreign policy advisor, Henry Kissinger, who combined with the president to act with secrecy, speed and surprise to bring about major policy changes: opening the door to Chinese diplomatic relations, reaching significant accords with the Soviet Union and terminating the gold standard. Although this style paid dividends for President Nixon, in the end it contributed to his demise. By "playing things close to the vest," he isolated himself from dialogue with others. Had he confided in a larger circle of advisors and friends, the Watergate scandal might not have occurred. But even with the scandal, he might have survived by listening to Washingtonians outside of his tight inner circle who thought he could survive by openly and freely admitting his complicity in Watergate and telling the nation he was sorry. They believed that because Nixon had won one of the greatest landslide victories in American history in 1972, a forgiving nation would welcome his continuation in office without the protracted and divisive political warfare brought on by impeachment proceedings.

2. Successful Transition

Charged with charting the path of a vast governmental complex, presidents must begin with a successful transition into office, but taking the reigns of power is not an easy task. Among the millions of federal employees, many may disagree with a president's policies and most have the best job security in the nation. How then can a temporary president, elected to serve only four years, lead a permanent bureaucracy? The answer is simple, but the process is difficult.

Before newly elected presidents can implement their policy objectives, they must achieve a successful transition into office. Presidents-elect cannot place too much emphasis on this enormous task, according to long-time presidential scholar Louis Koenig: "The environment of the modern Presidency makes imperative not only a rational method of succession but a smooth transition between the outgoing and the incoming Chief Executives."[7] Through successful transitions, presidents can begin to steer the executive branch and possibly the nation down the road they want to go. Without successful transitions, presidents will appear weak and their influence not as strong. So, in many ways, transitions offer presidents their first opportunity to make a good first impression on the bureaucracy.

Intimidating and *overwhelming* aptly describe the transition tasks facing presidents. Between their election in November and inauguration on January 20, presidents have approximately 5,000 positions to fill, approximately evenly divided between policy-making and non-policy-making staff, either by nomination and Senate confirmation or by appointment.[8] After the election, presidents-elect can expect to receive about 1,500 resumes and recommendations each day for these positions.[9] During his transition, John F. Kennedy wrote, "I must make appointments now; a year hence I will know who I really want to appoint."[10] Presidents must make these appointments, as Kennedy points out, when they are least able to do so. Yet they are like a rudder to enable presidents to steer the bureaucracy. In addition to the thousands of appointments, presidents-elect must also set forth their policy objectives for everything from energy and the environment to education and the economy.[11] Although cramped for time, successful presidential transitions proceed as much as possible at a deliberate pace, guided by past transitions.

Following Sound Principles. The presidential transitions of Ronald Reagan in 1980 and Bill Clinton in 1992 reveal three important principles. Presidents-elect should:

- Plan early, beginning even before their election, for the possibility of a transition;
- Delegate responsibility for their transitions to trusted advisers; and
- Appoint people with ideological beliefs similar to their own.

In his transition, Reagan followed these principles, creating according to some one of the best transitions in modern history as he "hit the ground running."[12] Clinton's transition, considered the antithesis to Reagan's, failed to follow these principles, causing many to say he "hit the ground walking."[13] An examination of the Reagan and Clinton transitions reveals why one succeeded and the other failed.

In having one of the most successful transitions in modern presidential history, Reagan not only followed the three principles, but in a sense, created them. To guarantee success, Reagan began planning early, very early, according to John P. Burke: "Reagan and his advisers began to think about a possible transition to the presidency even before Reagan had been nominated as his party's presidential candidate."[14] In addition, the early transition team worked closely with the campaign to plan policy objectives.[15] Although Reagan campaigned on certain themes, the transition team studied how to implement them, which allowed Reagan to start his formal transition immediately after his election.

Because of the massive task of appointing officials and preparing policy objectives, Reagan recognized the need to delegate. Once the director of the preelection transition effort, E. Pendleton James, completed his work, Reagan turned over the transition to his trusted friend Edwin Meese, who became his Attorney General, and Washington insider James Baker, who became his Secretary of the Treasury.[16] Together, Meese and Baker sorted through possible appointments and set policy objectives. And then as noted by James P. Pfiffner, they insisted that those appointed must agree with Reagan's ideology and policies: "The overall result of Reagan's selection process was an administration staffed with officials selected more systematically for their ideological loyalty to the president than any other recent administration."[17] Unlike previous administrations, Reagan's team made sure that the vast majority of appointees, even the low-level managerial appointments, agreed with the president's philosophy and policies. By increasing the number of Reagan loyalists in the bureaucracy, they improved their ability to lead it.

Clinton's 1992 presidential transition differed markedly from Reagan's 1980 transition. Notwithstanding the success of Reagan's transition, Clinton did not look to any of the principles used in 1980. Despite the need for early planning, Clinton felt it would hurt him politically. Already criticized by President George Bush Sr. for "measuring the drapes in the White House," Clinton did not want to undertake early planning for fear that it would seem "presumptive."[18]Although Clinton had a small team working on a possible transition, tensions ran high among the group, and there was virtually no communication between the transition team and the campaign.[19] Unlike the Reagan transition, the Clinton campaign did not coordinate objectives with the transition team. Immediately following his election, Clinton dismissed the leader of the transition, essentially starting over and demonstrating the failure of the early effort.[20] Although Clinton officially started his transition early, it lacked the support of even Clinton himself and no meaningful transition efforts began until after the election. His transition started on the wrong foot and never got off it.

Clinton also failed to delegate, instead opting to micromanage the transition, which created serious problems, according to Pfiffner: "The trouble with refusing to delegate authority to run the transition was that all decisions, major and minor, tended to gravitate to the top until they could be decided by the president-elect."[21] Even one of the foremost students of the presidency, Richard E. Neustadt, in a memorandum to Clinton aide Robert Reich, warned of the need to delegate to ensure a prompt and orderly transition of power.[22] Instead of delegating, Clinton put his fingerprints on every decision, holding up the announcements of many appointees until shortly before the inauguration.[23] His failure to delegate slowed a transition process already short on time. Making a massive number of appointments and decisions in a limited time makes delegation essential.

But Clinton not only failed to plan early and to delegate, he also failed to insist upon ideological loyalty among his appointees. Even though he considered ideology important, diversity trumped most considerations, according to Pfiffner: "For President Clinton the dominating theme of the personnel recruitment effort was diversity, which was summarized as the 'EGG' standards—ethnicity, gender, and geography."[24]

Because of this policy, Clinton neglected the ideological loyalty that benefited Reagan, thus lessening his influence within the government. By most accounts, Clinton's transition was a failure, because he failed to follow the keys to success found in the Reagan transition twelve years earlier. Although successful transitions help presidents to manage the bureaucracy by getting loyal officials in place and setting policy objectives, the follow-through or implementation is just as important and, like the transition, is not an easy task.

Choosing Good Managers. Inasmuch as the immense, vast, and far-reaching federal bureaucracy defies effective managerial control from one central authority, presidents can best serve themselves and the nation by choosing good managers to administer departments and agencies, especially in view of their not uncommon lack of managerial training and skill. Critics should not measure the managerial ability of presidents so much as their ability to choose good managers. Thus, the most important managerial decisions made by presidents are their choices to lead Cabinet departments and independent agencies.

Selecting Cabinet secretaries and the directors of independent agencies requires considerable wisdom in balancing a variety of interests: economic, historical, ideological, political, and social. Typically, a person chosen to head a Cabinet department, such as Education or Labor or Commerce, will mirror the interests represented by that department. Not to select such a person would invite the hostility of key groups that look to a department for leadership.

When weighing these interests, presidents also must decide if they will select persons of national and international reputation. For example, during his first administration, President George W. Bush picked strong-minded persons with national and international reputations, Colin Powell and Donald Rumsfeld, to head State and Defense, respectively. By contrast, President Richard M. Nixon did not pick persons whose reputations would enable them, if they chose to do so, to challenge his leadership. By choosing persons of high caliber and with significant reputations, presidents can place greater confidence in the quality of their advice and counsel, and in their leadership of departments and agencies. Moreover, persons of high stature possess greater freedom to tell presidents what they may not want to hear, but what they really need to know.

Presidents must recognize a weakness, however, in selecting especially strong and competent persons to head departments and agencies. As a Cabinet Secretary once said: "Members of the Cabinet are a president's natural enemies." How so? A president is one of only several superiors for a Cabinet secretary or agency director. Besides the president, secretaries and directors must respond to Congress, to interest groups, to their professional organizations and to the bureaucracy itself. In short, they must balance many competing interests, including the those of the president.

3. Organizational Model

Once presidents complete their transitions, they begin the task of leading the executive branch, which includes all of the cabinet departments and independent agencies, such as the National Aeronautics and Space Administration

(NASA). Additionally, presidents name persons to various boards and commissions, such as the J. William Fulbright Foreign Scholarship Board. To help them lead the bureaucracy, presidents have at their disposal those 5,000 or so appointments and nominations, otherwise known as political patronage. Some three million other employees in the bureaucracy come to their positions through the Civil Service and the Foreign Service.

Within the executive branch, but particularly the Executive Office of the President (EOP), presidential policy objectives become clear. Created in 1939 by the Administrative Reorganization Act, the EOP provides presidents with personnel directly under his control to help him manage the bureaucracy. Among the better-known components of the EOP are the White House Staff, National Security Council, Council of Economic Advisors, and Office of Management and Budget.

History provides lessons not only about how to design successful transitions, but also about how to lead the executive branch. Given the bureaucracy's vast size, one key to leadership stands out—delegation—according to Judith E. Michaels:

> Because government is so large and complex, the best way for a president to "control" the executive branch is to manage it indirectly, to delegate most issues that are not clearly presidential to department and agency heads. Presidents should lean on their cabinet secretaries; direct presidential involvement should be very selective.[25]

Political appointees, the ones chosen during the transition, are the keys to leading the bureaucracy. Through delegation, presidents can reach down into the bureaucracy to increase their control.

Delegating Responsibilities. Drown in detail or survive by delegating. Intense and competing pressures vie for the time of presidents. If presidents try to respond to all concerns and interests, major and minor, they will drown in detail. But if they delegate significant responsibilities to subordinates, they will free their time to concentrate on higher priorities.

Put another way, presidents are like either impressionist or realist painters. Impressionist presidents concentrate on painting a big picture that is coherent and understandable, whereas realist presidents focus more on the details of a picture. Included among the impressionist presidents are Franklin D. Roosevelt, Ronald Reagan, and George W. Bush, whereas Jimmy Carter stands out as an example of a realist president. As an impressionist president, Ronald Reagan had a basic set of principles that guided his approach to government and public policy. As he concentrated on the implementation of these principles, Reagan left other matters to subordinates. By contrast, Jimmy Carter sometimes devoted so much time to detail that he failed to see the big picture.

Successful delegation requires that presidents provide clear direction to subordinates and then monitor their performance. Harry S. Truman delegated the responsibility for conduct of the Korean War to General Douglas MacArthur, but when the president decided that the general had failed in this endeavor, he removed him from office.

Delegation, although critical to success, is not an easy task, which raises a crucial question: How can presidents delegate successfully? The answer is that it depends. Different presidents follow different managerial models. For example, Jimmy Carter followed a spokes-in-a-wheel model, but Ronald Reagan adhered first to a modified spokes-in-a-wheel model and then later to a hierarchical model.

Organizational Models Compared. No president since Carter has used the spokes-in-a-wheel model, which places the president at the managerial center.[26] In this model, spokes emanate from the president to various appointees, who report directly to the president,[27] but who does not have a chief of staff.[28] With the president thoroughly immersed in the details of management, the spokes-in-a-wheel model produces a "president-dependent" system that hinders administration.[29] Noting the problems this created for Carter, Burke observed: "While immersing himself in policy details, he did not have the skill or will to manage the organization processes from which they issued, nor had he vested power in anyone else to do it."[30] Although the spokes-in-a-wheel model accomplishes delegation, presidents confront an enormous burden of overseeing policy implementation, because they have no one below them to perform managerial oversight.

Recognizing both the assets and liabilities of the spokes-in-a-wheel model, Reagan modified it, which allowed both a chief of staff and a few senior staff members to report directly to him.[31] When he delegated a task, the chief of staff would oversee its implementation. If a problem or question arose, the chief of staff would direct that question to the appropriate White House staff member, Cabinet secretary, or agency director rather than taking it directly to the president. Whereas the president delegated policy objectives, he did not personally implement or directly oversee them. Later, he switched to a hierarchical model, placing much more authority in the hands of his chief of staff.[32]

In both the modified spokes-in-a-wheel and hierarchical models, presidents may find themselves too far removed from the management of government. President Reagan faced this charge[33] in his second administration during the Iran-Contra Affair, when his delegation of a policy objective to subordinates prompted the accusation that he was "out of touch" with his administration[34] and that subordinates had violated federal law. Ultimately, this charge led to protracted investigations by Congress and a Special Counsel.

Albeit necessary to successful management, particularly in a large bureaucracy, delegation has its limits. Presidents must delegate tasks, not power, as illustrated by the Nixon presidency. Based on problems during his first term, Nixon chose to change his managerial model. According to Richard P. Nathan:

> From the very outset, the Nixon Administration had been anti-bureaucracy. . . . The important difference was that, unlike many of its predecessors, the Nixon Administration did not come to terms with this initial attitude or find ways to sublimate it, as had the Eisenhower Administration eight years previously. There was no reduction in mistrust of the bureaucracy. On the contrary, these attitudes hardened to the point where unprecedented reorganizational steps were planned for the second term to take control of the machinery of domestic government.[35]

How did Nixon attempt to implement change? He created the so-called Administrative Presidency, which intended to change the bureaucracy and domestic programs through management, not through congressional legislation.[36] As previously noted, during his second term Nixon placed devoted and high-ranking political appointees, including White House staffers from his first term, in lower echelons of the bureaucracy to strengthen his control of the bureaucracy.[37] In *The Plot That Failed: Nixon and the Administrative Presidency*, Nathan recounts the story of one appointee:

> A close aid to John Mitchell in the first term, Donald E. Santarelli, named at the start of the second term as director of the Law Enforcement Assistance Administration in the Justice Department, was one of the few brave souls in what he thought was a private moment to speak about these new conditions. He said he was his own boss now and didn't check with anyone about his decisions. "There is no White House anymore." Santarelli was forced to resign because of the wide press coverage of his remarks, but many others who saw things the same way and behaved accordingly (although without saying so) stayed on.[38]

Knowing that White House consultation was unnecessary, Nixon's appointees had virtually no checks on them, which violated a fundamental tenet of delegation—accountability—made doubly damaging because of broad grants of power. During the Watergate scandal, Nixon and his senior staff diverted almost all of their attention to political survival, leaving little, if any, time for oversight of these powerful appointees in the bureaucracy.[39] So, his appointees had power, but without accountability for its exercise.

Testing Appointees' Ideas. Presidents John F. Kennedy and Lyndon B. Johnson failed to challenge the experts on Cuba and Vietnam. Kennedy accepted the experts' point of view that the Cuban people would rise up against Castro, if he permitted an invasion. They did not, and therefore the Bay of Pigs fiasco permanently marred his legacy. Johnson followed the experts' advice and counsel that countries in Southeast Asia would fall to communism like a row of dominoes, if the United States did not thwart their advance in Vietnam. This advice and counsel mortally wounded his presidency when the nation and his own party turned against him. In domestic policy, Johnson accepted the recommendations of social policy experts that led to the creation of his "Great Society" agenda, which included a "War on Poverty" and other ambitious and expensive social welfare projects. Now, over 30 years later, his ambitious agenda lies in ruins. His efforts to fight a war on two fronts, internationally against communism and domestically against poverty, generated inflationary pressures, budget deficits, campus turmoil, and urban riots. Presidents must subject expert opinion to intense scrutiny to ensure that it is in the national interest as well as in their own political interest. Critics now contend that President George W. Bush made a mistake similar to Presidents Kennedy and Johnson when he accepted the experts' view that the Iraqi people would welcome American troops with open arms.

Managerial Principles. Despite the fact that no fail-safe system exists to ensure a flawless delegation of authority and responsibility, presidents ought to follow four principles to make failure less likely. They should:

- Choose a managerial model that best corresponds with their needs. Since the massive demands on presidents now dictate a significant measure of delegation, they should adopt either a modified spokes-in-a-wheel model with a chief of staff or a hierarchical model with a chief of staff.
- Carefully study the managerial models of previous presidencies to learn from their strengths and weaknesses.
- Anticipate problems with whatever model they choose, standing ready to correct deficiencies as quickly as possible.
- Judiciously delegate tasks, not power, to ensure appropriate oversight and to preserve the power inherent in the presidential office. Put in simple terms, presidents should keep their appointees on a tight leash of tasks to perform rather than allow them to roam freely with broad grants of power.

Conclusion. To effectively manage the executive branch, presidents should have (1) a successful transition to power, and (2) a proper delegation of authority while in power. During the transition presidents should carefully select their appointees in part based on whether they would later like to delegate tasks to them. Thus, *delegation* is the bridge between a successful transition and a successful administration. Or, put another way, a successful transition should produce successful delegation.

4. Promotion of Ideas and Vision

Ideas and vision do not sell themselves. They require proper packaging and successful marketing. Effective presidents not only develop great ideas, but they also package and market them to Congress, the bureaucracy, interest groups, the media, and the public. Effective packaging and marketing can make the ideas almost irresistible, especially to members of Congress.

- George W. Bush had the idea of a different kind of conservatism, which he packaged and sold as "compassionate conservatism." Improving education, a major part of this package, he packaged and sold as "no child left behind." Politically, who can oppose "no child left behind"?
- In the same way, Lyndon Johnson's "Great Society" and "War on Poverty" put members of Congress on the defensive. After all, is anyone really against creating a "Great Society" or having a "War on Poverty"?
- Contrasts between Dwight D. Eisenhower and John F. Kennedy illustrate the importance of idea promotion. Eisenhower had a program known as Public Law 480, which used America's abundant agricultural production to help countries in need. Recognizing its ineffective packaging, Kennedy renamed it "Food for Peace." Similarly Kennedy recognized that an Eisenhower program to assist countries in the Western Hemisphere lacked sparkling packaging, so he created the "Alliance for Progress."

But that's not all there is to idea promotion. Besides macroscopic marketing of ideas, presidents must microscopically manage their forward progress, particularly in Congress. William Jefferson Clinton had a brilliant macroscopic marketing plan for national healthcare reform. While delivering a dazzling address to a Joint Session of Congress, he pulled out of his pocket and waved before the American people a plastic card, the size of a credit card, and said every American should have a healthcare card that would ensure their immediate healthcare in hospitals and other healthcare facilities. After his address, public opinion strongly favored healthcare reform, but he and his staff failed to microscopically monitor its passage through Congress, and the tide of public opinion turned against his proposal.

As the chief executive, presidents must manage the executive branch, including the massive American bureaucracy. But what about the legislative and judicial branches? Because the Founders separated the national government into three branches, which have powers to check one another, should presidents seek to manage the other branches to implement their vision for America? As the nation's elected leader, only presidents can serve as the voice of a nation. To play this role properly, they must manage all three branches of government, if they wish to implement their goals and objectives. So, presidential leadership necessarily entails management, not just of the executive branch but also of the legislative and judicial branches.

INFLUENCING THE LEGISLATIVE BRANCH

Presidents and Congress play a perpetual game of tug-of-war. Both want power, and both want prestige, but in their constant struggle for power and prestige, they act as though they cannot get along with one another, when in truth they cannot get along without one another. They are mutually dependent. Presidents need Congress to approve their policies and budgets, whereas Congress needs presidents to implement what they approve. How then should presidents manage their relationships with Congress? Successful presidents use nine methods.

1. The Presidential Veto

Since Article I, Section 7 of the Constitution grants to presidents the power to veto acts of Congress, either a veto or a threatened veto may serve as an excellent tool for managing Congress. Vetoes usually work best for presidents who are of the opposite political party of the majority in Congress as was the case with President George Bush, Sr. Frequently finding himself at odds with the congressional majority, he used the veto to manage his congressional relationships, according to Colin Campbell and Bert Rockman:

> By the summer of 1990, President Bush had established this authority as an important weapon in checking the initiatives of congressional Democrats. He had vetoed thirteen bills by that time, and Congress was unable to override one of them. The further threat of vetoes for legislation carried to the final weeks of the second session . . . added weight to the president's influence.[40]

Bush protected his objectives by using the veto to thwart the efforts of Congress to pass legislation contrary to his objectives, resulting in Bush gaining more influence with Congress. Thus, his use of the veto allowed Bush to cope with a hostile Congress.

In *Presidential Influence in Congress*, George C. Edwards III points out, however, that presidents should only use the veto in extreme circumstances:

Once exercised, a veto can only say no. At that point, the threat has failed and the chances of the president's legislative proposals passing in the forms that he desires are diminished. Moreover, the threat must be exercised with caution lest it be too often and too easily overcome.[41]

So presidents preserve the effectiveness of their veto power through judiciously using it. The mere threat of a veto may accomplish more than a veto itself. If the veto ceases to serve as a threat, then presidents lose a measure of influence and effectiveness with Congress.

If used correctly, however, the veto may serve as one of the most powerful weapons for presidents in managing the legislative branch. Although presidents can effectively block congressional action with the stroke of a pen, they should only veto a bill if it would boost their influence with Congress. Succinctly put, presidents may win a battle with a veto but lose the war for influence with Congress. Presidents should look on the veto power as just one of several methods to manage Congress.

2. Presidential Popularity

Presidential popularity also may help presidents manage Congress. According to Edwards, "presidential popularity sets the limits of what Washingtonians will do for or to the president; widespread popularity gives the president leeway and decreases resistance to policies."[42] Just as Congress will more likely support a popular president, so an unpopular president will incur greater difficulty in opposing Congress. Even Abraham Lincoln recognized the importance of popular support, stating, "Public sentiment is everything. With public sentiment, nothing can fail, without it nothing can succeed."[43]

Edwards suggests two reasons why presidential popularity enhances the standing of presidents with Congress. First, members of Congress believe that "they should accept instructions from their constituents."[44] If presidents enjoy high popularity among the people, members of Congress usually conclude that they should support what their constituents want. Furthermore, according to one study, "The public expects Congress to cooperate with the president and to expedite major aspects of his legislative programs."[45] Edwards sums up the argument this way: "If members of Congress respond to expectations (whether their own or the public's), they should increase their support for the president as the public increases its support for him."[46]

Second, presidential popularity functions as a political barometer for members of Congress, providing them "with a guide to the public's views,"[47] and an incentive to support presidential policies in sync with them. For example, members of Congress who oppose a popular president or who support an unpopular president can fatally erode their prospects for reelection.[48]

Many presidents have used their popularity to manage Congress. While still riding high from World War II fame as a five-star general, Dwight David Eisenhower enjoyed incredibly high popularity in 1955 when he wanted to stop Congress from passing a tax cut.[49] He sent Vice President Nixon to Capitol Hill with this message: "What will count is whether you were for or against the president."[50] Eisenhower knew that with broad popular support he could persuade Congress on this issue. On leaving office, Lyndon B. Johnson wrote in his memoirs: "Presidential popularity is a major source of strength in gaining cooperation from Congress."[51] And an aide of Jimmy Carter said: "No president whose popularity is as low as this President's has much clout on the Hill."[52]

3. Party Loyalty

As party leader, presidents can leverage their leadership to influence their party's members in Congress.[53] Customarily, presidents whose party holds the majority in Congress have considerably more influence. From 2001 to 2004, with his party in the majority, President George W. Bush used this leverage in getting Congress to pass key legislation, including tax reductions, education reform, changes in Medicare, and support for the War in Iraq. Why do members of a president's party in Congress support presidential initiatives?

- First, and quite obviously as members of the same party, they usually agree on the same policies.[54]
- Second, when members of a president's party disagree with presidential initiatives, they still often support them either out of a desire to make the president's administration look good or because of personal loyalty to their party and president.[55]
- Third, members of the president's party may support presidential initiatives out of sheer contempt for the opposing party, which they view as trying to undermine their president.[56]
- Fourth, presidents can exercise influence over party members through the magnetic lure of patronage, grants and contracts. Members of Congress, desiring reelection, know that the president can make them look good by doling out favors to their constituencies.

No factor is more important in predicting presidential success with the Congress than party loyalty. By gaining the support of their party in Congress, presidents can negotiate much more effectively with the opposition.[57]

4. Elections

Elections provide yet another opportunity for presidents to manage Congress. Every two years, the members of the House of Representatives as well as a third of the members of the Senate stand for election. Every four years, America elects a president. Both the congressional elections as well as the presidential election provide presidents a chance to manage Congress.

With party support so critical to a president, midterm congressional elections offer presidents an opportunity to change the look of Congress, as noted by Edwards:

> Once members of Congress are elected, they almost never change their party affiliation, and the rare instances when they do have not resulted from presidential urgings. Thus, if presidents are to alter the party composition of Congress, they must help to elect additional members of their party.[58]

The support of a popular president can carry a candidate to victory, but the support of an unpopular president can result in defeat. In 2002, a popular George W. Bush successfully campaigned for the election of Republicans to Congress, culminating in Republicans restoring their majority in the Senate and retaining their majority in the House. In 1966, Democratic candidates did not want the support of their president, Lyndon B. Johnson, whose popularity had dropped below 50 percent, and as a result he did not actively participate in the midterm elections.[59] Most candidates saw the president as a liability rather than an asset.

5. Presidential Honeymoon

Presidents also have an advantage with Congress following their election. For a few months following inauguration, presidents generally enjoy a "honeymoon" with Congress because of a supposed "mandate" of the people.[60] As previously mentioned, presidents must prepare to take advantage of this period to push as many of their campaign themes through Congress as possible.

6. Press

More than any other governmental institution, presidents enjoy access to the media. Rarely, if ever, does a presidential speech or appearance fail to make the news. With this access to the press, presidents can use it to advance causes in Congress. During the shutdown of the national government in 1995, President Clinton used the media to convince voters that the Republican majority in Congress, led by House Speaker Newt Gingrich and Senate Majority Leader Bob Dole, his challenger in the 1996 presidential election, instigated the unpopular shutdown.[61] Clinton used every opportunity to attack the Republicans, who lacked the same access to the press to mount a counter-attack. Subsequently, Republicans gave in to the president's demands to end the shutdown.

7. Negotiation

Separation of powers in the national government increases the importance of negotiation between the executive and legislative branches as the two vie for advantage and as diverse interest groups press their demands on both.[62] Even with all of their other ways for managing Congress, in the end presidents must negotiate an agreement acceptable to both,[63] which three sets of questions guide, according to Charles O. Jones:

- The issues: Who wants what? How do decision makers in each branch define social, economic, and political needs? Who controls the agenda?
- The president: What does he want? What are his resources? How does he view the presidency? The Congress?
- Congress: Which party is in the majority? What is the dominant congressional view of the presidency? Of the role of Congress?[64]

Although these questions remain the same for all presidents, presidents differ in how they negotiate.

Possessing finely honed negotiating skills acquired in part through his position as Senate Majority Leader,[65] President Lyndon B. Johnson developed techniques to work with Congress, such as acting fast, setting priorities, being persistent, and making party members look good.[66] Using these techniques, he pushed through Congress one of the largest legislative packages since the New Deal. Of course, an overwhelming Democratic majority buttressed his efforts. Later, however, Johnson lost support in Congress when his domestic programs and the War in Vietnam failed to achieve their objectives, even leading to riots and violence in the cities and on college campuses. As the War in Vietnam demanded more of his time, he began to neglect Congress,[67] which became like a scorned bride.

President Gerald R. Ford, who did not have Johnson's luxury of a friendly Congress, added the threat of a veto to his arsenal of weapons in negotiating with Congress. As noted by Jones: "The veto is definitely helpful to a minority president, particularly one with a limited program, who wants to resist the expansion of government."[68] By threatening to veto legislation, Ford could exercise more control over negotiations and often force a compromise.

8. The Vice President

Speaking of the office of the vice president, President John Adams said: "My country has in its wisdom contrived for me the most insignificant office that ever the invention of man contrived or his imagination conceived."[69] Although historically so regarded, the vice presidency has increased in importance from the 1950s until now. Beginning with President Eisenhower's increased use of Vice President Richard M. Nixon, each succeeding president has augmented vice presidential responsibilities. Now vice presidents, as illustrated by Richard Cheney, perform many policy and political chores that were beyond consideration not long ago. With Congress, he has served in a critical liaison role to win congressional approval of the president's program, drawing on his experience as a member of Congress to help the president.

Similarly, Vice President Dan Quayle played a comparable role for President Bush Sr., who used him as a liaison to Congress during the Gulf War. His influence was so significant that "according to three dozen congressmen from both parties interviewed by [*Washington Post* reporters] Broder and Woodward, the vice president gave them the impression that they had a direct channel to the White House."[70] Quayle used his contacts from his days as a Representative and Senator to push Bush's position on the Gulf War. When time came to seek congressional approval for the Gulf War, Quayle had done his homework to win a majority.[71] Recognizing his skills in dealing with Congress, Bush used Quayle to, in effect, manage Congress and get approval for the Gulf War.

9. Presidential Privileges

Often overlooked, yet very useful, in managing Congress are presidential privileges: parties at the White House, trips with the president on Air Force One, and invitations to bill signings, just to name a few. As related by Edwards about one Washington insider, "You can't use tact with a Congressman! A Congressman is a hog! You must take a stick and hit him on the snout!"[72] Because members of Congress like presidential attention, they may receive phone calls or invitations to the White House from the president to help bolster the president's cause in Congress.

President Johnson enhanced the art of extending privileges to members of Congress. He even made bill-signing ceremonies major extravaganzas. On one occasion, he used 60 pens and consumed 20 minutes to sign his name to one piece of legislation.[73] Why so many pens? Gifts for congressional supporters. With the vote for a controversial bill proposed by Johnson scheduled on Christmas Eve, he invited every member of Congress to the White House for a Christmas party the night before.[74] All presidents since Johnson have used presidential privileges, but none more so than Presidents Clinton and Bush Jr., who abundantly used White House "photo-ops" not only for themselves but also for members of Congress.

Conclusion

Jones likens the president and Congress to "two gears, each whirling at its own rate of speed. It is not surprising that, on coming together, they often clash."[75] With these two great institutions, designed by the Founders to live in conflict, presidents must learn how to manage Congress. Because presidents are not like a king or a dictator, who can lead by command, they must learn how to earn congressional support with discrete and indirect methods.

INFLUENCING THE JUDICIARY

From the U.S. Supreme Court to the various district and appellate courts across the country, the judicial branch plays an active role in American government. Like the legislative branch, the judicial and executive branches check each other, but unlike the other branches, the Founders gave judges lifetime tenure during good behavior to make them more politically independent. Today, however, the courts often serve as the final arbiter of important political issues of major impact on the president. Not only do they interpret the law, but they also can make the law by setting public policy through their rulings on critical political issues. So presidents need to manage the one branch of government designed to have a greater degree of political independence.

In response to the U.S. Supreme Court's vetoes of key elements in his New Deal, President Franklin D. Roosevelt unveiled a "court-packing" scheme to increase both the number of justices and his influence over the Court's decisions. Inasmuch as Article II, Section 2 grants presidents the power to nominate justices, subject to Senate confirmation, he recognized that this power permitted him to indirectly influence the Court's decisions by naming justices favorable to the New Deal. Although the Congress did not pass Roosevelt's "court-packing" scheme, the Supreme Court changed its position on the New Deal, leading to the saying that "A switch in time saved nine." The "court-packing" threat accomplished Roosevelt's objective. Once presidents make their judicial nominations, they lose control over them, which makes the selection of justices all the more important from the standpoint of indirectly influencing or managing the judiciary. Nominating judges favorable to a president's views functions as the principal means for presidents to manage the judiciary.

Although Supreme Court nominations are the most notable, presidents nominate judges at every level of the judiciary. In making these nominations, they customarily consider three criteria, according to Robert Scigliano: "professional qualifications, representational qualifications, and doctrinal qualifications."[76] Professionally, nominees need appropriate legal training and experience that manifests itself in a judicial temperament. Representationally, Scigliano says that nominees usually mirror America in various ways: "Those attributes which have been especially relevant as representational qualifications are political party affiliation, section of the country, religion, and, now perhaps, ethnicity."[77] Doctrinally, presidents typically name judges whose views mirror their own. The more presidents desire to shape the judiciary, the more important the doctrinal criterion becomes, and with that, the more controversial nominations become. For example:

- Richard M. Nixon lost Senate votes on two Southern nominations to the U.S. Supreme Court, Clement Haynsworth (South Carolina) and Harold Carswell (Florida), when the Senate's liberal Democratic majority thought that they were too Southern and too conservative. Nixon's "strict constructionist" views of Constitutional interpretation conflicted with the "loose constructionist" views of liberal Democrats. Nixon did not like such Supreme Court decisions as *Miranda v. Arizona* (1966), which expanded the rights of persons accused of crimes.
- Ronald Reagan lost his Supreme Court nomination of Robert Bork, whose belief that the Founders' intentions should guide judicial decision making conflicted with the Senate's liberal Democratic majority, which believed that changing times and circumstances should have greater influence on judicial decisions. Bork's view holds that failure to consider the Founders' "original intentions" makes constitutional interpretation like a ship at sea without a compass. The Senate's majority believed that to impose the Founders' views on succeeding generations prevented the Constitution from serving as a "living" document.
- George W. Bush suffered from successful Democratic filibusters of several of his nominees, including Charles Pickering and Miguel Estrada, whose conservative judicial views conflicted with liberal Democrats in the Senate for reasons similar to the Nixon and Reagan nominees.

Although Reagan lost the nomination of Robert Bork, he still changed the face of the judiciary through the application of doctrinal considerations.

As with his appointments within the executive branch, Reagan ensured that his judicial appointments agreed with his philosophy.[78] Sidney M. Milkis and Michael Nelson point out that:

> During the 1960s and 1970s, the courts had joined with liberal members of Congress and so-called public interest groups to broaden legal rules and procedures in ways that served African Americans, feminists, environmentalists, and other Democratic constituencies. The Reagan administration worked hard to disrupt this alliance. By the end of Reagan's second term, it appeared that he had appointed enough conservative judges to move the federal courts considerably to the right.[79]

When Reagan took office, he faced a hostile judiciary, but, through his nominations, he created a judiciary more in line with his policies.

Presidents also may influence the judiciary through the Justice Department's legal representations in court cases. The Solicitor General and the Attorney General may determine what cases they wish to prosecute, how they wish to defend a case, and what cases they wish to enter as a friend of the court by filing a brief with the court on behalf of a particular position.

As the branch of government farthest removed from the people, the judiciary may not bow directly to political pressure and public opinion, but it may respond indirectly to presidential influence through judicial nominations and legal representations of the Department of Justice.

CONCLUSION

Mastering the complexities of management by indirection through political leadership is the hallmark of successful presidents. Political persuasion to achieve goals usually works better than command decisions, which may create a defensive and hostile reaction from other parts of the government. Put another way, successful presidents manage primarily by indirection, exercising influence more than power, because an authoritarian manner makes them more vulnerable politically. Indirect methods, which require more nuance and subtlety, usually present the president as a more cooperative person. So, persuasion is the hallmark of indirect leadership, while command is the hallmark of direct leadership. Thus, the nation needs political presidents more than managerial presidents. But circumstances sometimes dictate direct leadership when no other options exist or when presidents need to demonstrate overt strength. Because the public holds presidents accountable for the implementation of their policies, presidents must exert influence not only over the Executive Branch but also over the Congress and the Courts, even though they lack the same measure of constitutional authority over those institutions.

Notes

[1]Judith E. Michaels, *The President's Call: Executive Leadership from FDR to George Bush* (Pittsburgh: University of Pittsburgh Press, 1997): 19.

[2]http://www.theatlantic.com/issues/2002/11/presidents.htm; http://capital2.capital.edu/faculty/jhall2/article008.htm; Clinton Rossiter, *The American Presidency* (New York: Harcourt Brace, 1956).

[3]James David Barber, *The Presidential Character: Predicting Performance in the White House* (Englewood Cliffs, NJ: Prentice Hall, 1972); Richard Ellis and Aaron Wildavsky, *Dilemmas of Presidential Leadership from Washington through Lincoln* (New Brunswick, NJ: Transaction, 1989); Fred I. Greenstein, *The Presidential Difference: Leadership Style from FDR to Clinton* (New York: The Free Press, 2000).

[4]Richard E. Neustadt, *Presidential Power: The Politics of Leadership* (New York: John Wiley, 1960).

[5]Barber, *The Presidential Character.*

[6]Richard P. Nathan, *The Plot That Failed: Nixon and the Administrative Presidency* (New York: John Wiley, 1975); Richard P. Nathan, *The Administrative Presidency* (New York: John Wiley, 1983).

[7]Louis W. Koening, *The Chief Executive* (New York: Harcourt, Brace & World, Inc., 1968): 81.

[8]James P. Pfiffner, *The Strategic Presidency,* 2nd ed. (Lawrence: University Press of Kansas, 1996): 56.

[9]Pfiffner, 57.

[10]Ibid.

[11]John P. Burke, *Presidential Transitions: From Politics to Practice* (Boulder, CO: Lynne Rienner Publishers, 2000): 12–13.

[12]Burke, 95.

[13]Pfiffner, 149.

[14]Burke, 95.

[15]Pfiffner, 95.

[16]Burke, 95, 97.

[17]Pfiffner, 65.

[18]Ibid., 150.

[19]Burke, 285.

[20]Burke, 286.

[21]Pfiffner, 151.

[22]Richard E. Neustadt, *Preparing to Be President: The Memos of Richard E. Neustadt* (Washington, DC: AEI Press, 2000): 125.

[23]Burke, 313.

[24]Pfiffner, 166.

[25]Michaels, 19.

[26]Colin Campbell, *Managing the Presidency: Carter, Reagan, and the Search for Executive Harmony* (Pittsburgh: University of Pittsburgh Press, 1986): 83.

[27]Ibid., 84.

[28]Ibid., 83.

[29]Burke, 68.

[30]Burke, 68.

[31]Campbell, *Managing*: 93, 109.

[32]Ibid., 93, 110.

[33]Burke, 156.

[34]Sidney M. Milkis and Michael Nelson, *The American Presidency: Origin & Development 1776–1998,* 3rd ed. (Washington, DC: Congressional Quarterly Press, 1999): 349.

[35]Nathan, *The Plot That Failed*, 82.

[36]Ibid., 93.

[37]Ibid., 74.

[38]Ibid., 76.

[39]Ibid.

[40]Colin Campbell and Bert A. Rockman, eds., *The Bush Presidency: First Appraisals,* "Strategy and Prospects of the Bush Presidency" by Charles Jones (Chatham, NJ: Chatham House Publishers, 1991): 61.

[41]George C. Edwards III, *Presidential Influence in Congress* (San Francisco: W.H. Freeman and Company, 1980): 24.

[42]Ibid., 86.

[43]Ibid.

[44]Edwards, 88.

[45]Ibid.

[46]Ibid.

[47]Ibid., 89.

[48]Ibid., 90.

[49]Ibid., 87.

[50]Ibid.

[51]Ibid., 88.

[52]Ibid.

[53]Ibid., 58.

[54]Ibid., 61.

[55]Ibid., 66.

[56]Ibid.

[57]Campbell, 156.

[58]Ibid., 66.

[59]Milkis and Nelson, 385.

[60]Charles O. Jones, *Separate But Equal Branches: Congress and the Presidency,* 2nd ed. (New York: Chatham House Publishers, 1999): 129.

[61]Milkis and Nelson, 385.

[62]Ibid., 129.

[63]Jones, 129.

[64]Ibid., 130.

[65]Ibid., 138.

[66]Ibid., 140–143.

[67]Jones, 143.

[68]Ibid., 149.

[69]Milkis and Nelson, 402.

[70]Paul G. Kengor, *Wreath Layer or Policy Player? The Vice President's Role in Foreign Policy* (Lanham, MD: Lexington Books, 2000): 190.

[71]Ibid., 192.

[72]Edwards, 159.

[73]Ibid.

[74]Ibid.,

[75]Jones, 128.

[76]Robert Scigliano, *The Supreme Court and the Presidency* (New York: Free Press, 1971): 105.

[77]Ibid., 110.

[78]Milkis and Nelson, 353.

[79]Ibid.,

Appendix

Topical Bibliography

On the Presidency Generally

Abbot, Philip. *The Challenge of the American Presidency*. Long Grove, IL: Waveland Press, 2003.

Arnold, Peri E. *Making the Managerial Presidency: Comprehensive Reorganization Planning 1905–1996*. Lawrence: University Press of Kansas, 1998.

Beschloss, Michael, ed. *American Heritage Illustrated History of the Presidents*. New York: Crown, 2000.

Borrelli, MaryAnne, and Janet M. Martin, eds. *The Other Elites: Women, Politics, and Power in the Executive Branch*. Boulder, CO: Lynne Rienner Publishers, 1997.

Brinkley, Alan, and David Dyer, eds. *The Reader's Companion to the American Presidency*. Boston: Houghton Mifflin, 2000.

Brown, Stuart Gerry. *The American President: Leadership, Partisanship, and Popularity*. New York: Macmillan, 1966.

Burke, John P. *Presidential Transitions: From Politics to Practice*. Boulder, CO: Lynne, Rienner, 2000.

Burke, John P., Fred Greenstein, Larry Berman and Richard Immerman. *How Presidents Test Reality*. New York: Russell Sage Foundation, 1989.

Cronin, Thomas E. *The State of the Presidency*. 2nd ed. Boston: Little, Brown, 1980.

Cronin, Thomas E., ed. *Rethinking the Presidency*. Boston: Little, Brown, 1982.

Cronin, Thomas E., and Michael A. Genovese. *The Paradoxes of the American Presidency*. 2nd ed. New York: Oxford University Press, 2003.

Davis, James W. *The American Presidency*. 2nd ed. Westport, CT: Praeger, 1995.

DeClerico, Robert. *The American President*. Englewood Cliffs: Prentice Hall, 2000.

DeGregorio, William A. *The Complete Book of U.S. Presidents*. New York: Random House Value Publishing, 2001.

Edwards, George C. III, John H. Kessel, and Bert A. Rockman, eds. *Researching the Presidency: Vital Questions, New Approaches*. Pittsburgh: University of Pittsburgh Press, 1993.

Gregg, Gary L. *The Presidential Republic: Executive Representation and Deliberative Democracy*. Lanham, MD: Rowman and Littlefield, 1997.

———, ed. *Thinking About the Presidency*. Lanham, MD: Rowman & Littlefield, 2005.

Grover, William F. *The President as Prisoner*. New York: State University of New York Press, 1989.

Hughes, Emmer John. *The Living Presidency*. New York: Coward, McCann & Geoghegan, 1973.

Johnson, Haynes, and David Broder. *The System*. Boston: Little, Brown, 1996.

Jones, Charles O. *Passages to the Presidency: From Campaigning to Governing*. Washington, DC: Brookings, 1998.

Kessel, John H. *Presidents, the Presidency, and the Political Environment.* Washington, DC: CQ Press, 2001.

Kunhardt, Philip B., Philip B. Kunhardt III, and Peter W. Kunhardt. *The American President.* New York: Riverhead Books, 1999.

Kumar, Martha Joynt, and Terry Sullivan. *The White House World: Transitions, Organization, and Office Operations.* College Station: Texas A & M University Press, 2003.

Martin, Janet M. *The Presidency and Women: Promise, Performance, and Illusion.* College Hill: Texas A & M University Press, 2003.

McPherson, James M., ed. *To The Best of My Ability.* New York: Dorling Kindersley, 2000.

Nelson, Lyle. *American Presidents.* Armonk, NY: M.E. Sharpe, 2003.

Nelson, Michael, ed. *The Presidency A to Z.* Washington, DC: CQ Press, 2003.

———. *The Presidency and the Political System.* 6th ed. Washington, DC: CQ Press, 2000.

Patterson, Thomas E. *Out of Order.* New York: Vintage Books, 1994.

Pious, Richard. *The American Presidency.* New York: Basic Books, 1979.

———. *The Presidency.* Boston: Allyn and Bacon, 1996.

Rossiter, Clinton. *The American Presidency.* New York: Harcourt, Brace, and World, 1956.

Schlesinger, Arthur M., Jr. *The Cycles of American History.* Boston: Houghton Mifflin, 1986.

Tatalovich, Raymond, Thomas S. Engeman and Michael Nelson, eds. *The Presidency and Political Science: Two Hundred Years of Constitutional Debate.* Baltimore: Johns Hopkins University Press, 2003.

Troy, Tevi. *Intellectuals and the American Presidency: Philosophers, Jesters, or Technicians?* Lanham, MD: Rowman & Littlefield, 2003.

Woodward, Augustus. *The Presidency of the United States.* New York: D. Van Veighton, 1825.

Urofsky, Melvin I., ed. *The American Presidents.* New York: Garland, 2000.

On Presidential History

Goldwin, Robert A. *100 Years of Emancipation.* Chicago: Rand McNally, 1964.

Cronin, Thomas E. *Inventing the American Presidency.* Lawrence: University Press of Kansas, 1989.

Ellis, Richard J., ed. *Founding the American Presidency.* Lanham, MD: Rowman and Littlefield, 1999.

MacDonald, Forrest. *The American Presidency: An Intellectual History.* Lawrence: University Press of Kansas, 1994.

Mansfield, Harvey, Jr. *Taming the Prince: The Ambivalence of the Modern Executive.* New York: Free Press, 1989.

McPherson, James, ed. *To the Best of My Ability.* New York: DK Publishing, 2001.

Milkis, Sidney M., and Michael Nelson. *The American Presidency: Origins and Development, 1776–2002,* 4th ed. Washington, DC: CQ Press, 2004.

Pauley, Matthew A. *I Do Solemnly Swear: The President's Constitutional Oath.* Lanham, MD: Rowman & Littlefield, 1999.

Relya, Harold C., ed. *The Executive Office of the President: A Historical, Biographical, and Bibliographical Guide.* Westport, CT: Greenwood Press, 1997.

Riccards, Michael P. *The Ferocious Engine of Democracy: A History of the American Presidency,* Vol. 1. Lanham, MD: Madison Books, 1995.

———. *The Ferocious Engine of Democracy: A History of the American Presidency,* Vol. 2. Lanham, MD: Madison Books, 1995.

On the Modern Presidency

Buchanan, Bruce, ed. *The State of the American Presidency.* Austin: University of Texas System, 2002.

Frendreis, John P., and Raymond Tatalovich. *The Modern Presidency and Economic Policy.* Itasca, IL: Peacock Publishers, 1994.

Genovese, Michael A. *The Presidency in an Age of Limits.* Westport, CT: Greenwood Press, 1993.

Gould, Lewis L. *The Modern American Presidency.* Lawrence: University Press of Kansas, 2003.

Hargrove, Erwin C. *The Power of the Modern Presidency.* New York: Knopf, 1974.

Maranto, Robert. *Politics and Bureaucracy in the Modern Presidency.* Westport, CT: Greenwood Press, 1993.

Nelson, Michael, ed. *The Evolving Presidency.* 2nd ed. Washington, DC: CQ Press, 2004.

Neustadt, Richard. *Presidential Power and the Modern Presidents.* New York: Free Press, 1991.

Peterson, Mark A. *Legislating Together: The White House and Capitol Hill from Eisenhower to Reagan.* Cambridge, MA: Harvard University Press, 1990.

Pfiffner, James P. *Character and the Modern Presidency.* Washington, DC: Brookings, 2001.

———. *The Modern Presidency.* New York: St. Martin's Press, 1994.

Rose, Richard. *The Postmodern President: The White House Meets the World.* Chatham, NJ: Chatham House, 1998.

Shaw, Malcolm. *The Modern Presidency: From Roosevelt to Reagan.* New York: Harper and Row, 1987.

Stuckey, M. *Strategic Failures in the Modern Presidency.* Albany: SUNY Press, 1997.

On Presidential Leadership

Abbot, Philip. *Strong Presidents: A Theory of Leadership.* Knoxville: University of Tennessee Press, 1996.

Blakesley, Lance. *Presidential Leadership: From Eisenhower to Clinton.* Chicago: Nelson-Hall, 1995.

Blondel, Jean. *Political Leadership.* London: Sage, 1987.

Burns, James MacGregor. *Leadership.* New York: Harper and Row, 1978.

———. *The Power to Lead: The Crisis of the American Presidency.* New York: Simon and Schuster, 1984.

———. *Presidential Government: The Crucible of Leadership.* Boston: Houghton Mifflin, 1973.

Crockett, David A. *The Opposition Presidency: Leadership and the Constraints of History.* College Station: Texas A & M University Press, 2002.

Ellis, Richard, and Aaron Wildavsky. *Dilemmas of Presidential Leadership.* New Brunswick, NJ: Transaction Publishers, 1989.

Ellis, Richard J. *Presidential Lightning Rods: The Politics of Blame Avoidance.* Lawrence: University Press of Kansas, 1994.

Genovese, Michael A. *The Presidential Dilemma: Leadership in the American System.* New York: HarperCollins, 1995.

Greenstein, Fred I., ed. *Leadership in the Modern Presidency.* Cambridge, MA: Harvard University Press, 1988.

———. *The Presidential Difference: Leadership Style from FDR to Clinton.* New York: Free Press, 2000.

Hargrove, Erwin C. *The President as Leader.* Lawrence: University Press of Kansas, 1999.

———. *Presidential Leadership: Personality and Political Style.* New York: Macmillan, 1966.

Kellerman, Barbara. *The Political Presidency: The Practice of Leadership.* New York: Oxford University Press, 1984.

Kernell, Samuel. *Going Public: New Strategies of Presidential Leadership.* 3rd ed. Washington, DC: CQ Press, 1997.

Lowi, Theodore J. *The Personal President: Power Invested, Promise Unfulfilled.* Ithaca, NY: Cornell University Press, 1985.

Neustadt, Richard E. *Presidential Power and the Modern Presidents: The Politics of Leadership from Roosevelt to Reagan.* New York: Free Press, 1990.

Renshon, Stanley A., ed. *One America: Political Leadership, National Identity, and the Dilemmas of Diversity.* Washington, DC: Georgetown University Press, 2001.

Rockman, Bert. *The Leadership Question: The Presidency and the American System*. New York: Praeger, 1984.

Smith, Hedrick. *The Power Game: How Washington Works*. New York: Ballantine, 1988.

Skowronek, Stephen. *The Politics President Make: Leadership from John Adams to George Bush*. Cambridge, MA: Harvard University Press, 1993.

Tatalovich, Raymond, and Bryon W. Daynes. *Presidential Power in the United States*. Belmont: Brooks/Cole, 1984.

On Presidential Leadership Styles

Burke, John P. *The Institutional Presidency*. Baltimore: Johns Hopkins University Press, 1992.

Covington, Cary R., and Lester G. Seligman. *The Coalitional Presidency*. Chicago: Dorsey Press, 1989.

Hess, Stephen. *Organizing the Presidency*. 3rd ed. Washington, DC: Brookings, 2002.

Johnson, Richard P. *Managing the White House*. New York: Harper-Collins, 1974.

Nathan, Richard P. *The Administrative Presidency*. New York: Wiley, 1983.

Pfiffner, James P. *The Strategic Presidency*. 2nd ed. Lawrence: University Press of Kansas, 1996.

———. *The Managerial Presidency*. 2nd ed. College Station: Texas A & M University Press, 1999.

———., ed. *The Strategic Presidency: Hitting the Ground Running*. 2nd ed. Lawrence: University Press of Kansas, 1996.

Schlesinger, Arthur M., Jr. *The Imperial Presidency*. rev. ed. Boston: Houghton Mifflin, 1989.

Stuckey, Mary E. *The President as Interpreter-in-Chief*. Chatham: Chatham House, 1991.

Sykes, Patricia Lee. *Presidents and Prime Ministers: Conviction Politics in the Anglo-American Tradition*. Lawrence, KS: University Press of Kansas, 2000.

Wayne, Stephen J. *The Legislative Presidency*. New York: Harper and Row, 1978.

Wildavsky, Aaron. *The Beleaguered Presidency*. New Brunswick, NJ: Transaction, 1991.

On the President and the Supreme Court

Abraham, Henry J. *The Judicial Process*, 6th ed. New York: Oxford University Press, 1993.

———. *Justices, Presidents, and Senators: A History of U.S. Supreme Court Appointments from Washington to Clinton*, 4th ed. Lanham, MD: Rowman and Littlefield, 1999.

Genovese, Michael. *Supreme Court, the Constitution, and Presidential Power*. Lanham, MD: Rowman & Littlefield, 1980.

Lasser, William. *The Limits of Judicial Power*. Chapel Hill: University of North Carolina Press, 1988.

Maltese, John Anthony. *The Selling of Supreme Court Nominees*. Baltimore: Johns Hopkins University Press, 1995.

Stephenson, Donald Grier, Jr. *Campaigns and the Court*. New York: Columbia University Press, 1999.

Wolfe, Christopher. *The Rise of Modern Judicial Review*. New York: Basic Books, 1986.

Yalof, David Alistair. *Pursuit of Justices: Presidential Politics and the Selection of Supreme Court Nominees*. Chicago: University of Chicago Press, 1999.

Yates, Jeff. *Popular Justice: Presidential Prestige and Executive Success in the Supreme Court*. New York: State University of New York Press, 2002.

On the President and Congress

Brinkley, Wilfred. *President and Congress*. New York: Knopf, 1947.

Bond, Jon R., and Richard Fleisher. *The President in the Legislative Arena*. Chicago: University of Chicago Press, 1990.

Conley, Richard S. *The Presidency, Congress, and Divided Government: A Postwar Assessment*. College Station: Texas A & M University Press, 2003.

Crabb, Cecil V., Jr., and Pat M. Holt. *Invitation to Struggle: Congress, the President, and Foreign Policy*, 4th ed. Washington, DC: CQ Press, 1992.

DeGrazia, Alfred. *Congress and the Presidency*. Washington, DC: American Enterprise Institute, 1967.

Edwards, George C., III. *At the Margins: Presidential Leadership of Congress*. New Haven, CT: Yale University Press, 1989.

———. *Presidential Influence in Congress*. San Francisco: W.H. Freeman, 1980.

Fisher, Louis. *Constitutional Conflicts between Congress and the President*, 3rd ed. Lawrence: University Press of Kansas, 1991.

Franck, Thomas M. *The Tethered Presidency: Congressional Restraints on Executive Power*. New York: New York University, 1981.

LeLoup, Lance T., and Steven A. Shull. *Congress and the President: The Policy Connection*. Belmont, CA: Wadsworth Publishing, 1993.

Mann, Thomas E., ed. *A Question of Balance: The President, the Congress, and Foreign Policy*. Washington, DC: Brookings, 1990.

Peterson, Mark A. *Legislating Together: The White House and Capitol Hill from Eisenhower to Reagan*. Cambridge, MA: Harvard University Press, 1990.

Peterson, Paul E., ed. *The President, the Congress, and the Making of Foreign Policy*. Norman: University of Oklahoma Press, 1994.

Spitzer, Robert J. *President and Congress: Executive Harmony at the Crossroads of American Government*. New York: McGraw-Hill, 1993.

Thurber, James A. *Dividend Democracy: Cooperation and Conflict Between the President and Congress*. Washington, DC: Congressional Quarterly Press, 1991.

————., ed. *Rivals for Power: Presidential-Congressional Relations*. Washington, DC: CQ Press, 1996.

Wayne, Stephen J. *The Legislative Presidency*. New York: Harper & Row, 1978.

On the President and Foreign Policy

Adler, David Gray, and Larry N. George, eds. *The Constitution and the Conduct of Foreign Policy*. Lawrence: University Press of Kansas, 1996.

Allison, Graham. The *Essence of Decision: Explaining the Cuban Missile Crisis*. New York: Addison-Wesley, 1999.

Destler, I. M. *Presidents, Bureaucrats, and Foreign Policy: The Politics of Organizational Reform*. Princeton: Princeton University Press, 1974.

George, Alexander L. *Presidential Decision Making in Foreign Policy: The Effective Use of Information and Advice*. Boulder, CO: Westview, 1980.

Mann, Thomas E. *A Question of Balance: The President, the Congress, and Foreign Policy*. Washington, DC: Brookings, 1990.

Warren, Sidney. *The President as a World Leader*. New York: McGraw-Hill, 1967.

On Campaigns and Nominations

Bartels, Larry. *Presidential Primaries and the Dynamics of Public Choice*. Princeton: Princeton University Press, 1988.

Bimber, Bruce, and Richard Davis. *Campaigning Online: The Internet and U.S. Elections*. New York: Oxford University Press, 2003.

Buchanan, Bruce. *Presidential Campaign Quality: Incentives and Reform*. Englewood Cliffs, NJ: Prentice Hall, 2004.

Busch, Andrew. *Outsiders and Openness in the Presidential Nominating System*. Pittsburgh: University of Pittsburgh Press, 1997.

Campbell, James E. *The American Campaign*. College Station: Texas A & M University Press, 2000.

Ceaser, James W. *Presidential Selection*. Princeton: Princeton University Press, 1979.

————. *Reforming the Reforms: A Critical Analysis of the Presidential Selection Process*. Princeton: Princeton University Press, 1982.

Chase, James S. *Emergence of the Presidential Nominating Convention, 1789–1832*. Urbana: University of Illinois Press, 1973.

Cook, Rhodes. *The Presidential Nominating Process: A Place for Us?* Lanham, MD: Rowman & Littlefield, 2003.

Donaldson, Gary A. *Liberalism's Last Hurrah: The Presidential Campaign of 1964.* Armonk: M. E. Sharpe, 2003.

Heard, Alexander and Michael Nelson, eds. *Presidential Selection.* Durham, NC: Duke University Press, 1987.

Conley, Patricia Heidotting. *Presidential Mandates: How Elections Shape the National Agenda.* Chicago: University of Chicago Press, 2001.

Jamieson, Kathleen. *Packaging the Presidency: A History and Criticism of Presidential Campaign Advertising*, 2nd ed. New York: Oxford University Press, 1988.

Mackenzie, Calvin, ed. *Innocent Until Nominated: The Breakdown of the Presidential Appointment Process.* Washington, DC: Brookings Institution Press, 2001.

Mayer, William B., ed. *In Pursuit of the White House 2000: How We Choose Our Presidential Nominees.* Chatham, NJ: Chatham House, 1999.

Mayer, William G. and Andrew Busch. *The Front-Loading Problem in Presidential Nominations.* Washington, DC: Brookings, 2003.

Ornstein, Norman J., and Thomas E. Mann, eds. *The Permanent Campaign and Its Future.* Washington, DC: American Enterprise Institute, 2000.

Rose, Gary L. ed. *Controversial Issues in Presidential Selection*, 2nd ed. Albany: State University Press of New York, 1994.

Wayne, Stephen J. *The Road to the White House 1996: The Politics of Presidential Elections.* New York: St. Martin's Press, 1997.

———. *The Road to the White House, 2000, The Post-Election Edition: The Politics of Presidential Elections.* New York: St. Martin's Press, 2001.

———. *The Road to the White House 2004: The Politics of Presidential Elections.* Belmont, Wadsworth Publishing, 2003.

On Campaign Finance

Ayres, Ian, and Bruce A. Ackerman. *Voting with Dollars: A New Paradigm for Campaign Finance.* New Haven, CT: Yale University Press, 2002.

Brown, Clifford Waters, Lynda W. Powell, and Clyde Wilcox. *Serious Money: Fundraising and Contributing in Presidential Nomination Campaigns.* New York: Cambridge University Press, 1995.

Corrado, Anthony. *Campaign Finance Reform: Beyond the Basics.* New York: Century Foundation Press, 2000.

———. *Campaign Finance Reform: A Sourcebook.* Washington, DC: The Brookings Institution, 1997.

Lewis, Charles. *The Buying of the Presidency.* New York: Harper Academic, 2004.

Lubenow, Gerald C. *A User's Guide to Campaign Finance Reform*. Lanham, MD: Rowman & Littlefield, 2001.

Malbin, Michael J., ed. *Life After Reform*. Lanham, MD: Rowman & Littlefield, 2003.

Smith, Bradley A. *Unfree Speech: The Folly of Campaign Finance Reform*. Princeton: Princeton University Press, 2001.

On Presidential Candidates

Hacker, Kenneth. *Presidential Candidate Images*. New York: Praeger, 2004.

Mayer, William G. *The Making of the Presidential Candidates*. Lanham, MD: Rowman & Littlefield, 2003.

Newman, Bruce I. *The Marketing of the President*. Thousand Oaks, CA: Sage Publications, 1994.

Schlesinger, Arthur M., ed. *Running for President: The Candidates and Their Images*. New York: Simon and Schuster, 1994.

Tenpas, Kathryn Dunn. *Presidents as Candidates: Inside the White House for the Presidential Campaign*. New York: Routledge Press, 2003.

On Elections

Abramson, Paul R., John H. Aldrich, and David W. Rhode. *Change and Continuity in the 1980 Elections*. Washington, DC: CQ Press, 1982.

———. *Change and Continuity in the 1984 Elections*. Washington, DC: CQ Press, 1986.

———. *Change and Continuity in the 1988 Elections*. Washington, DC: CQ Press, 1990.

———. *Change and Continuity in the 1992 Elections*. Washington, DC: CQ Press, 1994.

———. *Change and Continuity in the 1992 Elections, Revised Edition*. Washington, DC: CQ Press, 1995.

———. *Change and Continuity in the 1996 Elections*. Washington, DC: CQ Press, 1998.

———. *Change and Continuity in the 1996 and 1998 Elections*. Washington, DC: CQ Press, 1999.

Alexander, Herbert E. and Anthony Corrado. *Financing the 1992 Election*. Boulder, CO: Westview, 1995.

Asher, Herbert. *Presidential Elections and American Politics: Voters, Candidates, and Campaigns Since 1952*, 5th ed. New York: Harcourt Brace, 1992.

Campbell, Angus, Philip Converse, Warren Miller, and Donald Stokes. *The American Voter*. Abr. Ed. New York: Wiley, 1964.

Ceaser, James W. and Andrew Busch, eds. *Losing to Win: The 1996 Elections and American Politics.* Lanham, MD: Rowman & Littlefield, 1997.

―――. *Upside Down and Inside Out.* Lanham, MD: Rowman & Littlefield, 1993.

Crigler, Ann N., Marion R. Just, and Edward J. McCaffery. *Rethinking the Vote: The Politics and Prospects of American Election Reform.* New York: Oxford University Press, 2003.

Dershowitz, Alan M. *Supreme Injustice: How the Court Hijacked Election 2000.* New York: Oxford University Press, 2001.

Fair, Ray C. *Predicting Presidential Elections and Other Things.* Stanford: Stanford University Press, 2002.

Gillman, Howard. *The Votes That Counted: How the Court Decided the 2000 Presidential Election.* Chicago: The University of Chicago Press, 2003.

Goldstein, Michael L. *Guide to the 2004 Presidential Election.* Washington DC: CQ Press, 2003.

Nelson, Michael, ed. *The Elections of 1996.* Washington, DC: CQ Press, 1997.

―――. *The Elections of 2000.* Washington, DC: CQ Press, 2001.

Pelosi, Alexandra. *Sneaking into the Flying Circus.* New York: The Free Press, 2005.

Polsby, Nelson W. *Presidential Elections: Strategies and Structures of American Politics.* Lanham, MD: Rowman & Littlefield, 2003.

Pomper, Gerald M., ed. *The Election of 1996: Reports and Interpretations.* Chatham, NJ: Chatham House, 1997.

―――. *The Election of 2000: Reports and Interpretations.* Chatham, NJ: Chatham House, 2001.

Shade, William G., Ballard C. Campbell, and Craig R. Coenen, eds. *American Presidential Campaigns and Elections.* 3 vols. Armonk, NY: M.E. Sharpe, 2003.

Stonecash, Jeffrey M. *Political Polling.* Lanham, MD: Rowman & Littlefield, 2003.

Whitman, Mark, ed. *Florida 2000: A Sourcebook on the Contested Presidential Election.* Boulder, CO: Lynne Rienner Publishers, 2003.

On the Electoral College

Best, Judith. *The Case Against Direct Election of the President: A Defense of the Electoral College.* Ithaca, NY: Cornell University Press, 1975.

Glennon, Michael J. *When No Majority Rules: The Electoral College and Presidential Succession.* Washington, DC: CQ Press, 1992.

Gregg, Gary L., ed. *Securing Democracy.* Wilmington, DE: ISI Press, 2001.

Longley, Lawrence D. *The Politics of Electoral College Reform.* New Haven, CT: Yale University Press, 1972.

Pierce, Neal R. *The People's President: The Electoral College in American History and the Direct Vote Alternative.* New Haven, CT: Yale University Press, 1981.

Sayre, Wallace Stanley. *Voting for President: The Electoral College and the American Political System.* Washington, DC: Brookings Institution, 1970.

Zeidenstein, Harvey G. *Direct Election of the President.* Lexington, MA: Lexington Books, 1973.

On Impeachment

Van Tassel and Paul Finkelman. *Impeachable Offenses.* Washington, DC: CQ Press, 1999.

On Presidential Rhetoric and Communication

Campbell, K. and K. Jamieson. *Deeds Done in Words: Presidential Rhetoric and the Genres of Governance.* Chicago: University of Chicago Press, 1990.

Fields, Wayne. *Union of Words: A History of Presidential Eloquence.* New York: The Free Press, 1996.

Hart, R. *The Sound of Leadership: Presidential Communication in the Modern Age.* Chicago: University of Chicago Press, 1987.

Kernell, Samuel. *Going Public: New Strategies of Presidential Leadership,* 3rd ed. Washington, DC: CQ Press, 1997.

Kiewe, A., ed. *The Modern Presidency and the Crisis Rhetoric.* New York: Praeger, 1994.

Maltese, John Anthony. *Spin Control: The White House Office of Communication and the Management of Presidential News,* 2nd ed., rev. Chapel Hill: University of North Carolina Press, 1994.

Medhurst, M., ed. *Beyond the Rhetorical Presidency.* College Station: Texas A & M Press, 1996.

Tulis, Jeffrey K. *The Rhetorical Presidency.* Princeton: Princeton University Press, 1987.

Whitney, Gleaves, ed. *American Presidents: Their Farewell Messages to the Nation, 1796–2001.* Lanham, MD: Rowman & Littlefield, 2002.

On the Press and the Media

Foote, Joe. *Television Access and Political Power: The Networks, the Presidency, and the Loyal Opportunities.* New York: Praeger, 1990.

Grossman, Michael and Martha Kumar. *Portraying the President: The White House and the News Media.* Baltimore: John Hopkins University Press, 1981.

Patterson, Thomas E. *The Mass Media Election: How Americans Choose Their President.* New York: Praeger, 1980.

Rollins, Peter C. and John E. O'Connor. *Hollywood's White House: The American Presidency in Film and History.* Lexington: The University Press of Kentucky, 2003.

Sabato, Larry. *Feeding Frenzy: How Attack Journalism Has Transformed American Politics.* New York: Free Press, 1991.

Walsh, Kenneth T. *Feeding the Beast: The White House vs. the Press.* New York: Norton, 1997.

On Public Opinion and Polling

Beasley, Vanessa B. *You, the People: The Presidency and Public Opinion.* College Station: Texas A & M University Press, 2004.

Bennet, Linda L.M. and Stephen Earl Bennett. *Living with Leviathan.* Lawrence: University Press of Kansas, 1990.

Brace, Paul and Barbara Hinkley. *Follow the Leader: Opinion Polls and Modern Presidents.* New York: Basic Books, 1992.

Brody, Richard A. *Assessing the President: The Media, Elite Opinion, and Public Support.* Stanford: Stanford University Press, 1991.

Cohen, Jeffrey E. *Presidential Responsiveness and Public Policy-Making: The Public and the Policies That Presidents Choose.* Ann Arbor: University of Michigan Press, 1997.

Cornwall, Elmer E. *Presidential Leadership of Public Opinion.* Bloomington: Indiana University Press, 1965.

Edwards, George C., III. *The Public Presidency: The Pursuit of Popular Support.* New York: St. Martin's Press, 1983.

Eisinger, Robert A. *The Evolution of Presidential Polling.* New York: Cambridge, 2003.

Heith, Diane J. *Polling to Govern: Public Opinion and Presidential Leadership.* Stanford: Stanford University Press, 2003.

Jacobs, Lawrence R. and Robert Y. Shapiro. *Politicians Don't Pander: Political Manipulation and the Loss of Democratic Responsiveness.* Chicago: University of Chicago Press, 2000.

Towle, Michael J. *Out of Touch: The Presidency and Public Opinion.* College Station: Texas A & M University Press, 2004.

Verba, Sidney and Norman H. Nie. *Participation in America.* Chicago: University of Chicago Press, 1987.

On the Vice Presidency

Hatch, Louis Clinton. *A History of the Vice Presidency of the United States.* Westport, CT: Greenwood Press, 1970.

Kengor, Paul. *Wreath Layer or Policy Player?* Lanham, MD: Rowman & Littlefield, 2000.

Light, Paul C. *Vice-Presidential Power: Advice and Influence in the White House.* Baltimore: Johns Hopkins University Press, 1984.

Natoli, Marie. *American Prince, American Pauper: The Contemporary Vice Presidency in Perspective.* Westport, CT: Greenwood Press, 1985.

Tompkins, Dorothy Louis Culver. *Selection of the Vice President*. Berkeley: University of California, 1974.

Waugh, Edgar Wiggins. *Second Consul, the Vice Presidency, Our Greatest Political Problem*. Indianapolis: Bobbs-Merrill, 1956.

Young, David. *American Roulette: The History and Dilemma of the Vice Presidency*. New York: Holt, Rinehart and Winston, 1972.

On Presidential Scandals

Dunn, Charles W. *The Scarlet Thread of Scandal: Morality and the American Presidency*. Lanham, MD: Rowman & Littlefield, 2000.

Schultz, Jeffrey. *Presidential Scandals*. Washington, DC: CQ Press, 1999.

On Presidents and Issues

Anderson, David L. *Shadow on the White House: Presidents and the Vietnam War, 1945–1975*. Lawrence: University Press of Kansas, 1993.

Baumgartner, Jody C. and Naoko Kada. *Checking Executive Power: Presidential Impeachment in Comparative Perspective*. Westport, CT: Praeger, 2003.

Burke, John P., and Fred I. Greenstein. *How Presidents Test Reality: Decisions on Vietnam, 1954 and 1965*. New York: Russell Sage Foundation, 1991.

Dawson, Joseph III. *Commanders in Chief: Presidential Leadership in Modern Wars*. Lawrence: University Press of Kansas, 1993.

Koh, Harold H. *The National Security Constitution: Sharing Power after the Iran-Contra Affair*. New Haven, CT: Yale University Press, 1990.

Morgan, Ruth P. *The President and Civil Rights*. New York: St. Martin's Press, 1970.

Olson, Keith W. *Watergate: The Presidential Scandal That Shook America*. Lawrence: University Press of Kansas, 2003.

Shull, Steven A. *The President and Civil Rights Policy: Leadership and Change*. Westport, CT: Greenwood Press, 1989.

Talbott, Strobe. *The Russia Hand: A Memoir of Presidential Diplomacy*. New York: Random House, 2003.

On Presidential Appointments

Abraham, Henry. *Justices, Presidents, and Senators: A History of U.S. Supreme Court Appointments from Washington to Clinton*, 4th ed. Lanham, MD: Rowman and Littlefield, 1999.

Bernstein, Carl and Woodward, Bob. *All the President's Men*. New York: Simon & Schuster, 1987.

Mackenzie, Calvin G. *The Politics of Presidential Appointments*. New York: Free Press, 1981.

Maltese, John Anthony. *The Selling of Supreme Court Nominees*. Baltimore: Johns Hopkins University Press, 1995.

Yalof, David Alistair. *Pursuit of Justices: Presidential Politics and the Selection of Supreme Court Nominees*. Chicago: University of Chicago Press, 1999.

On Executive Staff and the Cabinet

Bennett, Anthony. *The American President's Cabinet: From Kennedy to Bush*. New York: St. Martin's Press, 1996.

Borrelli, MaryAnne. *The President's Cabinet: Gender, Power, and Representation*. Boulder, CO: Lynne Rienner Publishers, 2000.

Cohen, Jeffrey E. *The Politics of the U.S. Cabinet: Representation in the Executive Branch, 1789–1984*. Pittsburgh: University of Pittsburgh Press, 1988.

Kowert, Paul A. *Groupthink or Deadlock: When Do Leaders Learn from Their Advisors?* Albany: State University of New York Press, 2002.

Horn, Stephen. *The Cabinet and Congress*. New York: Columbia University Press, 1960.

Kernell, Samuel, and Samuel L. Popkin, eds. *Chief of Staff: Twenty-five Years of Managing the Presidency*. Berkeley: University of California Press, 1986.

Patterson, Bradley H., Jr. *The White House Staff: Inside the West Wing and Beyond*. Washington, DC: Brookings, 2000.

Reich, Robert. *Locked in the Cabinet*. New York: Knopf, 1997.

Warshaw, Shirley Anne. *Powersharing: White House-Cabinet Relations in the Modern Presidency*. Albany: State University of New York Press, 1996.

Weko, Thomas J. *The Politicizing Presidency: The White House Personnel Office, 1948–1994*. Lawrence: University Press of Kansas, 1995.

On Political Parties

Aldrich, John H. *Why Parties? The Origin and Transformation of Political Parties in America*. Chicago: University of Chicago Press, 1995.

Burns, James MacGregor. *The Deadlock of Democracy: Two-Party Politics in America*. Englewood Cliffs, NJ: Prentice Hall, 1978.

Cox, Gary W. and Samuel Kernell, eds. *The Politics of Divided Government*. Boulder, CO: Westview, 1991.

Darman, Richard. *Who's in Control? Polar Politics and the Sensible Center*. New York: Simon and Schuster, 1996.

Davis, James W. *The President as Party Leader*. New York: Praeger, 1992.

Fiorina, Morris. *Divided Government*. New York: Macmillan, 1992.

Mayhew, David R. *Divided We Govern: Party Control, Lawmaking, and Investigations, 1946–1990.* New Haven, CT: Yale University Press, 1991.

Milkis, Sidney M. *The President and the Parties: The Transformation of the American Political System.* New York: Oxford University Press, 1993.

On Presidential Powers

Cooper, Philip J. *By Order of the President: The Use and Abuse of Executive Direct Action.* Lawrence: University Press of Kansas, 2002.

Corwin, Edward S. *The President: Office and Powers, 1789–1984,* 5th ed. New York: New York University Press, 1984.

Fisher, Louis. *The Politics of Executive War Privilege.* Durham, NC: Carolina Academic Press, 2003.

————. *Presidential Spending Power.* Princeton: Princeton University Press, 1975.

————. *Presidential War Power.* Lawrence: University Press of Kansas, 1995.

Genovese, Michael A. *Power and the American Presidency, 1789–2000.* New York: Oxford University Press, 2000.

Heclo, Hugh, and Lester M. Salamon, eds. *The Illusion of Presidential Government.* Boulder, CO: Westview Press, 1981.

Howell, William G. *Power Without Persuasion: The Politics of Direct Presidential Action.* Princeton: Princeton University Press, 2003.

Jones, Charles O. *The Presidency in a Separated System.* Washington, DC: Brookings, 1994.

Mayer, Kenneth R. *With the Stroke of a Pen: Executive Orders and Presidential Power.* Princeton: Princeton University Press, 2001.

Rozell, Mark J. *Executive Privilege: Presidential Power, Secrecy, and Accountability,* 2nd ed. Lawrence: University Press of Kansas, 2002.

Spitzer, Robert J. *The Presidential Veto: Touchstone of the American Presidency.* Albany: State University of New York Press, 1988.

Watson, Richard A. *Presidential Vetoes and Public Policy.* Lawrence: University Press of Kansas, 1993.

On Presidential Personalities

Barber, James David. *The Presidential Character,* 4th ed. Englewood Cliffs, NJ: Prentice Hall, 1992.

George, Alexander, and Juliette George. *Presidential Personality & Performance.* Boulder, CO: Westview, 1998.

Hinckley, Barbara. *The Symbolic Presidency: How Presidents Portray Themselves.* New York: Routledge, 1990.

Greenstein, Fred I. *Personality and Politics: Problems of Evidence, Inference, and Conceptualization.* New York: Norton, 1975.

Pessen, Edward. *The Log Cabin Myth: The Social Backgrounds of the Presidents.* New York: New York University Press, 1996.

Pfiffner, James P. *The Character Factor.* College Station: Texas A & M University Press, 2004.

On Presidential Statistics

King, Gary, and Lyn Ragsdale. *The Elusive Executive: Discovering Statistical Patterns in a Presidency.* Washington, DC: CQ Press, 1988.

Ragsdale, Lyn. *Vital Statistics on the Presidency: Washington to Clinton.* Washington, DC: CQ Press, 1996.

On Presidential Politics and Policies

Baumgartner, Frank R., and Byron D. Jones. *Agendas and Instability in American Politics.* Chicago: University of Chicago Press, 1993.

Hargrove, Erwin C., and Michael Nelson. *Presidents, Politics, and Policy.* New York: Knopf, 1984.

Lammers, William W. *Presidential Politics: Patterns and Prospects.* New York: HarperCollins, 1976.

Pika, Joseph A. and John Anthony Maltese. *The Politics of the Presidency*, 6th ed. Washington, DC: CQ Press, 2004.

Ragsdale, Lyn. *Presidential Politics.* Boston: Houghton Mifflin, 1993.

Rudalevige, Andrew. *Managing the President's Program: Presidential Leadership and Policy Formulation.* Princeton: Princeton University Press, 2002.

Shull, Steven A., ed. *Presidential Policymaking: An End-of-Century Assessment.* Armonk: M.E. Sharpe, 1999.

On Economic Policies

Pfiffner, James P., ed. *The President and Economic Policy.* Philadelphia: Institute for the Study of Human Issues, 1986.

Porter, Roger B. *Presidential Decision Making: The Economic Policy Board.* New York: Cambridge University Press, 1980.

Stein, Herbert. *Presidential Economics: The Making of Economic Policy from Roosevelt to Reagan and Beyond*, 2nd rev. ed. Washington, DC: American Enterprise Institute, 1988.

On Domestic Policy

Lammers, William W. and Michael A. Genovese. *The Presidency and Domestic Policy: Comparing Leadership Styles, FDR to Clinton.* Washington, DC: CQ Press, 2001.

Light, Paul C. *The President's Agenda: Domestic Policy Choice from Kennedy to Clinton*, 3rd ed. Baltimore: Johns Hopkins University Press, 1999.

Shull, Steven A. *Domestic Policy Formation: Presidential-Congressional Partnership?* Westport, CT: Greenwood Press, 1983.

Warshaw, Shirley Anne. *The Domestic Presidency: Policy Making in the White House*. Boston: Allyn and Bacon, 1996.

On National Security Policy

Crabb, Cecil V., Jr., and Pat M. Holt. *Invitation to Struggle: Congress, the President, and Foreign Policy*, 4th ed. Washington, DC: CQ Press, 1992.

Watson, Robert P. et al., eds. *Presidential Doctrines: National Security From Woodrow Wilson to George W. Bush*. Hauppauge, NY: Nova Science Publishers, 2003.

On Religion and the Presidency

Bonnell, John Southerland. *Presidential Profiles: Religion in the Life of American Presidents*. Philadelphia: Westminster Press, 1971.

Dunn, Charles W. *American Political Theology*. New York: Praeger, 1984.

Hutcheson, Richard G. Jr. *God in the White House: How Religion Has Changed the Modern Presidency*. New York: Macmillan, 1998.

LoPatto, Paul. *Religion and the Presidential Election: American Political Parties and Elections*. New York: Praeger Publishers, 1995.

Pierard, Richard, et al. *Civil Religion and the Presidency*. Grand Rapids, MI: Zondervan, 2000.

On Comparisons Among Presidents

Brauer, Carl M. *Presidential Transitions: Eisenhower Through Reagan*. New York: Oxford University Press, 1986.

Campbell, Colin. *Managing the Presidency: Carter, Reagan, and the Search for Executive Harmony*. Pittsburgh: University of Pittsburgh Press, 1986.

Hart, John. *The Presidential Branch: From Washington to Clinton*, 2nd ed. Chatham: Chatham House, 1995.

Henderson, Philip G. *Managing the Presidency: The Eisenhower Legacy—From Kennedy to Reagan*. Boulder, CO: Westview, 1988.

Hult, Karen M. and Charles E. Walcott. *Empowering the White House: Governance Under Nixon, Ford, and Carter*. Lawrence: University Press of Kansas, 2004.

Leuchtenberg, William E. *In the Shadow of FDR: From Harry Truman to Ronald Reagan*. Ithaca, NY: Cornell University Press, 1983.

Pederson, William D. and Frank J. Williams, eds. *Franklin D. Roosevelt and Abraham Lincoln: Competing Perspectives on Two Great Presidencies.* Armonk: M.E. Sharpe, 2003.

Shull, Steven A., ed. *The Two Presidencies: A Quarter-Century Assessment.* Chicago: Nelson-Hall, 1991.

Simpson, Brooks D. *The Reconstruction Presidents.* Lawrence: University Press of Kansas, 1998.

Sundquist, James L. *Politics and Policy: The Eisenhower, Kennedy, and Johnson Years.* Washington, DC: Brookings, 1968.

Walcott, Charles E. and Karen M. Hult. *Governing the White House: From Hoover Through LBJ.* Lawrence: University Press of Kansas, 1993.

Wilson, Robert A., ed. *Character Above All: Ten Presidents from FDR to George Bush.* New York: Simone and Schuster, 1995.

On Presidential Greatness and Success

Dallek, Robert. *Hail to the Chief: The Making and Unmaking of American Presidents.* New York: Hyperion Books, 1996.

Fishel, Jeff. *Presidents and Promises: From Campaign Pledge to Presidential Performance.* Washington, DC: CQ Press, 1984.

Landy, Marc, and Sidney M. Milkis. *Presidential Greatness.* Lawrence: University Press of Kansas, 2001.

Murray, Robert K. and Tim H. Blessing. *Greatness in the White House.* University Park: Pennsylvania State University Press, 1994.

Simonton, Dean Keith. *Why Presidents Succeed.* New Haven, CT: Yale University Press, 1987.

On Presidential and Parliamentary Executives

Berkeley, Humphry. *The Power of the Prime Minister.* New York: Chilmark Press, 1968.

Wiseman, Herbert Victor. *Parliament and the Executive.* London: Routledge & K. Paul, 1966.

On the Future of the Presidency

Shapiro, Robert Y., Martha Joynt Kumar, and Lawrence R. Jacobs, eds. *Presidential Power: Forging the Presidency for the Twenty-first Century.* New York: Columbia University Press, 2000.

Watson, Robert P. and Ann Gordon, eds. *Anticipating Madam President.* Boulder, CO: Lynne Rienner Publishers, 2003.

On First Ladies

Anthony, Carl Sferraza. *First Ladies: The Saga of the Presidents' Wives and Their Power*. 2 vols. New York: Morrow, 1990.

Boller, Paul. *Presidential Wives: An Anecdotal History*, 2nd ed. New York: Oxford University Press, 2003.

Caroli, Betty Boyd. *The First Ladies*. New York: Oxford University Press, 1987.

———. *First Ladies: From Martha Washington to Laura Bush*. New York: Oxford University Press, 2003.

Gould, Lewis L., ed. *American First Ladies: Their Lives and Their Legacy*. New York: Routledge, 1996.

Gutin, Myra. *The President's Partner: The First Lady in the Twentieth Century*. Westport, CT: Greenwood Press, 1989.

Roberts, John B., II. *Rating the First Ladies: The Women Who Influenced the Presidency*. Sacramento: Citadel Press, 2003.

Troy, Gil. *Affairs of State: The Rise and Rejection of the Presidential Couple Since World War II*. Lawrence: University Press of Kansas, 1997.

———. *Mr. and Mrs. President: From the Trumans to the Clintons*, 2nd ed., rev. Lawrence: University Press of Kansas, 2000.

Watson, Robert P. *First Ladies of the United States*. Boulder, CO: Lynne Rienner Publishers, 2001.

———. *The Presidents' Wives: Reassessing the Office of First Lady*. Boulder, CO: Lynne Rienner Publishers, 2000.

Presidential Autobiographies and Biographies

On George Washington

Burns, James MacGregor, and Susan Dunn. *George Washington*. New York: Times Books, 2004.

Fitzpatrick, John Clement, ed. *The Diaries of George Washington 1748–1799*, 4 vols. Boston: Houghton Mifflin, 1925.

Higginbotham, Don. *George Washington: Uniting a Nation*. Lanham, MD: Rowman & Littlefield, 2002.

Langston, Thomas S. and Michael G. Sherman. *George Washington*. Washington, DC: CQ Press, 2003.

McDonald, Forrest. *The Presidency of George Washington*. Lawrence: University Press of Kansas, 1974.

Phelps, Glenn A. *George Washington and American Constitutionalism*. Lawrence: University Press of Kansas, 1993.

Schwartz, Barry. *George Washington: The Making of an American Symbol*. New York: Free Press, 1987.

Wills, Garry. *Cincinatus: George Washington and the Enlightenment*. Garden City, NY: Doubleday, 1984.

On John Adams

Brown, Ralph A. *The Presidency of John Adams*. Lawrence: University Press of Kansas, 1975.

Diggins, John Patrick and Arthur M. Schlesinger. *John Adams*. New York: Times Books, 2003.

Kurtz, Stephen G. *The Presidency of John Adams: The Collapse of Federalism 1795–1800*. Philadelphia: University of Pennsylvania Press, 1957.

McCullough, David. *John Adams*. New York: Simon & Schuster, 2002.

Morse, John Torrey. *John Adams*. New York: AMS Press, 1972.

Thompson, C. Bradley. *John Adams and the Spirit of Liberty*. Lawrence: University Press of Kansas, 2002.

On Thomas Jefferson

Appleby, Joyce, and Arthur M. Schlesinger. *Thomas Jefferson*. New York: Times Books, 2003.

Bernstein, R.B. *Thomas Jefferson*. New York: Oxford University Press, 2003.

Browne, Stephen Howard. *Jefferson's Call for Nationhood: The First Inaugural Address*. College Station: Texas A & M University Press, 2003.

Cunningham, Noble E. *In Pursuit of Reason: The Life of Thomas Jefferson*. Baton Rouge: Louisiana State University Press, 1987.

Dreisbach, Daniel L. *Thomas Jefferson and the Wall of Separation Between Church and State*. New York: New York University Press, 2003.

Ellis, Joseph J. *American Sphinx: The Character of Thomas Jefferson*. New York: Vintage, 1998.

Johnstone, Robert M. *Jefferson and the Presidency: Leadership in the Young Republic*. Ithaca, NY: Cornell University Press, 1978.

Holmes, Jerry. *Thomas Jefferson: A Chronology of His Thoughts*. Lanham, MD: Rowman & Littlefield, 2002.

Malone, Dumas. *Jefferson in His Time*. Boston: Little, Brown, 1948.

McDonald, Forrest. *The Presidency of Thomas Jefferson*. Lawrence: University Press of Kansas, 1976.

Matthews, Richard K. *The Radical Politics of Thomas Jefferson*. Lawrence: University Press of Kansas, 1994.

Peterson, Merrill. *The Jefferson Image in the American Mind*. New York: Oxford University Press, 1960.

Severance, John B. *Thomas Jefferson: Architect of Democracy*. Boston: Houghton Mifflin, Co., 1998.

Yarbough, Jean M. *American Virtues: Thomas Jefferson and the Character of a Free People*. Lawrence: University Press of Kansas, 1998.

On James Madison

Kernell, Samuel. *James Madison: The Theory and Practice of Republican Government*. Stanford: Stanford University Press, 2003.

Ketcham, Ralph. *James Madison: A Biography*. New York: Macmillan, 1971.

———. *Selected Writings of James Madison*. Indianapolis: Hackett Publishing Company, 2004.

Matthews, Richard K. *If Men Were Angels: James Madison and the Heartless Empire of Reason*. Lawrence: University Press of Kansas, 1997.

McCoy, Drew R. *The Last of the Fathers: James Madison and the Republican Legacy*. Cambridge, MA: Harvard University Press, 1989.

Rosen, Gary. *American Compact: James Madison and the Problem of Founding*. Lawrence: University Press of Kansas, 1999.

Rutland, Robert Allen. *The Presidency of James Madison*. Lawrence: University Press of Kansas, 1990.

Samples, John Curtis. *James Madison and the Future of Limited Government*. Washington, DC: Cato Institute, 2002.

Wills, Gary. *James Madison*. New York: Times Books, 2002.

On James Monroe

Ammon, Harry. *James Monroe: The Quest for National Identity*. New York: McGraw-Hill, 1971.

Cunningham Jr., Noble E. *The Presidency of James Monroe*. Lawrence: University Press of Kansas, 1996.

Morgan, George. *The Life of James Monroe*. New York: AMS Press, 1969.

Preston, Daniel, and Marlena C. DeLong. *The Papers of James Monroe*. Westport, CT: Greenwood Publishing, 2003.

Wilmerding, Lucius. *James Monroe: Public Claimant*. New Brunswick, NJ: Rutgers University Press, 1960.

On John Quincy Adams

East, Robert Abraham. *John Quincy Adams: The Critical Years 1785–1794*. New York: Brookman Associates, 1962.

Hargreaves, Mary W. M. *The Presidency of John Quincy Adams*. Lawrence: University Press of Kansas, 1985.

Hecht, Marie B. *John Quincy Adams: A Personal History of an Independent Man*. New York: Macmillan, 1972.

Nagel, Paul C. *John Quincy Adams: A Public Life, a Private Life*. Cambridge, MA: Harvard University Press, 1999.

Parsons, Lynn Hudson. *John Quincy Adams*. Lanham, MD: Rowman & Littlefield, 1999.

Remini, Robert V. *John Quincy Adams*. New York: Times Books, 2002.

On Andrew Jackson

Cole, Donald B. *The Presidency of Andrew Jackson*. Lawrence: University Press of Kansas, 1993.

Eaton, John Henry. *The Life of Andrew Jackson*. Tuscaloosa: University of Alabama Press, 1974.

Ellis, Richard E. *Andrew Jackson*. Washington, DC: CQ Press, 2003.

Latner, Richard B. *The Presidency of Andrew Jackson: White House Politics 1829–1837*. Athens: University of Georgia Press, 1979.

Remini, Robert V. *Andrew Jackson: The Course of American Democracy, 1833–1845*. Baltimore: Johns Hopkins University Press, 1998.

———. *The Life of Andrew Jackson*. New York: Perennial, 2001.

Schlesinger, Arthur. *The Age of Jackson*. Boston: Little, Brown, 1945.

On Martin Van Buren

Cole, Donald B. *Martin Van Buren and the American Political System*. Princeton: Princeton University Press, 1984.

Curtis, James C. *The Fox at Bay: Martin Van Buren and the Presidency*. Lexington: University Press of Kentucky, 1970.

Silbey, Joel H. *Martin Van Buren and the Emergence of American Popular Politics*. Lanham, MD: Rowman & Littlefield, 2002.

Van Buren, Martin. *The Autobiography of Martin Van Buren*. New York: A. M. Kelley, 1969.

Wilson, Major L. *The Presidency of Martin Van Buren*. Lawrence: University Press of Kansas, 1984.

On William Henry Harrison

Goebel, Dorothy Burne. *William Henry Harrison: A Political Biography*. Philadelphia: Porcupine Press, 1974.

Peterson, Norma Lois. *The Presidencies of William Henry Harrison and John Tyler*. Lawrence: University Press of Kansas, 1989.

On John Tyler

Merk, Fredrick. *Fruits of Propaganda in the Tyler Administration*. Cambridge, MA: Harvard University Press, 1971.

Monroe, Dan. *The Republican Vision of John Tyler*. College Station: Texas A&M University Press, 2003.

Morgan, Robert J. *A Whig Embattled: The Presidency Under John Tyler*. Hamden, CT: Archon Books, 1974.

Peterson, Norma Lois. *The Presidencies of William Henry Harrison and John Tyler*. Lawrence: University Press of Kansas, 1989.

On James Knox Polk

Bergeron, Paul H. *The Presidency of James K. Polk*. Lawrence: University Press of Kansas, 1987.

Haynes, Sam W. *James K. Polk and the Expansionist Impulse*. New York: Pearson Longman, 2001.

McCoy, Charles Allan. *Polk and the Presidency*. New York: Haskell House Publishers, 1973.

Seigenthaler, John. *James K. Polk*. New York: Times Books, 2003.

On Zachary Taylor

Bauer, K Jack. *Zachary Taylor: A Soldier, Planter, Statesman of the Old Southwest*. Baton Rouge: Louisiana State University Press, 1985.

McKinley, Silas Bent. *Old Rough and Ready: The Life and Times of Zachary Taylor*. New York: Vanguard Press, 1946.

Smith, Elbert B. *The Presidencies of Zachary Taylor and Millard Fillmore*. Lawrence: University Press of Kansas, 1988.

On Millard Fillmore

Farrell, John J. *Zachary Taylor and Millard Fillmore: Chronicles, Documents, and Bibliographical Aides*. Dobbs Ferry: Oceana Publications, 1971.

Rayback, Robert J. *Millard Fillmore: A Biography of a President*. Buffalo, NY: H. Stewart, 1959.

Smith, Elbert B. *The Presidencies of Zachary Taylor and Millard Fillmore*. Lawrence: University Press of Kansas, 1988.

On Franklin Pierce

Gara, Larry. *The Presidency of Franklin Pierce*. Lawrence: University Press of Kansas, 1991.

Hawthorne, Nathaniel. *Life of Franklin Pierce*. Phoenix, AZ: Freedonia Books, 2002.

On James Buchanan

Baker, Jean. *James Buchanan*. New York: Times Books, 2004.

Binder, Frederick M. *James Buchanan and the American Empire*. Cranbury, NJ: Associated University Presses, 1994.

Klein, Philip Shriver. *President James Buchanan: A Biography*. University Park: Penn State University Press, 1962.

Nelson, Michael, ed. *The Presidency and the Political System*, 4th ed. Washington, DC: Congressional Quarterly Press, 1995.

Smith, Elbert B. *The Presidency of James Buchanan*. Lawrence: University Press of Kansas, 1975.

On Abraham Lincoln

Donald, David Herbert. *Lincoln*. New York: Simon and Schuster, 1995.

———. *We Are Lincoln Men: Abraham Lincoln and His Friends*. New York: Simon and Schuster, 2003.

Gienapp, William E. *Abraham Lincoln and Civil War America*. New York: Oxford University Press, 2002.

Farber, Daniel. *Lincoln's Constitution*. Chicago: University of Chicago Press, 2003.

Goodwin, Doris Kearns. *Team of Rivals*. New York: Simon and Schuster, 2006.

Groth, Alexander J. *Lincoln: Authoritarian Savior*. Lanham, MD: Rowman & Littlefield, 1996.

Holzer, Harold. *Lincoln Seen and Heard*. Lawrence: University Press of Kansas, 2000.

Howells, William Dean. *The Life of Abraham Lincoln.* Bloomsburg: Indiana University Press, 1960.

Luthin, Reinhard Henry. *The Real Abraham Lincoln.* Englewood Cliffs, NJ: Prentice Hall, 1960.

McPherson, James M. *Abraham Lincoln and the Second American Revolution.* New York: Oxford University Press, 1992.

Neely, Mark E. *The Last Best Hope on Earth: Abraham Lincoln and the Promise of America.* Cambridge, MA: Harvard University Press, 1993.

Oates, Stephen B. *Abraham Lincoln: The Man Behind the Myths.* New York: Periennial, 1994.

Paludan, Phillip Shaw. *The Presidency of Abraham Lincoln.* Lawrence: University Press of Kansas, 1994.

Perret, Geoffrey. *Lincoln's War: The Untold Story of America's Greatest President as Commander in Chief.* New York: Random House, 2004.

Peterson, Merrill. *Lincoln in American Memory.* New York: Oxford, 1994.

Pinsker, Matthew. *Abraham Lincoln.* Washington, DC: CQ Press, 2002.

Potter, David M. *Lincoln and His Party in the Secession Crisis.* New Haven, CT: Yale University Press, 1942.

Rawley, James A. *Lincoln and Civil War Politics.* New York: Holt, Reinhart, and Winston, 1969.

Sandburg, Carl. *Abraham Lincoln: The Prairie Years and the War Years.* Toronto: Harvest Books, 2002.

Wright, John S. *Lincoln and the Politics of Slavery.* Reno: University of Nevada Press, 1970.

On Andrew Johnson

Benedict, Michael. *The Impeachment and Trial of Andrew Johnson.* New York: W.W. Norton, 1973.

Castel, Albert E. *The Politics of Andrew Johnson.* Lawrence: Regents Press of Kansas, 1979.

———. *The Presidency of Andrew Johnson.* Lawrence: University Press of Kansas, 1979.

Hearn, Chester G. *The Impeachment of Andrew Johnson.* Jefferson, NC: McFarland & Company, 2000.

McKitrick, Eric L. *Andrew Johnson and Reconstruction.* Chicago: University of Chicago Press, 1960.

Smith, Gene. *High Crimes and Misdemeanors: The Impeachment and Trial of Andrew Johnson.* New York: William Morrow, 1976.

Trefousse, Hans Louis. *Andrew Johnson: A Biography.* New York: Norton, 1989.

———. *Impeachment of a President: Andrew Johnson, the Blacks, and Reconstruction.* New York: Fordham University Press, 1999.

On Ulysses S. Grant

Coolidge, Louis Arthur. *Ulysses S. Grant*. New York: AMS Press, 1972.

Grant, Ulysses S. *Personal Memoirs of Ulysses S. Grant*. New York: Modern Library, 2000.

Kaltman, Al. *Cigars, Whiskey & Winning: Leadership Lessons from Ulysses S. Grant*. Englewood Cliffs, NJ: Prentice Hall, 1998.

Mantell, Martin E. *Johnson, Grant, and Politics of Reconstruction*. New York: Columbia University Press, 1973.

McFeely, William S. *Grant: A Biography*. New York: Norton, 1981.

Perret, Geoffrey. *Ulysses S. Grant: A Soldier and a President*. New York: Random House, 1997.

Simon, John Y. *The Papers of Ulysses S. Grant*. St. Louis: Southern Illinois University Press, 2003.

Simpson, Brooks D. *Let Us Have Peace: Ulysses S. Grant and the Politics of War and Reconstruction: 1861–1868*. Chapel Hill: University of North Carolina Press, 1997.

———. *Ulysses S. Grant: Triumph Over Adversity, 1822–1865*. New York: Houghton Mifflin Co, 2000.

Smith, Jean Edward. *Grant*. New York: Simon & Schuster, 2002.

On Rutherford B. Hayes

Hoogenboom, Ari Arthur. *The Presidency of Rutherford B. Hayes*. Lawrence: University Press of Kansas, 1988.

———. *Rutherford B. Hayes: Warrior and President*. Lawrence: University Press of Kansas, 1995.

Trefousse, Hans. *Rutherford B. Hayes: 1877–1881*. New York: Times Books, 2002.

Williams, Charles Richard. *The Life of Rutherford B. Hayes: The 19th President of the United States*. New York: Da Capo Press, 1971.

On James A. Garfield

Ackerman, Kenneth D. *The Dark Horse: The Surprise Election and Political Murder of President James A. Garfield*. New York: Carroll & Graf, 2003.

Booraem, Hendrik. *The Road to Respectability: James A. Garfield and His World 1844–1852*. Lewisburg, PA: Bucknell University Press, 1988.

Doenecke, Justus D. *The Presidencies of James A. Garfield and Chester A. Arthur*. Lawrence: University Press of Kansas, 1981.

Peskin, Allan. *Garfield: A Biography.* Kent, OH: Kent State University Press, 1998.

Taylor, John M. *Garfield of Ohio: The Available Man.* New York: Norton, 1970.

On Chester A. Arthur

Doenecke, Justus D. *The Presidencies of James A. Garfield and Chester A. Arthur.* Lawrence: University Press of Kansas, 1981.

Karabell, Zachary. *Chester Alan Arthur.* New York: Times Books, 2004.

Reeves, Thomas E. *Gentleman Boss: The Life of Chester Alan Arthur.* New York: Knopf, 1975.

On Grover Cleveland

Brodsky, Alyn. *Grover Cleveland: A Study in Character.* New York: Truman Talley Books, 2000.

Graff, Henry. *Grover Cleveland.* New York: Times Books, 2002.

Jeffers, H.P. *An Honest President: The Life and Presidencies of Grover Cleveland.* New York: Perennial, 2002.

Nevins, Allan. *Grover Cleveland: A Study in Courage.* New York: Dodd, Mead, and Company, 1932.

Tugwell, Rexford G. *Grover Cleveland.* New York: Macmillan, 1968.

Welch, Richard E. *The Presidency of Grover Cleveland.* Lawrence: University Press of Kansas, 1988.

On Benjamin Harrison

Sievers, Harry Joseph. *Benjamin Harrison*, 2nd ed. New York: University Publishers, 1968.

Socolofsky, Homer Edward. *The Presidency of Benjamin Harrison.* Lawrence: University Press of Kansas, 1987.

Spetter, Allan B. *The Presidency of Benjamin Harrison.* Lawrence: University Press of Kansas, 1987.

On William McKinley

Leech, Margaret. *In the Days of McKinley.* New York: Harper, 1959.

Gould, Lewis L. *The Presidency of William McKinley.* Lawrence: University Press of Kansas, 1980.

———. *The Spanish-American War and President McKinley.* Lawrence: University Press of Kansas, 1982.

Morgan, H. Wayne. *William McKinley and His America*. Syracuse: Syracuse University Press, 1963.

Olcott, Charles Sumner. *The Life of William McKinley*. New York: AMS Press, 1972.

Phillips, Kevin. *William McKinley*. New York: Times Books, 2003.

On Theodore Roosevelt

Auchincloss, Louis. *Theodore Roosevelt*. New York: Times Books, 2002.

Blum, John Morton. *The Republican Roosevelt*. Cambridge, MA: Harvard University Press, 1954.

Brands, H.W. *T.R. The Last Romantic*. New York: Basic Books, 1998.

Cadenhead, Edward. *Theodore Roosevelt: The Paradox of Progressivism*. Woodbury, NY: Barron's Educational Series, 1974.

Cooper, Milton Jr. *The Warrior and the Priest*. Cambridge, MA: Harvard University Press, 1983.

Dalton, Kathleen. *Theodore Roosevelt*. New York: Random House, 2004.

Di Nunzio, Mario R. *Theodore Roosevelt*. Washington, DC: CQ Press, 2003.

Gould, Lewis L. *The Presidency of Theodore Roosevelt*. Lawrence: University Press of Kansas, 1991.

Harbaugh, William Henry. *The Life and Times of Theodore Roosevelt*. New York: Oxford University Press, 1975.

Kraft, Betsy Harvey. *Theodore Roosevelt: Champion of the American Spirit*. Boston: Clarion Books, 2003.

McCullough, David. *Mornings on Horseback*. New York: Simon & Schuster, 1982.

Miller, Nathan. *Theodore Roosevelt. A Life*. New York: Morrow, 1993.

Morris, Edmund. *The Rise of Theodore Roosevelt*. New York: Coward, McCann, and Geoghegan, 1979.

———. *Theodore Rex*. New York: Random House, 2001.

Roosevelt, Theodore. *The Autobiography of Theodore Roosevelt*. New York: Octagon Books, 1975.

On William Howard Taft

Anderson, Donald F. *William Howard Taft: A Conservative's Conception of the Presidency*. Ithaca, NY: Cornell University Press, 1973.

Coletta, Paolo E. *The Presidency of William Howard Taft*. Lawrence: University Press of Kansas, 1973.

Minger, Ralph Eldin. *William Howard Taft and United States Foreign Policy*. Urbana: University of Illinois Press, 1975.

Pringles, Henry Fowles. *The Life and Times of William Howard Taft: A Biography*. New York: Harcourt, Brace, 1956.

Vivian, James F. *William Howard Taft*. New York: Praeger, 1990.

On Woodrow Wilson

Braeman, John. *Wilson*. Englewood Cliffs, NJ: Prentice Hall, 1972.

Brands, H.W. *Woodrow Wilson*. New York: Times Books, 2003.

Buckingham, Peter H. *Woodrow Wilson: A Bibliography of His Times and the Presidency*. Wilmington, DE: Scholarly Resources, 1990.

Clements, Kendrick A. *The Presidency of Woodrow Wilson*. Lawrence: University Press of Kansas, 1993.

————. *Woodrow Wilson: World Statesman*. Chicago: Ivan R. Dee, Inc., 1999.

————. *Woodrow Wilson*. Washington, DC: CQ Press, 2003.

Cooper, John Milton Jr. *Breaking the Heart of the World: Woodrow Wilson and the Fight for the League of Nations*. New York: Cambridge University Press, 2001.

Garraty, John A. *Woodrow Wilson: A Great Life in Brief*. Westport, CT: Greenwood Publishing Group, 1977.

George, Alexander, and Juliette George. *Woodrow Wilson and Colonel House: A Personality Study*. New York: John Day, 1956.

Gordon, Norman Levin. *Woodrow Wilson and World Politics*. New York: Oxford University Press, 1980.

Knock, Thomas J. *To End All Wars: Woodrow Wilson and the Quest for a New World Order*. New York: Oxford University Press, 1992.

Kraig, Robert Alexander. *Woodrow Wilson and the Lost World of the Oratorical Statesman*. College Station: Texas A & M University Press, 2004.

Levin, Phyllis Lee. *Edith and Woodrow: The Wilson White House*. New York: Scribner's, 2001.

Link, Arthur S. *Wilson*. Princeton: Princeton University Press, 1947.

Stid, Daniel D. *The President as Statesman: Woodrow Wilson and the Constitution*. Lawrence: University Press of Kansas, 1998.

Thompson, J.A. *Woodrow Wilson: Profiles in Power*. New York: Longman, 2002.

On Warren G. Harding

Anthony, Carl Sferrazza. *Florence Harding: The First Lady, the Jazz Age, and the Death of America's Most Scandalous President*. New York: William Morrow, 1998.

Chapple, Joe Mitchell. *Life and Times of Warren G. Harding: Our After War President*. Whitefish, MT: Kessinger Publishing Company, 2004.

Dean, John W. *Warren G. Harding*. New York: Times Books, 2004.

Downes, Randolph, Chandler. *The Rise of Warren G. Harding 1865–1920*. Columbus: Ohio State University Press, 1970.

Ferrell, Robert H. *The Strange Deaths of President Harding*. Columbia: University of Missouri Press, 1996.

Sinclair, Andrew. *The Available Man: The Life Behind the Masks of Warren Gamaliel Harding*. New York: Macmillan, 1965.

Trani, Eugene P. *The Presidency of Warren G. Harding*. Lawrence: University Press of Kansas, 1977.

On Calvin Coolidge

Abels, Jules. *In the Time of Silent Cal*. New York: Putnam, 1969.

Coolidge, Calvin. *An Autobiography of Calvin Coolidge*. New York: Cosmopolitan Book Corporation, 1929.

Ferrell, Robert H. *The Presidency of Calvin Coolidge*. Lawrence: University Press of Kansas, 1998.

Lathem, Edward Connery. *Meet Calvin Coolidge: The Man Behind the Myth*. Brattleboro, VT: Stephen Greene Press, 1960.

McCoy, Donald R. *Calvin Coolidge: The Quiet President*. New York: Macmillan, 1967.

White, William A. *A Puritan in Babylon*. New York: Macmillan, 1938.

On Herbert Hoover

Burner, David. *Herbert Hoover: A Public Life*. New York: Knopf, 1979.

Clements, Kendrick A. *Hoover, Conservation, and Consumerism*. Lawrence: University Press of Kansas, 2000.

Fausold, Martin L. *The Hoover Presidency: A Reappraisal*. Albany: State University of New York Press, 1979.

———. *The Presidency of Herbert C. Hoover*. Lawrence: University Press of Kansas, 1985.

Ferrell, Robert H. *The Presidency of Calvin Coolidge*. Lawrence: University Press of Kansas, 1998.

Haynes, John Earl, ed. *Calvin Coolidge and the Coolidge Era*. Washington, DC: Library of Congress, 1998.

Hoover, Herbert. *Memoirs, 2 vols*. New York: Macmillan, 1951.

Nash, George. *The Life of Herbert Hoover*. New York: W.W. Norton, 1983.

Sobel, Robert. *Coolidge: An American Enigma*. Washington, DC: Regnery, 1998.

Wilson, Joan Hoff. *Herbert Hoover: Forgotten Progressive*. Boston: Little, Brown and Co., 1975.

On Franklin D. Roosevelt

Black, Conrad. *Franklin Delano Roosevelt: Champion of Freedom*. New York: Public Affairs Press, 2004.

Burns, James MacGregor. *Roosevelt: The Lion and the Fox.* New York: Harcourt, Brace, Jovanovich, 2003.

———. *Roosevelt: Soldier of Freedom.* New York: Harcourt, Brace, Jovanovich, 1970.

Dallek, Robert. *Franklin D. Roosevelt and American Foreign Policy.* New York: Oxford University Press, 1995.

Dickinson, Matthew J. *Bitter Harvest: FDR and the Growth of the Presidential Branch.* New York: Cambridge University Press, 1997.

Evans, Hugh E. *The Hidden Campaign: FDR's Health and the 1944 Election.* Armonk, NY: M.E. Sharpe, 2002.

Freedman, Russell. *Franklin Delano Roosevelt.* New York: Clarion Books, 1990.

Freidel, Frank. *Franklin D. Roosevelt.* Boston: Little, Brown, 1952.

Freidel, Frank B. *Franklin D. Roosevelt: A Rendezvous with Destiny.* Boston: Little, Brown, 1990.

Hoopes, Townsend and Douglass Brinkley. *FDR and the Creation of the U.N.* New Haven, CT: Yale University Press, 1997.

Houck, Davis W. and Amos Kiewe. *FDR's Body Politics: The Rhetoric of Disability.* College Station: Texas A & M University Press, 2003.

Howard, Thomas C. and William D. Pederson, eds. *Franklin D. Roosevelt and the Formation of the Modern World.* Armonk, NY: M.E. Sharpe, 2002.

Howard, Thomas C. and Frank J. Williams, eds. *Franklin D. Roosevelt and Abraham Lincoln.* Armonk, NY: M.E. Sharpe, 2002.

Jackson, Robert H. *That Man: An Insider's Portrait of Franklin D. Roosevelt.* New York: Oxford University Press, 2003.

Jenkins, Roy. *Franklin Delano Roosevelt.* New York: Times Books, 2003.

Leuchtenburg, William E. *Franklin D. Roosevelt and the New Deal, 1932–1940.* New York: Harper and Row, 1963.

Maney, Patrick J. *The Roosevelt Presence: The Life and Legacy of FDR.* Berkley: University of California Press, 1998.

McElvaine, Robert S. *Franklin Delano Roosevelt.* Washington, DC: CQ Press, 2002.

McJimsey, George. *The Presidency of Franklin Delano Roosevelt.* Lawrence: University Press of Kansas, 2000.

Shaw, Stephen K., William D. Pederson, and Frank J. Williams, eds. *Franklin D. Roosevelt and the Transformation of the Supreme Court.* Armonk, NY: M.E. Sharpe, 2003.

Schlesinger, Arthur Meier. *The Age of Roosevelt.* Boston: Houghton, Mifflin, 1957.

Wolf, Thomas P., William D. Pederson, and Byron W. Daynes, eds. *Franklin D. Roosevelt and Congress.* Armonk, NY: M.E. Sharpe, 2000.

Young, Nancy Beck, William D. Pederson, and Byron W. Daynes, eds. *Franklin D. Roosevelt and the Shaping of American Political Culture.* Armonk, NY: M.E. Sharpe, 2001.

On Harry S. Truman

Donovan, Robert J. *Conflict and Crisis: The Presidency of Harry S. Truman.* New York: Norton, 1977.

Ferrell, Robert H. *Harry S. Truman*, Washington, DC: CQ Press, 2003.

Hamby, Alonzo L. *Beyond the New Deal: Harry S. Truman and American Liberalism.* New York: Columbia University Press, 1973.

———. *Man of the People: A Life of Harry S. Truman.* New York: Oxford University Press, 1995.

Hogan, Michael J. *A Cross of Iron: Harry S. Truman and the Origins of the National Security State, 1945–1954.* Cambridge: Cambridge University Press, 1998.

Lacey, Michael, ed. *The Truman Presidency.* New York: Cambridge University Press, 1989.

McCoy, Donald R. *The Presidency of Harry S. Truman.* Lawrence: University Press of Kansas, 1984.

McCullough, David. *Truman.* New York: Simon & Schuster, 1993.

Moskin, J. Robert. *Mr. Truman's War: The Final Victories of World War II and the Birth of the Postwar World.* Lawrence: University Press of Kansas, 2002.

Truman, Harry S. *Memoirs, 2 vols.* Garden City, NY: Doubleday, 1955.

On Dwight D. Eisenhower

Ambrose, Stephen E. *Eisenhower: Soldier and President.* New York: Touchstone Books, 1991.

———. *The Supreme Commander: The War Years of General Dwight D. Eisenhower.* Jackson: University Press of Mississippi, 1999.

Brownell, Herbert with John P. Burke. *Advising Ike.* Lawrence: University Press of Kansas, 1993.

Eisenhower, Dwight D. *The White House Years.* Garden City, NY: Doubleday, 1965.

Greenstein, Fred I. *The Hidden-Hand Presidency: Eisenhower as Leader.* Baltimore: Johns Hopkins University Press, 1994.

Lasby, Clarence G. *Eisenhower's Heart Attack: How Ike Beat Heart Disease and Held on to the Presidency.* Lawrence: University Press of Kansas, 1997.

Neal, Steve. *The Eisenhowers.* Lawrence: University Press of Kansas, 1984.

Pach, Chester J., Jr., and Elmo Richardson. *The Presidency of Dwight D. Eisenhower.* Lawrence: University Press of Kansas, 1979.

Sloan, John W. *Eisenhower and the Management of Prosperity.* Lawrence: University Press of Kansas, 1991.

Wicker, Tom. *Dwight D. Eisenhower.* New York: Times Books, 2002.

On John F. Kennedy

Bagnall, Joseph Albert. *The Kennedy Option.* Lanham, MD: Rowman & Littlefield, 2002.

Bass, Warren. *Support Any Friend: Kennedy's Middle East and the Making of the US-Israel Alliance.* New York: Oxford University Press, 2003.

Benson, Thomas W. *Writing JFK: Presidential Rhetoric and the Press in the Bay of Pigs Crisis.* College Station: Texas A & M University Press, 2003.

Brogan, Hugh. *Kennedy.* London and New York: Longman, 1996.

Burns, James MacGregor. *John Kennedy: A Political Profile.* New York: Harcourt, Brace, 1960.

Carty, Thomas. *A Catholic in the White House?* New York: Palgrave Macmillan, 2004.

Dallek, Robert. *An Unfinished Life: John F. Kennedy.* Lebanon: Little Brown & Company, 2003.

Freedman, Lawrence. *Kennedy's Wars: Berlin, Cuba, Laos, and Vietnam.* New York: Oxford University Press, 2003.

Giglio, James N. *The Presidency of John F. Kennedy.* Lawrence: University Press of Kansas, 1991.

Giglio, James N. and Stephen G. Rabe. *Debating the Kennedy Presidency.* Lanham, MD: Rowman & Littlefield, 2003.

Kennedy, John Fitzgerald. *Profiles of Courage.* New York: Ballantine, 1978.

Miroff, Bruce. *Pragmatic Illusions: The Presidential Politics of John. F. Kennedy.* New York: David McKay, 1976.

Reeves, Richard. *President Kennedy: Profile of Power.* New York: Simon and Schuster, 1993.

Schlesinger, Arthur M., Jr. *A Thousand Days: John F. Kennedy in the White House.* Boston: Houghton Mifflin, 1965.

Stern, Sheldon M. *Averting the "Final Failure": John F. Kennedy and the Secret Cuban Missile Crisis Meetings.* Stanford, CA: Stanford University Press, 2003.

On Lyndon B. Johnson

Anderson, James E. and Jared E. Haelton. *Managing Macroeconomic Policy: The Johnson Presidency.* Austin: University of Texas Press, 1986.

Barrett, David M. *Uncertain Warriors.* Lawrence: University Press of Kansas, 1993.

Bernstein, Irving. *Guns or Butter: The Presidency of Lyndon Johnson.* New York: Oxford University Press, 1996.

Bornet, Vaughn Davis. *The Presidency of Lyndon B. Johnson.* Lawrence: University Press of Kansas, 1983.

Califano, Joseph A. *The Triumph and Tragedy of Lyndon Johnson: The White House Years.* College Hill: Texas A & M University Press, 2000.

Caro, Robert A. *The Years of Lyndon Johnson: Master of the Senate.* New York: Knopf, 2003.

———. *The Years of Lyndon Johnson: Means of Ascent.* New York: Knopf, 1990.

———. *The Years of Lyndon Johnson: Path to Power.* New York: Knopf, 1983.

Castel, Albert E. *The Presidency of Lyndon B. Johnson.* Lawrence: University Press of Kansas, 1979.

Cowger, Thomas W. and Sherwin J. Markman, eds. *Lyndon Johnson Remembered: An Intimate Portrait of a Presidency.* Lanham, MD: Rowman & Littlefield, 2003.

Dallek, Robert. *Flawed Giant: Lyndon Johnson and His Times, 1961–1973.* New York: Oxford University Press, 1996.

———. *Lyndon B. Johnson: Portrait of a President.* New York: Oxford University Press, 2003.

Graff, Henry. *The Tuesday Cabinet.* Englewood Cliffs, NJ: Prentice Hall, 1970.

Hennggeler, Paul R. *In His Steps: Lyndon Johnson and the Kennedy Mystique.* Chicago: Ivan R. Dee, Inc., 1991.

Kearns, Doris. *Lyndon Johnson and the American Dream.* New York: Harper and Row, 1976.

Langston, Thomas S. *Lyndon Baines Johnson.* Washington, DC: CQ Press, 2002.

Reedy, George. *Lyndon B. Johnson: A Memoir.* Kansas City: Andrews McMeel Publishing, 1985.

Schulman, Bruce J. *Lyndon Johnson and American Liberalism.* New York: Bedford/St. Martin's, 1995.

Thompson, Kenneth W. *The Johnson Presidency: Twenty Intimate Perspectives.* Lanham, MD: Rowman & Littlefield, 1986.

Valenti, Jack. *A Very Human President.* New York: Norton, 1975.

On Richard M. Nixon

Emery, Frederick. *Watergate: The Corruption of American Politics and the Fall of Richard Nixon.* New York: Time Books, 1994.

Genovese, Michael A. *The Nixon Presidency: Power and Politics in Turbulent Times.* Westport, CT: Greenwood Press, 1990.

———. *The Watergate Crisis.* Westport, CT: Greenwood Press, 1999.

Greenberg, David. *Nixon's Shadow: The History of an Image.* New York: W.W. Norton & Company, 2003.

Kimball, Jeffrey. *Nixon's Vietnam War.* Lawrence: University Press of Kansas, 1998.

Kutler, Stanley. *The Wars of Watergate.* New York: Alfred A. Knopf, 1990.

Matusow, Allen J. *Nixon's Economy: Booms, Busts, Dollars, and Votes.* Lawrence: University Press of Kansas, 1998.

Mazlish, Bruce. *In Search of Nixon: A Psychohistorical Inquiry.* Baltimore: Pelican, 1973.

Morgan, Iwan. *Nixon.* New York: Oxford, 2002.

Nixon, Richard. *R.N: The Memoirs of Richard Nixon.* New York: Simon & Schuster, 1990.

Pynn, Ronald E. *Watergate and the American Political Process.* New York: Praeger, 1975.

Reeves, Richard. *President Nixon: Alone in the White House.* New York: Simon and Schuster, 2001.

Small, Melvin. *The Presidency of Richard Nixon.* Lawrence: University Press of Kansas, 1999.

Strober, Gerald S. *Nixon: An Oral History of His Presidency.* New York: HarperCollins, 1994.

White, Theodore H. *Breach of Faith: The Fall of Richard Nixon.* New York: Anteneum, 1975.

Woodward, Bob. *The Final Days.* New York: Simon and Schuster, 1976.

On Gerald R. Ford

Cannon, James M. *Time and Chance: Gerald Ford's Appointment with History.* Ann Arbor: University of Michigan Press, 1997.

Ford, Gerald R. *A Time to Heal.* New York: Harper and Row, 1979.

Greene, John Robert. *The Presidency of Gerald R. Ford.* Lawrence: University Press of Kansas, 1995.

Schapsmeier, Edward L. *Gerald R. Ford's Date With Destiny: A Political Biography.* New York: Peter Lang Publishing, 1989.

On Jimmy Carter

Ariail, Dan, and Cheryl Heckler-Feltz. *The Carpenter's Apprentice: The Spiritual Biography of Jimmy Carter.* Grand Rapids, MI: Zondervan, 1996.

Bourne, Peter G. *Jimmy Carter: A Comprehensive Biography from Plains to Postpresidency.* New York: Scribner's, 1997.

Carter, Jimmy. *Keeping Faith: Memoirs of a President.* New York: Bantam, 1982.

Fink, Gary M., and Hugh Davis Graham, eds., *The Carter Presidency: Policy Choices in the Post–New Deal Era.* Lawrence: University Press of Kansas, 1998.

Hargrove, Erwin C. *Jimmy Carter as President: Leadership and the Politics of the Public Good.* Baton Rouge: Louisiana State University Press, 1988.

Hayward, Steven. *The Real Jimmy Carter.* Washington, DC: Regnery Publishing, 2004.

Glad, Betty. *Jimmy Carter: In Search of the Great White House.* New York: W. W. Norton & Company, 1980.

Kaufman, Burton I. *The Presidency of James Earl Carter, Jr.* Lawrence: University Press of Kansas, 1993.

Kucharsky, David. *Man from Plains: The Mind and Spirit of Jimmy Carter.* New York: HarperCollins, 1977.

Lynn, Laurence E., Jr. and David F. Whitman. *The President as Policymaker: Jimmy Carter and Welfare Reform.* Philadelphia: Temple University Press, 1981.

Mazlish, Bruce. *Jimmy Carter: A Character Portrait.* New York: Simon & Schuster, 1980.

Rosenbaum, Herbert D. and Alexej Ugrinsky, eds., *The Presidency and Domestic Policies of Jimmy Carter.* Westport, CT: Greenwood Press, 1994.

Wooten, James. *Dasher: The Roots and Rising of Jimmy Carter.* New York: Summit Books, 1978.

On Ronald Reagan

Berman, Larry, ed. *Looking Back on Reagan's Presidency.* Baltimore: Johns Hopkins University Press, 1990.

Boyarsky, Bill. *Ronald Reagan: His Life and Rise to the Presidency.* New York: Random House, 1981.

Brownlee, W. Elliot and Hugh Davis Graham. *The Reagan Presidency.* Lawrence: University Press of Kansas, 2003.

Busch, Andres. *Reagan and the Politics of Freedom.* Lanham, MD: Rowman & Littlefield, 2001.

Cannon, Lou. *President Reagan: A Role of a Lifetime.* New York: Simon and Schuster, 1991.

Conley, Richard S. *Reassessing the Reagan Presidency.* Lanham, MD: Rowman & Littlefield, 2003.

Edwards, Lee. *Ronald Reagan: A Political Biography.* Houston: Nordland Publishing International, 1980.

Hayward, Steven F. *The Age of Reagan: The Fall of the Old Liberal Order, 1964–1980.* New York: Random House, 2001.

Kengor, Paul. *God and Ronald Reagan.* New York: Regan Books, 2004.

Niskanen, William A. *Reaganomics.* New York: Oxford University Press, 1988.

Pemberton, William E. *Exit with Honor: The Life and Presidency of Ronald Reagan.* Armonk, NY: M.E. Sharp, 1997.

Reagan, Ronald. *An American Life: The Autobiography.* New York: Simon and Schuster, 1990.

Schaller, Michael. *Reckoning with Reagan: America and Its President in the 1980s.* New York: Oxford University Press, 1992.

Sloan, John W. *The Reagan Effect: Economics and Presidential Leadership.* Lawrence: University Press of Kansas, 1999.

Stockman, David. *The Triumph of Politics: Why the Reagan Revolution Failed.* New York: Harper and Row, 1986.

Strober, Deborah Hart, and Gerald S. Strober. *Reagan: The Man and His Presidency.* Boston: Houghton Mifflin, 1998.

Thompson, Kenneth W. *The Reagan Presidency: Ten Intimate Perspectives of Ronald Reagan.* Lanham, MD: Rowman & Littlefield, 1997.

Wallison, Peter J. *Ronald Reagan: The Power of Conviction and the Success of His Presidency.* Boulder, CO: Westview Press, 2002.

On George Herbert Walker Bush

Bush, George. *Looking Forward.* New York: Bantam Books, 1988.

Greene, John Robert. *The Presidency of George Bush.* Lawrence: University Press of Kansas, 2000.

King, Nicholas. *George Bush: A Biography.* New York: Dodd, Mead, 1980.

Kolb, Charles. *White House Daze.* New York: Maxwell Macmillan International, 1994.

Mervin, David. *George Bush and the Guardianship Presidency.* New York: St. Martin's Press, 1998.

Parmet, Herbert S. *George Bush: The Life of a Lone Star Yankee.* New York: Scribner's, 1997.

Thompson, Kenneth W., ed. *The Bush Presidency: Ten Intimate Perspectives of George Bush.* Lanham, MD: Rowman & Littlefield, 1997.

———., ed. *The Bush Presidency-Part II: Ten Intimate Perspectives of George Bush.* Lanham, MD: Rowman & Littlefield, 1998.

On William Jefferson Clinton

Adler, David Gray and Michael A. Genovese. *The Presidency and the Law: The Clinton Legacy.* Lawrence: University Press of Kansas, 2002.

Allen, Charles F. *The Comeback Kid: The Life and Career of Bill Clinton.* New York: Carol Publishing Group, 1992.

Benjamin and Steven Simon. *The Age of Sacred Terror.* New York: Random House, 2002.

Berman, William C. *From the Center to the Edge: The Politics and Policies of the Clinton Presidency.* Lanham, MD: Rowman and Littlefield, 2001.

Clinton, Bill. *My Life.* New York: Knopf, 2004.

Hohenberg, John. *The Bill Clinton Story: Winning the Presidency.* New York: Syracuse University Press, 1994.

Johnson, Haynes. *The Best of Times: America in the Clinton Years.* New York: Harcourt, 2001.

Klein, Joe. *The Natural: The Misunderstood Presidency of Bill Clinton.* New York: Doubleday, 2002.

Maraniss, David. *First in His Class: The Biography of Bill Clinton.* New York: Simon and Schuster, 1995.

Morris, Dick. *Behind the Oval Office: Winning the Presidency in the Nineties.* New York: Random House, 1997.

Renshon, Stanley A. *High Hopes: The Clinton Presidency and the Politics of Ambition.* New York: New York University Press, 1996.

Walker, Martin. *The President We Deserve: Bill Clinton: His Rise, Falls, and Comebacks.* New York: Crown, 1996.

Woodward, Bob. *The Agenda.* New York: Simon & Schuster, 1994.

On George W. Bush

Bartlett, Bruce R. *Imposter,* New York: Doubleday, 2006.

Campbell, Colin and Bert A. Rockman. *The George W. Bush Presidency.* Washington, DC: CQ Press, 2004.

Daadler, Ivo H. and James M. Lindsay. *America Unbound: The Bush Revolution in Foreign Policy.* Washington, DC: Brookings Institution Press, 2003.

Frum, David. *The Right Man.* New York: Random House, 2003.

Gregg, Gary L. and Mark J. Rozell, eds. *Considering the Bush Presidency.* New York: Oxford University Press, 2003.

Kengor, Paul. *God and George W. Bush.* New York: Regan Books, 2004.

Mansfield, Stephen. *The Faith of George W. Bush.* New York: J.P. Tarcher, 2003.

Mitchell, Elizabeth. *W: Revenge of the Bush Dynasty.* New York: Berkley Publishing Group, 2003.

Woodward, Bob. *Bush at War.* New York: Simon & Schuster, 2003.

———. *Plan of Attack.* New York: Simon & Schuster, 2004.

PERSONAL HISTORY OF AMERICAN PRESIDENTS

President	Term	State	Religion	First Office Age/ Inauguration Age	College	Occupation	Pre-Presidential Position
1. Washington	1789–97	VA	Episcopalian	17/57	None	Farmer/Surveyor	Commander in Chief
2. Adams, J.	1797–1801	MA	Unitarian	39/61	Harvard	Farmer/Lawyer	Vice President
3. Jefferson	1801–09	VA	No Specific	26/58	William & Mary	Farmer/Lawyer	Vice President
4. Madison	1809–17	VA	Episcopalian	25/58	Princeton	Farmer	Secretary of State
5. Monroe	1817–25	VA	Episcopalian	24/59	William & Mary	Lawyer/Farmer	Secretary of State
6. Adams, J.Q.	1825–29	MA	Unitarian	27/58	Harvard	Lawyer	Secretary of State
7. Jackson	1829–37	TN	Presbyterian	21/62	None	Lawyer	U.S. Senator
8. Van Buren	1837–41	NY	Dutch Reformed	30/55	None	Lawyer	Vice President
9. Harrison, W.H.	1841	IN	Episcopalian	26/68	Hampden-Sydney	Military	Minister to Columbia
10. Tyler	1841–45	VA	Episcopalian	21/51	William & Mary	Lawyer	Vice President
11. Polk	1845–49	TN	Presbyterian	28/50	U. of N. Carolina	Lawyer	Governor
12. Taylor	1849–50	KY	Episcopalian	None/65	None	Military	General
13. Fillmore	1850–53	NY	Unitarian	28/50	None	Lawyer	Vice President
14. Pierce	1853–57	NH	Episcopalian	25/48	Bowdoin	Lawyer	U.S. District Attorney
15. Buchanan	1857–61	PA	Presbyterian	11/65	Dickinson	Lawyer	Minister to Great Britain
16. Lincoln	1861–65	IL	No Specific	25/52	None	Lawyer	U.S. Representative
17. Johnson, A.	1865–69	TN	No Specific	20/57	None	Tailor	Vice President
18. Grant	1869–77	OH	Presbyterian	None/47	West Point	Military	General
19. Hayes	1877–81	OH	Methodist	36/55	Kenyon	Lawyer	Governor
20. Garfield	1881	OH	Disciples of Christ	28/50	Williams	Educator/Lawyer	U.S. Senator
21. Arthur	1881–85	NY	Episcopalian	31/51	Union	Lawyer	Vice President
22. Cleveland	1885–89	NY	Presbyterian	26/48	None	Lawyer	Governor
23. Harrison, B.	1889–93	IN	Presbyterian	24/56	Miami of Ohio	Lawyer	U.S. Senator
24. Cleveland	1893–97	NY	Presbyterian	26/48	None	Lawyer	Governor
25. McKinley	1897–1901	OH	Methodist	26/54	Allegheny	Lawyer	Governor
26. Roosevelt, T.	1901–09	NY	Dutch Reformed	24/43	Harvard	Lawyer, Author	Vice President

(continued)

PERSONAL HISTORY OF AMERICAN PRESIDENTS (*continued*)

President	Term	State	Religion	First Office Age/ Inauguration Age	College	Occupation	Pre-Presidential Position
27. Taft	1909–13	OH	Unitarian	24/52	Yale	Lawyer	Secretary of War
28. Wilson	1913–21	NJ	Presbyterian	54/56	Princeton	Educator	Governor
29. Harding	1921–23	OH	Baptist	35/56	OH Central	Newspaper Editor	U.S. Senator
30. Coolidge	1923–29	MA	Congregationalist	26/51	Amherst	Lawyer	Vice President
31. Hoover	1929–33	CA	Quaker	43/55	Stanford	Mining Engineer	Secretary of Commerce
32. Roosevelt, F.	1933–45	NY	Episcopalian	28/49	Harvard	Lawyer	Governor
33. Truman	1945–53	MO	Baptist	38/61	None	Clerk, Store Owner	Vice President
34. Eisenhower	1953–61	NY	Presbyterian	None/63	West Point	Military	President, Columbia University
35. Kennedy	1961–63	MA	Roman Catholic	29/43	Harvard	Newspaper Reporter	U.S. Senator
36. Johnson, L.	1963–69	TX	Disciples of Christ	28/55	SW Texas State Teacher's College	Educator	Vice President
37. Nixon	1969–74	NY	Quaker	34/56	Whittier	Lawyer	Vice President
38. Ford	1974–77	MI	Episcopalian	36/61	U. of Michigan	Lawyer	Vice President
39. Carter	1977–81	GA	Baptist	38/52	U.S. Naval Academy	Farmer/Businessman	Governor
40. Reagan	1981–89	CA	Presbyterian	55/69	Eureka	Entertainer	Governor
41. Bush	1989–93	TX	Episcopalian	42/64	Yale	Businessman	Vice President
42. Clinton	1993–2001	AR	S. Baptist	30/46	Georgetown	Lawyer	Governor
43. Bush, G.W.	2001–	TX	Methodist	48/54	Yale	Businessman	Governor

PRESIDENTIAL ELECTION RESULTS, 1789–2004

Year	Presidents Other Candidates	Party	Popular Vote	Electoral Vote
1789	**George Washington**			**69**
	John Adams			34
	Others			35
1793	**George Washington**			**132**
	John Adams			77
	George Clinton			50
	Others			5
1796	**John Adams**	**Federalist**		**71**
	Thomas Jefferson	Democratic-Republican		68
	Thomas Pinckney	Federalist		59
	Aaron Burr	Democratic-Republican		30
	Others			48
1800	**Thomas Jefferson**	**Democratic-Republican**		**73**
	Aaron Burr	Democratic-Republican		73
	John Adams	Federalist		65
	Charles C. Pinckney	Federalist		64
1804	**Thomas Jefferson**	**Democratic-Republican**		**162**
	Charles C. Pinckney	Federalist		14
1808	**James Madison**	**Democratic-Republican**		**122**
	Charles C. Pinckney	Federalist		47
	George Clinton	Independent-Republican		6
1812	**James Madison**	**Democratic-Republican**		**128**
	DeWitt Clinton	Federalist		89
1816	**James Monroe**	**Democratic-Republican**		**183**
	Rufus King	Federalist		34
1820	**James Monroe**	**Democratic-Republican**		**231**
	John Quincy Adams	Independent-Republican		1
1824	**John Quincy Adams**	**Democratic-Republican**	**108,740 (30.5%)**	**84**
	Andrew Jackson	Democratic-Republican	153,544 (43.1%)	99
	Henry Clay	Democratic-Republican	47,136 (13.2%)	37
	William H. Crawford	Democratic-Republican	46,618 (13.1)	41
1828	**Andrew Jackson**	**Democratic**	**647,231 (56.0%)**	**178**
	John Quincy Adams	National Republican	509,097 (44.0%)	83
1832	**Andrew Jackson**	**Democratic**	**687,502 (55.0%)**	**219**
	Henry Clay	National Republican	530,189 (42.4%)	49
	William Wirt	Anti-Masonic		7
	John Floyd	National Republican	33,108 (2.6)	11
1836	**Martin Van Buren**	**Democratic**	**761,549 (50.9%)**	**170**
	William H. Harrison	Whig	549,567 (36.7%)	73
	Hugh L. White	Whig	145,396 (9.7%)	26
	Daniel Webster	Whig	41,287 (2.7%)	14
1840	**William H. Harrison**	**Whig**	**1,275,017 (53.1%)**	**234**
	Martin Van Buren	Democratic	1,128,702 (46.9%)	60
1844	**James K. Polk**	**Democratic**	**1,337,243 (49.6%)**	**170**
	Henry Clay	Whig	1,299,068 (48.1%)	105
	James G. Birney	Liberty	63,300 (2.3%)	0
1848	**Zachary Taylor**	**Whig**	**1,360,101 (47.4%)**	**163**
	Lewis Cass	Democratic	1,220,544 (42.5%)	127
	Martin Van Buren	Free Soil	291,163 (10.1%)	0

YEAR	PRESIDENTS OTHER CANDIDATES	PARTY	POPULAR VOTE	ELECTORAL VOTE
1852	**Franklin Pierce**	**Democratic**	**1,601,474 (50.9%)**	**254**
	Winfield Scott	Whig	1,386,578 (44.1%)	42
1856	**James Buchanan**	**Democratic**	**1,838,169 (45.4%)**	**174**
	John C. Fremont	Republican	1,335,264 (33.0%)	114
	Millard Fillmore	American	874,534 (21.6%)	8
1860	**Abraham Lincoln**	**Republican**	**1,865,593 (39.8%)**	**180**
	Stephen A. Douglas	Democratic	1,381,713 (29.5%)	12
	John C. Breckinridge	Democratic	848,356 (18.1%)	72
	John Bell	Constitutional Union	592,906 (12.6%)	79
1864	**Abraham Lincoln**	**Republican**	**2,206,938 (55.0%)**	**212**
	George B. McClellan	Democratic	1,803,787 (45.0%)	21
1868	**Ulysses S. Grant**	**Republican**	**3,013,421 (52.7%)**	**214**
	Schuyler Colfax			
	Horatio Seymour	Democratic	2,706,829 (47.3%)	80
1872	**Ulysses S. Grant**	**Republican**	**3,596,745 (55.6%)**	**286**
	Horace Greeley	Democratic	2,843,446 (43.9%)	66
1876	**Rutherford B. Hayes**	**Republican**	**4,036,571 (48.0%)**	**185**
	Samuel J. Tilden	Democratic	4,284,020 (51.0%)	184
1880	**James A. Garfield**	**Republican**	**4,449,053 (48.3%)**	**214**
	Winfield S. Hancock	Democratic	4,442,035 (48.2%)	155
	James B. Weaver	Greenback-Labor	380,578 (3.4%)	
1884	**Grover Cleveland**	**Democratic**	**4,874,986 (48.5%)**	**219**
	James G. Blaine	Republican	4,851,931 (48.2%)	182
	Benjamin F. Butler	Greenback-Labor	175,370 (1.8%)	
1888	**Benjamin Harrison**	**Republican**	**5,444,337 (47.8%)**	**233**
	Grover Cleveland	Democratic	5,540,050 (48.6%)	168
1892	**Grover Cleveland**	**Democratic**	**5,554,414 (46.0%)**	**277**
	Benjamin Harrison	Republican	5,190,802 (43.0%)	145
	James B. Weaver	Peoples	1,027,329 (8.5%)	22
1896	**William McKinley**	**Republican**	**7,035,638 (50.8%)**	**271**
	William J. Bryan	Democratic; Populist	6,467,946 (46.7%)	176
1900	**William McKinley**	**Republican**	**7,219,530 (51.7%)**	**292**
	William J. Bryan	Democratic; Populist	6,356,734 (45.5%)	155
1904	**Theodore Roosevelt**	**Republican**	**7,628,834 (56.4%)**	**336**
	Alton B. Parker	Democratic	5,084,401 (37.6%)	140
	Eugene V. Debs	Socialist	402,460 (3.0%)	0
1908	**William H. Taft**	**Republican**	**7,679,006 (51.6%)**	**321**
	William J. Bryan	Democratic	6,409,106 (43.1%)	162
	Eugene V. Debs	Socialist	420,820 (2.8%)	0
1912	**Woodrow Wilson**	**Democratic**	**6,286,820 (41.8%)**	**435**
	Theodore Roosevelt	Progressive	4,126,020 (27.4%)	88
	William H. Taft	Republican	3,483,922 (23.2%)	8
	Eugene V. Debs	Socialist	897,011 (6.0%)	0
1916	**Woodrow Wilson**	**Democratic**	**9,129,606 (49.3%)**	**277**
	Charles E. Hughes	Republican	8,538,211 (46.1%)	254
1920	**Warren G. Harding**	**Republican**	**16,152,200 (61.0%)**	**404**
	James M. Cox	Democratic	9,147,353 (34.6%)	127
	Eugene V. Debs	Socialist	919,799 (3.5%)	0
1924	**Calvin Coolidge**	**Republican**	**15,725,016 (54.1%)**	**382**
	John W. Davis	Democratic	8,384,586 (28.8%)	136
	Robert M. LaFollette	Progressive	4,822,856 (16.6%)	13

Year	Presidents Other Candidates	Party	Popular Vote	Electoral Vote
1928	**Herbert C. Hoover**	**Republican**	**21,392,190 (58.2%)**	**444**
	Alfred E. Smith	Democratic	15,016,443 (40.8%)	87
1932	**Franklin D. Roosevelt**	**Democratic**	**22,809,638 (57.3)**	**472**
	Herbert C. Hoover	Republican	15,758,901 (39.6%)	59
	Norman Thomas	Socialist	881,951 (2.2%)	0
1936	**Franklin D. Roosevelt**	**Democratic**	**27,751,612 (60.7%)**	**523**
	Alfred M. Landon	Republican	16,681,913 (36.4%)	8
	William Lemke	Union	891,958 (1.9%)	0
1940	**Franklin D. Roosevelt**	**Democratic**	**27,243,466 (54.7%)**	**449**
	Wendell L. Wilkie	Republican	22,304,755 (44.8%)	82
1944	**Franklin D. Roosevelt**	**Democratic**	**25,602,505 (52.8%)**	**432**
	Thomas E. Dewey	Republican	22,006,278 (44.5%)	99
1948	**Harry S. Truman**	**Democratic**	**24,105,812 (49.5%)**	**303**
	Thomas E. Dewey	Republican	21,970,065 (45.1%)	189
	J. Strom Thurmond	States' Rights	1,169,063 (2.4%)	39
	Henry A. Wallace	Progressive	1,157,172 (2.4%)	0
1952	**Dwight D. Eisenhower**	**Republican**	**33,936,234 (55.2%)**	**442**
	Adlai E. Stevenson	Democratic	27,314,992 (44.5%)	89
1956	**Dwight D. Eisenhower**	**Republican**	**35,590,472 (57.4%)**	**457**
	Adlai E. Stevenson	Democratic	26,022,752 (42.0%)	73
1960	**John F. Kennedy**	**Democratic**	**34,227,096 (49.9%)**	**303**
	Richard M. Nixon	Republican	34,108,546 (49.6%)	219
1964	**Lyndon B. Johnson**	**Democratic**	**43,126,233 (61.1%)**	**486**
	Barry Goldwater	Republican	27,174,989 (38.5%)	52
1968	**Richard M. Nixon**	**Republican**	**31,783,783 (43.4%)**	**301**
	Hubert H. Humphrey	Democratic	31,271,839 (42.7%)	191
	George C. Wallace	American Independent	9,899,557 (13.5%)	46
1972	**Richard M. Nixon**	**Republican**	**46,632,189 (61.3%)**	**520**
	George McGovern	Democratic	28,422,015 (37.3%)	17
1976	**Jimmy Carter**	**Democratic**	**40,828,587 (50.1%)**	**297**
	Gerald R. Ford	Republican	39,147,613 (48.0%)	240
1980	**Ronald Reagan**	**Republican**	**42,941,145 (51.0%)**	**489**
	Jimmy Carter	Democratic	34,663,037 (41.0%)	49
	John B. Anderson	Independent	5,551,551 (6.6%)	0
1984	**Ronald Reagan**	**Republican**	**53,428,357 (59%)**	**525**
	Walter F. Mondale	Democratic	36,930,923 (41%)	13
1988	**George Bush**	**Republican**	**48,881,011 (53%)**	**426**
	Michael Dukakis	Democratic	41,828,350 (46%)	111
1992	**Bill Clinton**	**Democratic**	**38,394,210 (43%)**	**370**
	George Bush	Republican	33,974,386 (38%)	168
	H. Ross Perot	Independent	16,573,465 (19%)	0
1996	**Bill Clinton**	**Democratic**	**45,628,667 (49%)**	**379**
	Bob Dole	Republican	37,869,435 (41%)	159
	H. Ross Perot	Reform	7,874,283 (8%)	0
2000	**George W. Bush**	**Republican**	**50,456,169 (48%)**	**271**
	Al Gore	Democrat	50,996,116 (48%)	266
	Ralph Nader	Green	2,767,176 (3%)	0
2004	**George W. Bush**	**Republican**	**62,040,610 (51%)**	**286**
	John Kerry	Democrat	59,028,444 (48%)	251

RELIGIOUS AFFILIATIONS OF PRESIDENTS

DENOMINATION	NUMBER OF PRESIDENTS	PERCENT OF PRESIDENTS	PERCENT OF CURRENT U.S. POP.	RATIO % OF PRES. TO % OF POP.
Episcopalian	11	26.20%	1.7%	15.4
Presbyterian	9	21%	2.8%	5.1
Baptist	4	9.5%	18.0%	0.5
Unitarian	4	9.50%	0.2%	47.5
Methodist	3	9.5%	8.0%	1.5
Disciples of Christ	3	7.10%	0.4%	18.7
Dutch Reformed	2	4.80%	0.1%	48.0
Quaker	2	4.80%	0.7%	6.9
Catholic	1	2.40%	26.0%	0.1
Congregationalist/ United Church of Christ	1	2.40%	0.6%	4.0

RELIGION	PRESIDENTS
Episcopalian	George Washington
	James Madison
	James Monroe
	William Henry Harrison
	John Tyler
	Zachary Taylor
	Franklin Pierce
	Chester A. Arthur
	Franklin Delano Roosevelt
	Gerald Ford
	George H. W. Bush
Presbyterian	Andrew Jackson
	James Knox Polk
	Ulysses S. Grant
	James Buchanan
	Grover Cleveland
	Benjamin Harrison
	Woodrow Wilson
	Dwight D. Eisenhower
	Ronald Reagan
Methodist	Rutherford B. Hayes
	William McKinley
	George W. Bush
Baptist	Warren G. Harding
	Harry S. Truman
	Jimmy Carter
	William Jefferson Clinton
Unitarian	John Adams
	John Quincy Adams
	Millard Fillmore
	William Howard Taft
Disciples of Christ	James A. Garfield
	Lyndon Baines Johnson
No Specific Denomination	Thomas Jefferson
	Abraham Lincoln
	Andrew Johnson
Dutch Reformed	Martin Van Buren
	Theodore Roosevelt
Quaker	Herbert Hoover
	Richard M. Nixon
Congregationalist	Calvin Coolidge
Catholic	John F. Kennedy

Constitution of the United States

We the people of the United States, in order to form a more perfect union, establish justice, insure domestic tranquility, provide for the common defense, promote the general welfare, and secure the blessings of liberty to ourselves and our posterity, do ordain and establish this Constitution for the United States of America.

Article I

Section 1.   All legislative powers herein granted shall be vested in a Congress of the United States, which shall consist of a Senate and House of Representatives.

Section 2.   The House of Representatives shall be composed of members chosen every second year by the people of the several states, and the electors in each state shall have the qualifications requisite for electors of the most numerous branch of the state legislature.

No person shall be a Representative who shall not have attained to the age of twenty five years, and been seven years a citizen of the United States, and who shall not, when elected, be an inhabitant of that state in which he shall be chosen.

Representatives and direct taxes shall be apportioned among the several states which may be included within this union, according to their respective numbers, which shall be determined by adding to the whole number of free persons, including those bound to service for a term of years, and excluding Indians not taxed, three fifths of all other Persons. The actual Enumeration shall be made within three years after the first meeting of the Congress of the United States, and within every subsequent term of ten years, in such manner as they shall by law direct. The number of Representatives shall not exceed one for every thirty thousand, but each state shall have at least one Representative; and until such enumeration shall be made, the state of New Hampshire shall be entitled to choose three, Massachusetts eight, Rhode Island and Providence Plantations one, Connecticut five, New York six, New Jersey four, Pennsylvania eight, Delaware one, Maryland six, Virginia ten, North Carolina five, South Carolina five, and Georgia three.

When vacancies happen in the Representation from any state, the executive authority thereof shall issue writs of election to fill such vacancies.

The House of Representatives shall choose their speaker and other officers; and shall have the sole power of impeachment.

Section 3.   The Senate of the United States shall be composed of two Senators from each state, chosen by the legislature thereof, for six years; and each Senator shall have one vote.

Immediately after they shall be assembled in consequence of the first election, they shall be divided as equally as may be into three classes. The seats of the Senators of the first class shall be vacated at the expiration of the second year, of the second class at the expiration of the fourth year, and the third class at the expiration of the sixth year, so that one third may be chosen every second year; and if vacancies happen by resignation, or otherwise, during the recess of the legislature of any state, the executive thereof may make temporary appointments until the next meeting of the legislature, which shall then fill such vacancies.

No person shall be a Senator who shall not have attained to the age of thirty years, and been nine years a citizen of the United States and who shall not, when elected, be an inhabitant of that state for which he shall be chosen.

The Vice President of the United States shall be President of the Senate, but shall have no vote, unless they be equally divided.

The Senate shall choose their other officers, and also a President pro tempore, in the absence of the Vice President, or when he shall exercise the office of President of the United States.

The Senate shall have the sole power to try all impeachments. When sitting for that purpose, they shall be on oath or affirmation. When the President of the United States is tried, the Chief Justice shall preside: And no person shall be convicted without the concurrence of two thirds of the members present.

Judgment in cases of impeachment shall not extend further than to removal from office, and disqualification to hold and enjoy any office of honor, trust or profit under the United States: but the party convicted shall nevertheless be liable and subject to indictment, trial, judgment and punishment, according to law.

Section 4.   The times, places and manner of holding elections for Senators and Representatives, shall be prescribed in each state by the legislature thereof; but the Congress may at any time by law make or alter such regulations, except as to the places of choosing Senators.

The Congress shall assemble at least once in every year, and such meeting shall be on the first Monday in December, unless they shall by law appoint a different day.

Section 5.   Each House shall be the judge of the elections, returns and qualifications of its own members, and a majority of each shall constitute a quorum to do business; but a smaller number may adjourn from day to day, and may be authorized to compel the attendance of absent members, in such manner, and under such penalties as each House may provide.

Each House may determine the rules of its proceedings, punish its members for disorderly behavior, and, with the concurrence of two thirds, expel a member. Each House shall keep a journal of its proceedings, and from time to time publish the same, excepting such parts as may in their judgment require secrecy; and the yeas and nays of the members of either House on any question shall, at the desire of one fifth of those present, be entered on the journal.

Neither House, during the session of Congress, shall, without the consent of the other, adjourn for more than three days, nor to any other place than that in which the two Houses shall be sitting.

Section 6.   The Senators and Representatives shall receive a compensation for their services, to be ascertained by law, and paid out of the treasury of the United States. They shall in all cases, except treason, felony and breach of the peace, be privileged from arrest during their attendance at the session of their respective Houses, and in going to and returning from the same; and for any speech or debate in either House, they shall not be questioned in any other place.

No Senator or Representative shall, during the time for which he was elected, be appointed to any civil office under the authority of the United States, which shall have been created, or the emoluments whereof shall have been increased during such time: and no person holding any office under the United States, shall be a member of either House during his continuance in office.

Section 7.   All bills for raising revenue shall originate in the House of Representatives; but the Senate may propose or concur with amendments as on other Bills.

Every bill which shall have passed the House of Representatives and the Senate, shall, before it become a law, be presented to the President of the United States; if he approve he shall sign it, but if not he shall return it, with his objections to that House in which it shall have originated, who shall enter the objections at large on their journal, and proceed to reconsider it. If after such reconsideration two thirds of that House shall agree to pass the bill, it shall be sent, together with the objections, to the other House, by which it shall likewise be reconsidered, and if approved by two thirds of that House, it shall become a law. But in all such cases the votes of both Houses shall be determined by yeas and nays, and the names of the persons voting for and against the bill shall be entered on the journal of each House respectively. If any bill shall not be returned by the President within ten days (Sundays excepted) after it shall have been presented to him, the same shall be a law, in like manner as if he had signed it, unless the Congress by their adjournment prevent its return, in which case it shall not be a law.

Every order, resolution, or vote to which the concurrence of the Senate and House of Representatives may be necessary (except on a question of adjournment) shall be presented to the President of the United States; and before the same shall take effect, shall be approved by him, or being disapproved by him, shall be repassed by two thirds of the Senate and House of Representatives, according to the rules and limitations prescribed in the case of a bill.

Section 8.   The Congress shall have power to lay and collect taxes, duties, imposts and excises, to pay the debts and provide for the common defense and general welfare of the United States; but all duties, imposts and excises shall be uniform throughout the United States;

To borrow money on the credit of the United States;

To regulate commerce with foreign nations, and among the several states, and with the Indian tribes;

To establish a uniform rule of naturalization, and uniform laws on the subject of bankruptcies throughout the United States;

To coin money, regulate the value thereof, and of foreign coin, and fix the standard of weights and measures;

To provide for the punishment of counterfeiting the securities and current coin of the United States;

To establish post offices and post roads;

To promote the progress of science and useful arts, by securing for limited times to authors and inventors the exclusive right to their respective writings and discoveries;

To constitute tribunals inferior to the Supreme Court;

To define and punish piracies and felonies committed on the high seas, and offenses against the law of nations;

To declare war, grant letters of marque and reprisal, and make rules concerning captures on land and water;

To raise and support armies, but no appropriation of money to that use shall be for a longer term than two years;

To provide and maintain a navy;

To make rules for the government and regulation of the land and naval forces;

To provide for calling forth the militia to execute the laws of the union, suppress insurrections and repel invasions;

To provide for organizing, arming, and disciplining, the militia, and for governing such part of them as may be employed in the service of the United States, reserving to the states respectively, the appointment of the officers, and the authority of training the militia according to the discipline prescribed by Congress;

To exercise exclusive legislation in all cases whatsoever, over such District (not exceeding ten miles square) as may, by cession of particular states, and the acceptance of Congress, become the seat of the government of the United States, and to exercise like authority over all places purchased by the consent of the legislature of the state in which the same shall be, for the erection of forts, magazines, arsenals, dockyards, and other needful buildings;—And

To make all laws which shall be necessary and proper for carrying into execution the foregoing powers, and all other powers vested by this Constitution in the government of the United States, or in any department or officer thereof.

Section 9.   The migration or importation of such persons as any of the states now existing shall think proper to admit, shall not be prohibited by the

Congress prior to the year one thousand eight hundred and eight, but a tax or duty may be imposed on such importation, not exceeding ten dollars for each person.

The privilege of the writ of habeas corpus shall not be suspended, unless when in cases of rebellion or invasion the public safety may require it.

No bill of attainder or ex post facto Law shall be passed.

No capitation, or other direct, tax shall be laid, unless in proportion to the census or enumeration herein before directed to be taken.

No tax or duty shall be laid on articles exported from any state.

No preference shall be given by any regulation of commerce or revenue to the ports of one state over those of another: nor shall vessels bound to, or from, one state, be obliged to enter, clear or pay duties in another.

No money shall be drawn from the treasury, but in consequence of appropriations made by law; and a regular statement and account of receipts and expenditures of all public money shall be published from time to time.

No title of nobility shall be granted by the United States: and no person holding any office of profit or trust under them, shall, without the consent of the Congress, accept of any present, emolument, office, or title, of any kind whatever, from any king, prince, or foreign state.

Section 10.   No state shall enter into any treaty, alliance, or confederation; grant letters of marque and reprisal; coin money; emit bills of credit; make anything but gold and silver coin a tender in payment of debts; pass any bill of attainder, ex post facto law, or law impairing the obligation of contracts, or grant any title of nobility.

No state shall, without the consent of the Congress, lay any imposts or duties on imports or exports, except what may be absolutely necessary for executing its inspection laws: and the net produce of all duties and imposts, laid by any state on imports or exports, shall be for the use of the treasury of the United States; and all such laws shall be subject to the revision and control of the Congress.

No state shall, without the consent of Congress, lay any duty of tonnage, keep troops, or ships of war in time of peace, enter into any agreement or compact with another state, or with a foreign power, or engage in war, unless actually invaded, or in such imminent danger as will not admit of delay.

Article II

Section 1.   The executive power shall be vested in a President of the United States of America. He shall hold his office during the term of four years, and, together with the Vice President, chosen for the same term, be elected, as follows:

Each state shall appoint, in such manner as the Legislature thereof may direct, a number of electors, equal to the whole number of Senators and

Representatives to which the State may be entitled in the Congress: but no Senator or Representative, or person holding an office of trust or profit under the United States, shall be appointed an elector.

The electors shall meet in their respective states, and vote by ballot for two persons, of whom one at least shall not be an inhabitant of the same state with themselves. And they shall make a list of all the persons voted for, and of the number of votes for each; which list they shall sign and certify, and transmit sealed to the seat of the government of the United States, directed to the President of the Senate. The President of the Senate shall, in the presence of the Senate and House of Representatives, open all the certificates, and the votes shall then be counted. The person having the greatest number of votes shall be the President, if such number be a majority of the whole number of electors appointed; and if there be more than one who have such majority, and have an equal number of votes, then the House of Representatives shall immediately choose by ballot one of them for President; and if no person have a majority, then from the five highest on the list the said House shall in like manner choose the President. But in choosing the President, the votes shall be taken by States, the representation from each state having one vote; A quorum for this purpose shall consist of a member or members from two thirds of the states, and a majority of all the states shall be necessary to a choice. In every case, after the choice of the President, the person having the greatest number of votes of the electors shall be the Vice President. But if there should remain two or more who have equal votes, the Senate shall choose from them by ballot the Vice President.

The Congress may determine the time of choosing the electors, and the day on which they shall give their votes; which day shall be the same throughout the United States.

No person except a natural born citizen, or a citizen of the United States, at the time of the adoption of this Constitution, shall be eligible to the office of President; neither shall any person be eligible to that office who shall not have attained to the age of thirty five years, and been fourteen years a resident within the United States.

In case of the removal of the President from office, or of his death, resignation, or inability to discharge the powers and duties of the said office, the same shall devolve on the Vice President, and the Congress may by law provide for the case of removal, death, resignation or inability, both of the President and Vice President, declaring what officer shall then act as President, and such officer shall act accordingly, until the disability be removed, or a President shall be elected.

The President shall, at stated times, receive for his services, a compensation, which shall neither be increased nor diminished during the period for which he shall have been elected, and he shall not receive within that period any other emolument from the United States, or any of them.

Before he enter on the execution of his office, he shall take the following oath or affirmation:—"I do solemnly swear (or affirm) that I will faithfully execute the office of President of the United States, and will to the best of my ability, preserve, protect and defend the Constitution of the United States."

Section 2.   The President shall be commander in chief of the Army and Navy of the United States, and of the militia of the several states, when called into the actual service of the United States; he may require the opinion, in writing, of the principal officer in each of the executive departments, upon any subject relating to the duties of their respective offices, and he shall have power to grant reprieves and pardons for offenses against the United States, except in cases of impeachment.

He shall have power, by and with the advice and consent of the Senate, to make treaties, provided two thirds of the Senators present concur; and he shall nominate, and by and with the advice and consent of the Senate, shall appoint ambassadors, other public ministers and consuls, judges of the Supreme Court, and all other officers of the United States, whose appointments are not herein otherwise provided for, and which shall be established by law: but the Congress may by law vest the appointment of such inferior officers, as they think proper, in the President alone, in the courts of law, or in the heads of departments.

The President shall have power to fill up all vacancies that may happen during the recess of the Senate, by granting commissions which shall expire at the end of their next session.

Section 3.   He shall from time to time give to the Congress information of the state of the union, and recommend to their consideration such measures as he shall judge necessary and expedient; he may, on extraordinary occasions, convene both Houses, or either of them, and in case of disagreement between them, with respect to the time of adjournment, he may adjourn them to such time as he shall think proper; he shall receive ambassadors and other public ministers; he shall take care that the laws be faithfully executed, and shall commission all the officers of the United States.

Section 4.   The President, Vice President and all civil officers of the United States, shall be removed from office on impeachment for, and conviction of, treason, bribery, or other high crimes and misdemeanors.

Article III

Section 1.   The judicial power of the United States, shall be vested in one Supreme Court, and in such inferior courts as the Congress may from time to time ordain and establish. The judges, both of the supreme and inferior courts, shall hold their offices during good behaviour, and shall, at stated times, receive for their services, a compensation, which shall not be diminished during their continuance in office.

Section 2.   The judicial power shall extend to all cases, in law and equity, arising under this Constitution, the laws of the United States, and treaties made, or which shall be made, under their authority;—to all cases affecting ambassadors, other public ministers and consuls;—to all cases of admiralty and maritime jurisdiction;—to controversies to which the United States shall be a party;—to controversies between two or more states;—between a state and citizens of another state;— between citizens of different states;—between citizens of the same state claiming lands under grants of different states, and between a state, or the citizens thereof, and foreign states, citizens or subjects.

In all cases affecting ambassadors, other public ministers and consuls, and those in which a state shall be party, the Supreme Court shall have original jurisdiction. In all the other cases before mentioned, the Supreme Court shall have appellate jurisdiction, both as to law and fact, with such exceptions, and under such regulations as the Congress shall make.

The trial of all crimes, except in cases of impeachment, shall be by jury; and such trial shall be held in the state where the said crimes shall have been committed; but when not committed within any state, the trial shall be at such place or places as the Congress may by law have directed.

Section 3.   Treason against the United States, shall consist only in levying war against them, or in adhering to their enemies, giving them aid and comfort. No person shall be convicted of treason unless on the testimony of two witnesses to the same overt act, or on confession in open court.

The Congress shall have power to declare the punishment of treason, but no attainder of treason shall work corruption of blood, or forfeiture except during the life of the person attainted.

Article IV

Section 1.   Full faith and credit shall be given in each state to the public acts, records, and judicial proceedings of every other state. And the Congress may by general laws prescribe the manner in which such acts, records, and proceedings shall be proved, and the effect thereof.

Section 2.   The citizens of each state shall be entitled to all privileges and immunities of citizens in the several states.

A person charged in any state with treason, felony, or other crime, who shall flee from justice, and be found in another state, shall on demand of the executive authority of the state from which he fled, be delivered up, to be removed to the state having jurisdiction of the crime.

No person held to service or labor in one state, under the laws thereof, escaping into another, shall, in consequence of any law or regulation therein, be discharged from such service or labor, but shall be delivered up on claim of the party to whom such service or labor may be due.

Section 3.   New states may be admitted by the Congress into this union; but no new states shall be formed or erected within the jurisdiction of any other state; nor any state be formed by the junction of two or more states, or parts of states, without the consent of the legislatures of the states concerned as well as of the Congress.

The Congress shall have power to dispose of and make all needful rules and regulations respecting the territory or other property belonging to the United States; and nothing in this Constitution shall be so construed as to prejudice any claims of the United States, or of any particular state.

Section 4.   The United States shall guarantee to every state in this union a republican form of government, and shall protect each of them against invasion; and on application of the legislature, or of the executive (when the legislature cannot be convened) against domestic violence.

Article V

The Congress, whenever two thirds of both houses shall deem it necessary, shall propose amendments to this Constitution, or, on the application of the legislatures of two thirds of the several states, shall call a convention for proposing amendments, which, in either case, shall be valid to all intents and purposes, as part of this Constitution, when ratified by the legislatures of three fourths of the several states, or by conventions in three fourths thereof, as the one or the other mode of ratification may be proposed by the Congress; provided that no amendment which may be made prior to the year one thousand eight hundred and eight shall in any manner affect the first and fourth clauses in the ninth section of the first article; and that no state, without its consent, shall be deprived of its equal suffrage in the Senate.

Article VI

All debts contracted and engagements entered into, before the adoption of this Constitution, shall be as valid against the United States under this Constitution, as under the Confederation.

This Constitution, and the laws of the United States which shall be made in pursuance thereof; and all treaties made, or which shall be made, under the authority of the United States, shall be the supreme law of the land; and the judges in every state shall be bound thereby, anything in the Constitution or laws of any State to the contrary notwithstanding.

The Senators and Representatives before mentioned, and the members of the several state legislatures, and all executive and judicial officers, both of the United States and of the several states, shall be bound by oath or affirmation, to support this Constitution; but no religious test shall ever be required as a qualification to any office or public trust under the United States.

Article VII

The ratification of the conventions of nine states, shall be sufficient for the establishment of this Constitution between the states so ratifying the same.

Done in convention by the unanimous consent of the states present the seventeenth day of September in the year of our Lord one thousand seven hundred and eighty seven and of the independence of the United States of America the twelfth. In witness whereof We have hereunto subscribed our Names,

George Washington, President and deputy from Virginia

Amendments

(The first ten amendments were ratified in 1791)

Amendment I

Congress shall make no law respecting an establishment of religion, or prohibiting the free exercise thereof; or abridging the freedom of speech, or of the press; or the right of the people peaceably to assemble, and to petition the government for a redress of grievances.

Amendment II

A well regulated militia, being necessary to the security of a free state, the right of the people to keep and bear arms, shall not be infringed.

Amendment III

No soldier shall, in time of peace be quartered in any house, without the consent of the owner, nor in time of war, but in a manner to be prescribed by law.

Amendment IV

The right of the people to be secure in their persons, houses, papers, and effects, against unreasonable searches and seizures, shall not be violated, and no warrants shall issue, but upon probable cause, supported by oath or affirmation, and particularly describing the place to be searched, and the persons or things to be seized.

Amendment V

No person shall be held to answer for a capital, or otherwise infamous crime, unless on a presentment or indictment of a grand jury, except in cases arising in the land or naval forces, or in the militia, when in actual service in time of war or public danger; nor shall any person be subject for the same offense to be twice put in jeopardy of life or limb; nor shall be compelled in any criminal case to be a witness against himself, nor be deprived of life, liberty, or property, without due process of law; nor shall private property be taken for public use, without just compensation.

Amendment VI

In all criminal prosecutions, the accused shall enjoy the right to a speedy and public trial, by an impartial jury of the state and district wherein the crime shall have been committed, which district shall have been previously ascertained by law, and to be informed of the nature and cause of the accusation; to be confronted with the witnesses against him; to have compulsory process for obtaining witnesses in his favor, and to have the assistance of counsel for his defense.

Amendment VII

In suits at common law, where the value in controversy shall exceed twenty dollars, the right of trial by jury shall be preserved, and no fact tried by a jury, shall be otherwise reexamined in any court of the United States, than according to the rules of the common law.

Amendment VIII

Excessive bail shall not be required, nor excessive fines imposed, nor cruel and unusual punishments inflicted.

Amendment IX

The enumeration in the Constitution, of certain rights, shall not be construed to deny or disparage others retained by the people.

Amendment X

The powers not delegated to the United States by the Constitution, nor prohibited by it to the states, are reserved to the states respectively, or to the people.

Amendment XI (1798)

The judicial power of the United States shall not be construed to extend to any suit in law or equity, commenced or prosecuted against one of the United States by citizens of another state, or by citizens or subjects of any foreign state.

Amendment XII (1804)

The electors shall meet in their respective states and vote by ballot for President and Vice-President, one of whom, at least, shall not be an inhabitant of the same state with themselves; they shall name in their ballots the person voted for as President, and in distinct ballots the person voted for as Vice-President, and they shall make distinct lists of all persons voted for as President, and of all persons voted for as Vice-President, and of the number of votes for each, which lists they shall sign and certify, and transmit sealed to the seat of the government of the United States, directed to the President of the Senate;—The President of the Senate shall, in the presence of the Senate and House of Representatives, open all the certificates and the votes shall then be counted;—the person having the greatest number of votes for President, shall be the President, if such number be a majority of the whole number of electors appointed; and if no person have such majority, then from the persons having the highest numbers not exceeding three on the list of those voted for as President, the House of Representatives shall choose immediately, by ballot, the President. But in choosing the President, the votes shall be taken by states, the representation from each state having one vote; a quorum for this purpose shall consist of a member or members from two-thirds of the states, and a majority of all the states shall be necessary to a choice. And if the House of Representatives shall not choose a President whenever the right of choice shall devolve upon them, before the fourth day of March next following, then the Vice-President shall act as President, as in the case of the death or other constitutional disability of the President. The person having the greatest number of votes as Vice-President, shall be the Vice-President, if such number be a majority of the whole number of electors appointed, and if no person have a majority, then from the two highest numbers on the list, the Senate shall choose the Vice-President; a quorum for the purpose shall consist of two-thirds of the whole number of Senators, and a majority of the whole number shall be necessary to a choice. But no person constitutionally ineligible to the office of President shall be eligible to that of Vice-President of the United States.

Amendment XIII (1865)

Section 1. Neither slavery nor involuntary servitude, except as a punishment for crime whereof the party shall have been duly convicted, shall exist within the United States, or any place subject to their jurisdiction.

Section 2.   Congress shall have power to enforce this article by appropriate legislation.

Amendment XIV (1868)

Section 1.   All persons born or naturalized in the United States, and subject to the jurisdiction thereof, are citizens of the United States and of the state wherein they reside. No state shall make or enforce any law which shall abridge the privileges or immunities of citizens of the United States; nor shall any state deprive any person of life, liberty, or property, without due process of law; nor deny to any person within its jurisdiction the equal protection of the laws.

Section 2.   Representatives shall be apportioned among the several states according to their respective numbers, counting the whole number of persons in each state, excluding Indians not taxed. But when the right to vote at any election for the choice of electors for President and Vice President of the United States, Representatives in Congress, the executive and judicial officers of a state, or the members of the legislature thereof, is denied to any of the male inhabitants of such state, being twenty-one years of age, and citizens of the United States, or in any way abridged, except for participation in rebellion, or other crime, the basis of representation therein shall be reduced in the proportion which the number of such male citizens shall bear to the whole number of male citizens twenty-one years of age in such state.

Section 3.   No person shall be a Senator or Representative in Congress, or elector of President and Vice President, or hold any office, civil or military, under the United States, or under any state, who, having previously taken an oath, as a member of Congress, or as an officer of the United States, or as a member of any state legislature, or as an executive or judicial officer of any state, to support the Constitution of the United States, shall have engaged in insurrection or rebellion against the same, or given aid or comfort to the enemies thereof. But Congress may by a vote of two-thirds of each House, remove such disability.

Section 4.   The validity of the public debt of the United States, authorized by law, including debts incurred for payment of pensions and bounties for services in suppressing insurrection or rebellion, shall not be questioned. But neither the United States nor any state shall assume or pay any debt or obligation incurred in aid of insurrection or rebellion against the United States, or any claim for the loss or emancipation of any slave; but all such debts, obligations and claims shall be held illegal and void.

Section 5.   The Congress shall have power to enforce, by appropriate legislation, the provisions of this article.

Amendment XV (1870)

Section 1.   The right of citizens of the United States to vote shall not be denied or abridged by the United States or by any state on account of race, color, or previous condition of servitude.

Section 2.   The Congress shall have power to enforce this article by appropriate legislation.

Amendment XVI (1913)

The Congress shall have power to lay and collect taxes on incomes, from whatever source derived, without apportionment among the several states, and without regard to any census of enumeration.

Amendment XVII (1913)

The Senate of the United States shall be composed of two Senators from each state, elected by the people thereof, for six years; and each Senator shall have one vote. The electors in each state shall have the qualifications requisite for electors of the most numerous branch of the state legislatures.

When vacancies happen in the representation of any state in the Senate, the executive authority of such state shall issue writs of election to fill such vacancies: Provided, that the legislature of any state may empower the executive thereof to make temporary appointments until the people fill the vacancies by election as the legislature may direct.

This amendment shall not be so construed as to affect the election or term of any Senator chosen before it becomes valid as part of the Constitution.

Amendment XVIII (1919)

Section 1.   After one year from the ratification of this article the manufacture, sale, or transportation of intoxicating liquors within, the importation thereof into, or the exportation thereof from the United States and all territory subject to the jurisdiction thereof for beverage purposes is hereby prohibited.

Section 2.   The Congress and the several states shall have concurrent power to enforce this article by appropriate legislation.

Section 3.   This article shall be inoperative unless it shall have been ratified as an amendment to the Constitution by the legislatures of the several states, as provided in the Constitution, within seven years from the date of the submission hereof to the states by the Congress.

Amendment XIX (1920)

The right of citizens of the United States to vote shall not be denied or abridged by the United States or by any state on account of sex.

Congress shall have power to enforce this article by appropriate legislation.

Amendment XX (1933)

Section 1. The terms of the President and Vice President shall end at noon on the 20th day of January, and the terms of Senators and Representatives at noon on the 3d day of January, of the years in which such terms would have ended if this article had not been ratified; and the terms of their successors shall then begin.

Section 2. The Congress shall assemble at least once in every year, and such meeting shall begin at noon on the 3d day of January, unless they shall by law appoint a different day.

Section 3. If, at the time fixed for the beginning of the term of the President, the President elect shall have died, the Vice President elect shall become President. If a President shall not have been chosen before the time fixed for the beginning of his term, or if the President elect shall have failed to qualify, then the Vice President elect shall act as President until a President shall have qualified; and the Congress may by law provide for the case wherein neither a President elect nor a Vice President elect shall have qualified, declaring who shall then act as President, or the manner in which one who is to act shall be selected, and such person shall act accordingly until a President or Vice President shall have qualified.

Section 4. The Congress may by law provide for the case of the death of any of the persons from whom the House of Representatives may choose a President whenever the right of choice shall have devolved upon them, and for the case of the death of any of the persons from whom the Senate may choose a Vice President whenever the right of choice shall have devolved upon them.

Section 5. Sections 1 and 2 shall take effect on the 15th day of October following the ratification of this article.

Section 6. This article shall be inoperative unless it shall have been ratified as an amendment to the Constitution by the legislatures of three-fourths of the several states within seven years from the date of its submission.

Amendment XXI (1933)

Section 1. The eighteenth article of amendment to the Constitution of the United States is hereby repealed.

Section 2. The transportation or importation into any state, territory, or possession of the United States for delivery or use therein of intoxicating liquors, in violation of the laws thereof, is hereby prohibited.

Section 3. This article shall be inoperative unless it shall have been ratified as an amendment to the Constitution by conventions in the several states, as provided in the Constitution, within seven years from the date of the submission hereof to the states by the Congress.

Amendment XXII (1951)

Section 1. No person shall be elected to the office of the President more than twice, and no person who has held the office of President, or acted as President, for more than two years of a term to which some other person was elected President shall be elected to the office of the President more than once. But this article shall not apply to any person holding the office of President when this article was proposed by the Congress, and shall not prevent any person who may be holding the office of President, or acting as President, during the term within which this article becomes operative from holding the office of President or acting as President during the remainder of such term.

Section 2. This article shall be inoperative unless it shall have been ratified as an amendment to the Constitution by the legislatures of three-fourths of the several states within seven years from the date of its submission to the states by the Congress.

Amendment XXIII (1961)

Section 1. The District constituting the seat of government of the United States shall appoint in such manner as the Congress may direct:

A number of electors of President and Vice President equal to the whole number of Senators and Representatives in Congress to which the District would be entitled if it were a state, but in no event more than the least populous state; they shall be in addition to those appointed by the states, but they shall be considered, for the purposes of the election of President and Vice President, to be electors appointed by a state; and they shall meet in the District and perform such duties as provided by the twelfth article of amendment.

Section 2.   The Congress shall have power to enforce this article by appropriate legislation.

Amendment XXIV (1964)

Section 1.   The right of citizens of the United States to vote in any primary or other election for President or Vice President, for electors for President or Vice President, or for Senator or Representative in Congress, shall not be denied or abridged by the United States or any state by reason of failure to pay any poll tax or other tax.

Section 2.   The Congress shall have power to enforce this article by appropriate legislation.

Amendment XXV (1967)

Section 1.   In case of the removal of the President from office or of his death or resignation, the Vice President shall become President.

Section 2.   Whenever there is a vacancy in the office of the Vice President, the President shall nominate a Vice President who shall take office upon confirmation by a majority vote of both Houses of Congress.

Section 3.   Whenever the President transmits to the President pro tempore of the Senate and the Speaker of the House of Representatives his written declaration that he is unable to discharge the powers and duties of his office, and until he transmits to them a written declaration to the contrary, such powers and duties shall be discharged by the Vice President as Acting President.

Section 4.   Whenever the Vice President and a majority of either the principal officers of the executive departments or of such other body as Congress may by law provide, transmit to the President pro tempore of the Senate and the Speaker of the House of Representatives their written declaration that the President is unable to discharge the powers and duties of his office, the Vice President shall immediately assume the powers and duties of the office as Acting President.

Thereafter, when the President transmits to the President pro tempore of the Senate and the Speaker of the House of Representatives his written declaration that no inability exists, he shall resume the powers and duties of his office unless the Vice President and a majority of either the principal officers of the executive department or of such other body as Congress may by law provide, transmit within four days to the President pro tempore of the Senate and the Speaker of the House of Representatives their written declaration that the President is unable to discharge the powers and duties of his office. Thereupon Congress shall decide the issue, assembling within forty-eight hours for that purpose if not in session. If the Congress, within twenty-one days after receipt of the latter written declaration, or, if Congress is not in session, within twenty-one days after Congress is required to assemble, determines by two-thirds vote of both Houses that the President is unable to discharge the powers and duties of his office, the Vice President shall continue to discharge the same as Acting President; otherwise, the President shall resume the powers and duties of his office.

Amendment XXVI (1971)

Section 1.   The right of citizens of the United States, who are 18 years of age or older, to vote, shall not be denied or abridged by the United States or any state on account of age.

Section 2.   The Congress shall have the power to enforce this article by appropriate legislation.

Amendment XXVII (1992)

No law varying the compensation for the services of the Senators and Representatives shall take effect until an election of Representatives shall have intervened.

Index